Between mother and daughter

...st profound ...eir teenage ...show how ...nce, but to develop a deeper bond, a lasting bond that will carry through their en... ...l experiences the ...oth mother ...."

This Book is Due in

21 Days

...e is Yours—
...tionships,

"Refreshingly candid and chock-full of helpful suggestions and interesting tidbits. If you are a teenage girl or the mother of a teenage daughter, I encourage you to run, not walk, to get your copy!"

—Sue Patton Thoele, psychotherapist and author of *The Courage to Be Yourself, The Woman's Book of Courage,* and *Heart Centered Marriage*

"This wonderful book is easy to read and apply in everyday life. Some of the best advice, which we can all use a little of now and then, is about arguing, misunderstanding, fights, and lingering, bad feelings. Every parent of a teen needs to negotiate this territory, and this book provides extremely helpful advice, tips, and support. I highly recommend it for any parent with an adolescent of any age."

—Vimala McClure, author of *The Tao of Motherhood* and *The Path of Parenting*

"Every parent of a teenager must read and reread this book. Its value is boundless, especially the fact that it isn't written from the perspective of how to 'deal with' or 'manage' our children. Judy's relationship with Amanda will be inspirational to parents who aren't afraid to listen to their children, learn from their children, and be a friend to their children."

—Hugh and Gayle Prather, parents, ministers, and authors of *Spiritual Parenting, I Will Never Leave You,* and *Spiritual Notes to Myself*

between
mother & daughter

between
mother & daughter

A teenager and her mom share
the secrets of a strong relationship

Judy Ford and Amanda Ford

Foreword by Carmen Renee Berry

Afterword by Mavis Gruver

CONARI PRESS
Berkeley, California

Conari Press books are distributed by Publishers Group West.

ISBN: 1-57324-164-4

Cover photography: Theresa Vargo, Mill Valley, CA
Cover design: Ame Beanland
Interior design: Suzanne Albertson

Library of Congress Cataloging-in-Publication Data
Ford, Judy, 1944–
     Between mother & daughter : a teenager and her mom share the secrets of a strong relationship / Judy Ford and Amanda Ford.
          p.   cm.
     ISBN 1-57324-164-4
     1. Mothers and daughters.   2. Parent and teenager.   3. Teenage girls—family relationships.   4. Parenting.   I. Ford, Amanda.   II. Title.
III. Title: Between mother and daughter.
HQ755.85.F677   1999   99-23770
306.874'3—dc21   CIP

Printed in the United States of America on recycled paper.

99 00 01 02 03   Malloy   10 9 8 7 6 5 4 3 2 1

For Mothers and Daughters

everywhere.

May we forever consider the

spirited girl

in ourselves and each other.

between
mother & daughter

W hen I was sixteen, my parents bought me a Mustang Mach I, avocado green with a black interior. Definitely the hottest car among my circle of friends. To prove that point, I accepted a challenge thrown to me by another teenager who had a new car: to race down a residential street in Pasadena one Friday night. The group of teenagers witnessing the dare divided up between us, thereby demonstrating their confidence in one or the other of us. My car was filled to capacity, and there was no question in my mind that I would leave my challenger in the dust, which I did. As my elated passengers cheered the victory, I spent just a little too much time gloating while looking in the rearview mirror at the shrinking image of my competitor. I looked up to see an orange-painted sawhorse that held up a "Caution: Road Work Ahead" sign, just in time to avoid hitting it dead on but not in time to keep it from shearing off my driver-side mirror. As I surveyed the damage on my beloved car, my sense of victory was short-lived.

Driving home that night I was filled with dread. I certainly didn't want to find out what my parents' reaction would be upon learning that I had a) been racing with other kids in my car, and b) I had damaged the car I had assured them I was responsible enough to receive from them. So, the next morning, early, before any damage could be noticed, I took the car to a repair shop and got it fixed on the spot. I thought I was free and clear.

Unfortunately, I wasn't very good at being bad. Without thinking, I came home and dropped the receipt from the repair shop on the floor of my room (where most of my belongings lived). My mother always respected my space. She never searched my room like some mothers did. Never read my diary. In fact, she wasn't snooping when she found the receipt. She simply looked down while standing in my room talking with me, and there it was, declaring my guilt.

I don't know if it was because I rarely did anything like this, or because she couldn't believe I would go to all that trouble just to get myself caught, but she just rolled her eyes when she saw the receipt. I didn't even need to confess; she figured out the gist of my misdeed all on her own.

I was such a good girl that I never quite embraced adolescence when I was a teenager. Adolescence is often defined in terms of specific ages (thirteen to nineteen) or in terms of grades in school (junior through senior high school). I prefer to see adolescence as a necessary transitional phase that must be successfully navigated to move into adulthood. I wish, like Amanda Ford, I could report that I'd completed this transition by the time I went off to college. Quite honestly, I believe my adolescent tasks were finally resolved sometime in my early thirties. It took me a long time after I received my high school diploma to have a sense of myself as an adult woman, to make my own decisions, and to hide the receipts when I was trying to get away with something.

Perhaps one of the impediments to moving into adulthood was the idea that I had to separate from my parents. I tried repeatedly to leave them—geographically, emotionally, spiritually—only to find myself indelibly tied to them all the same. It wasn't until I learned how to redefine my relationship with my mother and father, rather than separate from them, that I no longer related to my parents in an adolescent way—as reference points against which to rebel. Only then did I develop an effective adult-to-adult relationship with them.

Had I the opportunity to learn from Amanda and Judy's experiences, maybe years could have been shaved off this elongated process. These authors have discovered and beautifully written about the multifaceted process of redefining instead of severing their relationship. *Between Mother and Daughter* is an extremely helpful guide through the tumultuous transition that all women must traverse, whether they be thirteen or thirty-three. Filled with authentic emotion and down-to-earth ideas for conflict resolution, it captures the essence of what all mothers and daughters face when the nature of the relationship must be reinvented.

The adolescent process is new to both mother and daughter; neither knows what she is in for or what it all means. The exercises in the book help promote understanding and reduce the risks of misinterpretation. After all, all that daughters are trying to do is grow up, and mothers, as best as they can, are trying to help that happen.

As a former psychotherapist, and now a massage therapist, I was delighted by the work Amanda and Judy have done regarding the body image of the blossoming adolescent. Most if not all the women I have worked with in massage therapy during the past ten years struggle with some level of loathing toward their own bodies. Some of their deepest emotional wounds come from misguided advice or intrusive actions or critical comments from their mothers.

If our own mothers do not accept our bodies, how can we? Tugs of war over weight, nutrition, and dress leave lasting impressions on young women. Certainly the reaction we received when we first started our periods, finally got to shave our legs, and shopped for that first bra are intertwined with the very fabric of a woman's being. Whether we see ourselves as beautiful or ugly, alluring or repulsive, stems from reactions we saw in our mother's eyes. I hope that every mother of a teenage daughter will open her heart to what is written here.

I can still remember as an adolescent, not too many years ago, pushing my mother away with all my might. Now, as an adult, there is no person with whom I'd rather spend time than my mom. After I grew up, something amazing happened to my mother. She miraculously mutated into a delightful, wise, funny, and emotionally adept friend. I'd like to tell myself that she's the one who changed, but I know that I finally resolved important issues and allowed her into my life in a new way. To all those mothers and daughters who are frustrated with each other, let me bear witness to the fact that the transition is well worth the effort. Inside that strict, overcontrolling mother-monster and that sassy, rebellious daughter-demon are two women who one day will look back on this era with a sigh of relief and perhaps some laughter, and will enjoy each other immensely once again.

Two Voices—Two Viewpoints

*B*etween *Mother and Daughter* was written by the two of us—
nineteen-year-old Amanda, a college student, and mother
Judy, a family therapist—to help both mothers and teenage
daughters create the strongest, most loving relationships possible.
We wrote it because we know very well that the adolescent years are
full of challenges for both mother and daughter, and we believe that
by understanding each other's perspective, you will become better
prepared to find good solutions.

Between Mother and Daughter is about navigating and negotiating
this pivotal time in order to create a healthy and happy mother-
daughter relationship. It's an invitation to both mothers and daughters to open your minds and hearts and see the possibilities for
improving your relationship.

Between Mother and Daughter is not so much an advice book—
although we do give practical tips—as it is an insider's view of the
absolute nitty-gritty of the mother-daughter struggle. We start with
the premise that mothers and daughters want a happy, strong connection but often struggle to stay close during the teen years. We
have seen many mothers and daughters flounder because they were
unwilling to understand what life was like from the other's perspective, or they made false assumptions about each other and were
unable to work through their differences; sadly, many have
remained estranged. *Between Mother and Daughter* can help you avoid
these pitfalls.

We wrote *Between Mother and Daughter* so that teenage girls might better understand their changing feelings toward their mothers and learn how to communicate their needs and desires in a constructive way. Mothers will get a firsthand view of the struggles and inner turmoil that their daughters are experiencing. In the end, both mothers and daughters will see that having a good relationship is *not* impossible. You both have the power to stay connected and make positive changes in your relationship.

We begin each chapter with a true scenario, straightforward and unadorned, and then take turns discussing each issue from our own particular perspective. Although this book is written in two distinct voices, one addressing mothers and the other teenage girls, we encourage you to read both parts. By reading the mother's point of view, daughters may be able to better understand why her mother does what she does. By reading the daughter's point of view, mothers will gain an inside glimpse of the special challenges teenage girls face as they grow up.

Reading each other's part will help you understand how both people can work together to create a rewarding relationship. Just as your relationship is made up of two people, this book has two parts, and it's incomplete if one viewpoint is left unread. Hearing both sides of the story will help you work with each other to create a mutually satisfying relationship.

There is no one right way to have a relationship—there are as many ways as there are mothers and daughters. Each relationship is unique. The ideas presented in this book are not the only ideas; they are just some ideas. While we share the steps we've taken, we don't intend for you to follow our path exactly. Instead, we invite you to use the ideas we present as a starting point to find the solutions that match your relationship. As you read, keep an open mind and be willing to try new things. Some of our solutions may work for you step-by-step, while others may simply provide a starting point that leads you to new ways of relating. Let our story spark ideas within you about how to achieve your ideal mother-daughter relationship.

Each chapter is filled with mother and daughter tips, to-do lists, discussion ideas, or quizzes. Although not everything will apply directly to you, our experience shows that following these suggestions will help point you in a positive direction. We can truly say, "We've been there, we've done that." Be open to our suggestions, and brainstorm with each other; you can find the communication style and solutions that will benefit your unique relationship.

After reading *Between Mother and Daughter* and practicing some of these skills, we are confident that you can keep your relationship intact through the turbulence of the adolescent years. You will learn from each other and grow together and when your struggles are over, you will be left with a strong bond and will have created a legacy that will continue forever. We strongly believe that it's possible for both mothers and daughters to treasure the coming-of-age years, and we wish you both renewed enthusiasm to tackle the sometimes seemingly impossible task of enjoying one another.

PART 1

Staying Connected

1

Roots to Support Her and Wings to Fly

But I'm Her Mother!

"Your daughter is in critical condition," Dr. Stewart said. "She'll be transported to Children's Hospital as soon as the neo-natal emergency team arrives."

"Why? What's wrong?" I asked, still whirling from the emergency C-section I'd just undergone.

"Meconium aspiration syndrome," he said. "She needs to be on a respirator."

"Can I see her?" I pleaded.

Covered from head to toe in sticky, greenish goo, weighing 5 pounds 14 ounces, Amanda was, I could see, the most beautiful and smartest baby. Although her breathing was labored, her spunk and determination were strong. Tiny, tired, and sick, and only 19 inches long, she was magnificent. With a twinkle in her eye and a sparkling personality, she had an enormous spirit. Instantly I wanted to get to know her, comfort her, kiss her, whisper in her ear, make it all better, but there wasn't time. The special-equipped ambulance was waiting. There was nothing for me to do, the nurse said, except to recover my strength.

"But I'm her mother," I pleaded, as if that fact alone was enough to shield her from the uncertainty ahead. As they rolled her away in the life-saving incubator, I gasped. It didn't seem fair that I was unable to protect my darling baby girl. No one could ease the agony of this premature separation. However, this episode taught me an enormous lesson about the relationship I would develop with my daughter—ultimately Amanda's life was out of my hands. I shivered as it slowly dawned on me how many challenges she'd face in her life that I couldn't control.

Immediately after her birth, I was thrown into the seemingly contradictory task of caring intensely while graciously letting go. In order for her to receive the best medical attention, I signed the permission slip for her to be transported across town without me. Only one hour old, Amanda was already a separate individual with a will and destiny of her own. Little did I know how many times over the next nineteen years I'd encounter that fact.

Mothering is a mysterious task. First you create an intimate, all-consuming attachment with your daughter, then you spend the rest of your life learning to let her go. Providing food, love, and shelter, you are your daughter's life-source. Although she is a separate person from you, as a baby, your daughter is so thoroughly dependent on you that she is a part of you. As your daughter grows older, this intense closeness lessens and takes on a more subtle dimension. She still depends on you, but not in the same way. Navigating this gradual release while still remaining connected can be difficult, particularly as she reaches her teen years. That's when conflict between you may be intense and when mothers (and daughters too) bemoan the lack of connection.

At first you take care of your daughter's every need, but gradually this shifts as she grows up. First you carry her in a backpack; soon she's walking on her own. Abruptly, during the teen years, it seems as if she doesn't need you at all any more. You're no longer your daughter's life source as she pushes for more independence. Painful as it is to go through, that's the way it's meant to be. It's your sacred duty to give your daughter roots to support her and wings to fly.

Parents can only give good advice or put them on the right paths, but the final forming of a person's character lies in their own hands.

—Anne Frank

This is much easier to do when she's four years old and she only wants to climb the ladder and go down the slide by herself while you "sit over there." It's harder when she wants to stay out past midnight or doesn't think you need to meet her date's parents. It's much easier to keep your relationship thriving when at eight she writes you notes and says how much she loves you than when she's thirteen, rolling her eyes and sighing at every comment you make. When she was a little girl, she wanted you to read her bedtime stories; now she insists you knock before entering her room. Once she told you everything, now she doesn't say a word. Sometimes it seems that she doesn't want you in her life at all, that she doesn't need you any more.

When your daughter reaches adolescence, you may miss your sweet little girl with the sunny disposition. It's not because you don't want your daughter to grow up, but because there are days, even months, when you wonder if you will ever have a harmonious connection again. All mothers desire to have a strong relationship with their daughters, but when our daughters begin to pull away and are talking back or pouting, it is hard for us to tell if that is what they want as well.

Be assured that your adolescent daughter needs you as much as she always has, but in a new way. She's growing up and cannot tolerate being treated like a child. What worked at ten is antiquated only two years later. Unfortunately many mothers and daughters get stuck in a vicious circle, reacting in the same old way to one another. Their minds are closed, they're stuck in a rut. It doesn't have to be that way—the teen years are full of glorious

There is nothing more thrilling in this world than to have a child that is yours, and yet is mysteriously a stranger.

—Agatha Christie

opportunities to get to know each other better and have more heart-to-heart connection.

I wish every mother and daughter could look each other in the eye and honestly say, "I like you." Getting your daughter to love you is not a triumph, because every girl loves her mother. You know that you have really succeeded when your adolescent daughter tells her friends that she really *likes* you. It is not often that an adolescent girl chooses to spend time with her mother or openly shares details of her day. These things come with the respect, openness, and trust that are formed in friendship, not in a relationship where the mother is solely in charge.

As a mother who has a delightful relationship with her teenage daughter and as a counselor to thousands of other mothers, let me reassure you that you too can have a fulfilling connection—as long as you're willing to grow, learn, and experiment.

RAINY DAY PROJECT

Make a collage poster of the two of you. Include baby pictures, school pictures, and pictures of each of you as teens. Add poems, jokes, and inspiring words that have meaning for you both. Hang it up and let it be a reminder of your one-of-a-kind relationship.

The Little Girl in the Photo Album

Several times during my teenage years, my mother would get nostalgic and drag me on a trip down memory lane with her. Sitting on the couch with dozens of old picture albums and scrapbooks, she would flip through pages filled with photos, drawings, and letters, hoping that I would soon join her in the joys of reminiscing.

"Look at this one," she would say, handing me a drawing of two people, both without bodies and with arms coming out of their heads where their ears should be. "It's me and you playing ball," she would say. "Don't you remember? You drew it for me."

"No, I don't remember at all."

She would continue by pulling out piles of old papers. "Let me read you these." I never found the notes that read, "I love you, Mom" or "Mom, you are the best" particularly profound or moving, but as my mother read, her eyes would light up with excitement and joy.

"Remember when you used to write me all these cute little notes?" she would ask.

"Mom, I was like five years old," I would say, a bit irritated by her question. "Do you really expect me to remember?"

She always chose to ignore these statements and would continue. "Oh, look at you there!" my mother would say, pointing out a little girl who was dressed up in a Cookie Monster costume. "You were so adorable!"

The bright-eyed, blonde child in those pictures was a stranger to me. I didn't know her. I never quite understood why my mother would show me all of those old photos and letters. It was as if she hoped they would strike some chord within me and bring me to remember something that I had obviously forgotten.

For my mother, there was sentimental value attached to every item in those books, but it was different for me. Looking at pictures of me as a child brought joy to my mother's heart; for me, it merely brought back a few blurry snapshots of a life I used to live. It was real to her, yet so obscure to me. Treasuring the days when I insisted on following her wherever she went and wrote her notes professing my desire to be just like her when I grew up, my mother remembers being the center of my world. However, I don't remember what it felt like to be that child in those pictures. I don't remember worshipping her as she swears I once did.

My memories of relating to my mother go back only as far as the seventh grade; for me, that is when our relationship began. I can clearly remember the excitement that filled me when she dropped me off at my first junior high dance and my irritation at her when she made me get off the phone at 9 P.M. on school nights. For me, my adolescent years, not my childhood, make up the foundation of our relationship.

I know from my own experiences and from talking with dozens of other girls that, once they become teenagers, many girls get frustrated with their mothers. Complaining that their mothers don't understand them, that they are too strict, that they don't trust them, and that they are embarrassing, most teenage girls have seemingly endless lists of things that bug them about their mothers. We often blame our mothers for all the difficulties in our relationship, saying, "If she would only do this differently, we would get along better." Putting most of the responsibility on our mothers' shoulders, we expect *them* to change so that the relationship moves in a positive direction. However, if you want to have a good relationship with your mother, you must be willing to do your part. Believe it or not, you have the ability to make a positive change in your relationship with your mother.

Just because you and your mother have disagreements and don't ever seem to get along doesn't mean that there is no hope for a good relationship. First, it helps to realize that all girls have difficulties in their relationships with their mothers, particularly during the teen years. My mother and I are not perfect. We fight and argue, we disagree and have struggles just like every other teenage girl and her mother. However, we have worked hard to learn how to deal with our problems and to create a relationship that is fulfilling for us both.

Family life is a training ground. Learn to get along at home and you can get along everywhere.

—Harriet Ruchlin

If you wanted to have a heart-to-heart mother-daughter talk, where would you want to have it?

1. At home
2. In the car
3. At a quiet restaurant
4. On a walk
5. Other

I wrote this book to give other teenage girls insight into my relationship with my mother and a chance to learn from the things that I did right, as well as my mistakes. I don't pretend to be the perfect daughter or claim know all the "secrets" to getting along with your mother. I can be a brat, and at times I've been difficult. I've picked fights with Mom; I've gone behind her back and done things that she specifically told me not to do; I've told her, "I had a great day at school today," when, really, I had skipped all my classes and spent the day with my friends at the mall.

So, you see, I am not perfect and I know what it's like to be a teenage girl who's struggling to get along with her mother. I don't have all the solutions to problems that you may have, but I do have insight. I am nineteen now and in college. Away from home, I can look back on our relationship in a new light. I can understand what mistakes I made when relating to my mother, I know what things worked for us and what things didn't work. I can look back and say, "Here's what I could have done differently."

After reading *Between Mother and Daughter*, I hope your feelings of desperation and hopelessness disappear. I hope you will have learned how to teach your mother how to relate to you as the young woman you now are, not as the little girl in the photo album you once were.

2

Your Evolving Relationship

Drive Me to the Mall, Please

"You can drop me off up there," I said, pointing to the corner ahead of us. "But, honey, that's two blocks away from the mall," Mom replied, surprised that I wanted to be let out of the car so far from my destination. "Don't you want me to drop you off closer?"

"No, thanks. I'll just walk."

"It's not a problem," she replied. "Where are you meeting Jamie? I'll just drop you off there. You know, I really don't like you walking all that way alone."

"Mother, I'm thirteen. I think I can walk a few blocks by myself!" I crossed my fingers, hoping that she would let me out at the corner and wouldn't insist on driving me all the way to the mall. "I want to walk. You don't need to take me the whole way."

My mother looked at me and sighed. She was obviously frustrated, but she pulled over to the corner anyway.

"Can I have some money?" I asked. "After we're finished at the mall, Jamie and I are going to take the bus to see a movie."

"I have an idea," my mother said, her eyes lighting up. "I have some shopping I can do at the mall. I'll go and do mine while you girls do yours, then we can meet up and I'll take you both to the movie and out to dinner."

"No thanks, Mom. We wanna take the bus." I could tell she was disappointed, but did she honestly believe I would want to go to the movies with her? I see her every day; why doesn't she understand that I just want to be with my friends?

Reaching for her purse, Mom took a deep breath. "You know," she said, "when you were little, you loved to hang out with your mother. You always wanted to be with me. I couldn't even go to the mailbox without you wanting to tag along."

Rolling my eyes, I responded, "I'm not little anymore."

She grabbed a twenty-dollar bill from her purse and handed it to me. Then she said, "At least we know you still need me for some things. How would you get to the mall if you didn't have your mother? And where would you get money?"

"I'd take the bus and I'd get a job," I said matter-of-factly. Then jumping out of the car, I said, "Thanks, Mom. I'll see you later." I began my two-block walk to the mall.

❋ She's Growing Up

One of the first clues that your daughter has started individuation—pulling away from her mother in order to find her own identity—is when she wants you to drive her places so that she can be with her friends.

It doesn't stop there. You cheerfully drive your daughter where she wants to go, and instead of being thankful for what you've done, she is distant and cold. You ask her if she had fun skiing, if she handed in her homework assignment, or what movie she saw with her friends, and she gets irritated. Devoting more of her energy to hanging out with her friends, she spends less time with you. She doesn't tell you as much as you'd like her to. Some days she doesn't want to have anything to do with you at all. Suddenly you are no longer number one with her and are left on the outside looking in.

I vividly remember my response to Amanda's insistence that I drop her off so she could walk the two blocks to the mall by herself. I was proud of her spirit and independence; in fact, many times I encouraged her try new things and venture out on her own. I didn't want her to be tied to my apron strings, so whenever she wanted to have an adventure I'd say, "Sounds good, try it." At thirteen, she was taking the bus to the slopes for all-day skiing and lessons. I wanted her to go after what she wanted, to know her own mind, and to be able to stick up for herself. I'd raised her to have good self-esteem; I boasted to friends about her accomplishments and cheered her on when she demonstrated a new level of competence.

I have so much I can teach her. I would say you might encounter defeats but you must never be defeated. I would teach her to love a lot. Laugh a lot at the silliest things and be very serious. I would teach her to love life, I could do that.

—Maya Angelou, on the possibility of having a daughter

Up until that moment, however, I'd never considered how her determination to be her own person would impact me. I hadn't considered how her thrust toward independence would shatter my security. Her determination to spend an afternoon with her best friend left me feeling like I'd had been stripped of my life's purpose. Walking two blocks to the mall was a victory of autonomy for her, but for me it was a reminder of my vulnerability and a shaking of my "Mommy" identity. Until that moment I hadn't realized how much I depended on Amanda—not only because she added meaning and purpose to my life—but because she was good company. She was fun to be with, and for twelve years she'd been my cheerful companion and buddy. Her needing me gave me a reason to get up in the morning. Though I understood her need to be with her friends, that afternoon I didn't want her to go to the mall and movie without me. I tried several times to coax her into letting me tag along, but she sensed my clinging and jumped out the car as quickly as possible. She was diplomatic, but that didn't stop me from trying to manipulate her by asking, "What would you do without me?" I didn't like myself for using a guilt trip, but I couldn't stop myself. I handed her twenty dollars and didn't even try to hide my disappointment. Ashamed, frustrated, angry, sad, abandoned, and lonely, I barely knew what to do with myself. For the rest of the afternoon, I was agitated and couldn't get my bearings. When she came home, I probed for every little detail—"Did you like the movie?" "What did you have for lunch?" "How was the bus ride?" She answered with one-syllable words, went straight to her room, shut the door, and called her friends to relive the excitement of her day. My day seemed utterly flat and boring by comparison; our relationship was approaching a new phase, and I didn't like it.

In the adolescent years, girls and moms can argue over the slightest things. As your daughter proclaims her new self, she'll see things differently than you. "I wasn't mad at her, but Lynn was convinced I was," said Haddie. "I was only reminding her not to forget her lunch, but she said I was nagging." She may take her frustrations out on you. If she's run into difficulty at school, instead of sharing her predicament, she might snap at you or want to be left alone. Once, she ran to you for comfort; now, she wants to go to her room and recover on her own. She no longer turns to you to fix her problems.

As mothers, we know this will happen; after all, we went through it ourselves with our mothers. But we don't expect this change to come all at once or to affect us so deeply. It hurts, scares, and confuses us. How can they push us aside so easily? Will we ever be friends again? What will I do now?

At times like this, it's important to remember that the transition from adoring her mother to creating her own life is not easy for your daughter either. All girls want to involve their mothers in their lives, but they are not sure how, when, or to what extent, and they aren't sure how to express this.

When a girl reaches a certain age, she wants to experience life on her own and distinguish herself from her mother. It's when our daughters begin to lead their own lives that we seem to go crazy. Intellectually, I understood Amanda's need to separate herself from me and even supported it. I thought I was doing a fine job; after all, at thirteen, she was more independent than I had been. But she still clamored for more privacy and autonomy. I knew that she still needed my involvement and mothering, but I was not sure how, when, or how much.

It's a difficult transition for everyone. Our confusion over how to moderate the separation and maintain a good relationship creates confusion and frustration in our daughters. A daughter has no idea why, as she grows older, her mother seems to curtail her freedom. To her, there should be a natural transition from childhood to adolescence. As she gets older and more capable, she thinks she should be given all the freedom she needs. You give her as much as you are ready to give, which is often more than what you want her to have in the first place, yet she is convinced that the opposite is happening and complains that you treat her like a child.

By the time a girl reaches adolescence, she's already become independent in many ways. The role that she now wants and needs you to play has changed. She still wants you in her life, she just wants you involved differently. Your daughter's mixed messages are signs that she is unsure how to express this new need. She hasn't figured out how to find the balance between being a daughter and being an independent young woman. You are both going through these new struggles and trying to master behaviors that are foreign to both of you.

Mothers always ask, "What happened to my sweet little girl?" All that has happened to her is that she is growing up.

✳ What's a Mother to Do?

Don't Take It Personally

Above all else, don't take these events personally. Remember when your little girl was two years old and didn't want you to dress her any longer? "I can do it by myself," she said. Even though it took her twice as long to get dressed and when she finally did her pants were on backwards, you stepped back and let her do it. You were patient, understanding, and perhaps even proud of her determination. Often you were amused at the combinations she would choose, but you knew she was on a course to conquer shirts and socks, so you nodded encouragingly. When she'd let you, you gladly assisted in pulling her shirt over her head or slipping on her mismatched socks. You knew that dressing herself was one of the many steps she'd make toward autonomy. Your daughter's ability to take care of herself in a new way even allowed you a few bonuses, like the fact that you now had more time to dress yourself.

There's no need to take her adolescent independence personally either. The separation is not about you. It's not about whether or not you are a good mother or whether or not she loves you. Just as she tried on several different outfits before she decided on the perfect one, she must now check out everything from hairstyles to friends to hobbies to career options before she is able to select the best one. Try to sit back and let her do it on her own. She may do things that you know you could assist her in doing better, but try not to jump in to help unless you are invited. There are times when you must jump in, like if she is doing drugs or having unprotected sex, but for the most part, let her have a say in the matters that affect her. This way she'll learn about the consequences of her own actions. She needs these teen years for practice before she leaves your nest for good.

When Amanda first reached adolescence, I once said to her, "I hope that you and I will always have a good relationship. I want to work together with you so that we can always be friends." Let your daughter know over and over again, "I want to have a good relationship with you. I want to learn too." Few of us were really ready for parenting when we had our children. In fact, most parents grow up as they raise their children. Not many of us are prepared to have a teenage daughter; we must learn how to relate to her as she grows up. Tell her, "I've never been a mother of a teenage girl before, and I'm trying to figure it out."

"This stood out in my head," Amanda remembers. "I remembered this statement during the times when we would fight and the times when I didn't think that she understood me. She made it clear to me that she was willing to make an effort. Knowing that she was working with me, not against me, made a huge difference in our relationship."

What can you do? Even if you've already raised a daughter successfully, *this* daughter is unique. Be positive, and tell her that you want a good relationship with her and that you know it is possible. You are now laying the foundation for your adult relationship, and your mature selves are unfolding. Opposing this natural transition will make life with your daughter more difficult. The more we resist, the harder she fights. Many mother-daughter arguments, even as adults, are caused because the mother doesn't understand the woman her daughter has become. When fights do happen, remind yourselves, "We're both learning." The process is full of trials, tirades, and triumphs. As you master these new mothering skills, you and your daughter will learn how adaptable you both are and this will have incredible advantages for both of you.

> *When the bond between mother and daughter is strong and the mother has been an effective role model, then the daughter can experience her mother within herself as an inner strength.*
>
> —*Josephine Evetts-Secker*

FOR MOTHERS AND DAUGHTERS

If you could improve two things about your relationship, what would they be?

Leave Me Alone

Once I began junior high, my life took on a whole new form. I knew it would. Turning thirteen, I was excited that I had finally entered the stage I had long awaited—I had become a teenager. The first day of junior high, I was introduced to a new way of life, one that I had heard stories and seen movies about. A world where people went to school dances and wore stylish clothes, hung out with their friends without their parents around and talked on the phone for hours at a time. I knew then that my life would never be the same.

Despite all the changes I had anticipated, there was one thing that I never expected. I never thought I would suddenly dislike my mother. I had seen on television and read in magazines about how teenage girls always fought with their mothers, but I didn't think that I would ever be as irrational as those girls. However, once I reached junior high, I began to realize what caused mothers and daughters to argue and I started to understand why so often teenage girls got frustrated and began to dislike their mothers. As my own desire for independence started pulling me away from my mother, I realized that disagreements were inevitable. I saw that having a good relationship with her would not come naturally; it would take effort.

Once you become a teenager, you begin to get a taste of adult life. You are given more freedom and start to enjoy doing things on your own. You no longer need, or want, your mother around like you did earlier. Once, you begged your mother to come along on the class field trip, but now you would just die if she even thought about chaperoning the school dance. Ready to take charge of your life in a new way, you want to make decisions on your own. You decide what you will eat for lunch, what clubs and sports you want to join, and which elective classes you want to take the following semester. Friends you have chosen for yourself come into your life, not ones who are your friends simply because your parents are friends. You have new feelings and experiences you don't want to share with your mother. You used to tell your mother everything; now you have secrets from her. You begin to understand what it feels like to be an independent person with your own feelings and thoughts. The older you get and the more freedom you experience, the stronger your pull for independence.

The world begins to open up to you in a whole new way, but unfortunately, this newfound desire to be free can also cause a real strain on your relationship with your mother. You feel like you are able to do many things on your own, yet she continues to hold you back. She insists on helping you make decisions, asks about every detail of your day, and never lets you be alone.

It may even seem like your mother becomes more strict as you get older. It's not because she is trying to control your life, or because she doesn't want you to have any fun, but because she is worried. Maybe her feelings have been hurt because she is no longer so important in your life, maybe she is worried that you will make a mistake and regret it for the rest of your life, maybe she is not sure how to be the mother of a teenage girl. When you begin to pull away, your mother's instinctual reaction is to pull you closer.

I used to feel that my mom treated me more like a child when I was thirteen than she did when I was eight. I realize now it wasn't because my mom didn't recognize that I was growing up, but rather that she *did* see it and was scared. She was worried about losing the close relationship we once shared and wanted to protect me from any harm that might come my way or from mistakes I might make.

My mother has always been overprotective. As a child, I just accepted her worrying as a normal mother activity. As I got older, though, her constant reminders to "Be careful," "Call me as soon you get there," or "Use your best judgment" really began to get on my nerves. It angered me that she didn't think I could make good decisions on my own. Sometimes I resented her for trying to run my life. Even though I knew deep down that my mother was only acting this way because she loved me, it bothered me just the same. I would get easily annoyed at her questions and there were many times when she drove me absolutely crazy.

"I can't stand it when my mother asks me a million questions about my day when I come home from school," says fourteen-year-old Malia. "I'll tell her about some of the things that I did during the day, but that's never enough. She always wants to know more."

Sam, age sixteen, says, "My mother never lets me go anywhere unless she has met the people that I'm going out with, knows exactly where I'm going to be, and has a number where she can reach me if she needs to."

"There's not one particular thing that bugs me about my mom," says fifteen-year-old Jenna. "Just the way that she acts gets on my nerves. She talks too loud in public and whenever I have friends over, she asks them stupid questions. She's just so embarrassing!"

There have been many times in my life when I wished that my mother would leave me alone or times when I believed I would be completely happy if I never saw her again. I wanted to get away from her questions, her overprotective nature, and her nagging. At times, I couldn't stand a single thing about my mother; just the sound of her calling my name from upstairs would make my skin crawl.

The more independence I wanted from my mother, the more faults I found in her. I would use the things about my mother that I didn't like to separate myself from her. Throughout my teenage years I began to notice parts of my mother in myself. My mannerisms, my favorite foods, my opinions about things, and even many of my clothing tastes obviously came from my mother. I hated this! When people would say, "You look so much like your mother," I would reply, "I don't think I look anything like her. She has dark hair and dark eyes and I have blonde hair and blue eyes!" I didn't want to be seen as similar to my mother; I wanted to be viewed as an independent young woman with the ability to think and make decisions on my own. I wanted distance from her in order to try new things in life without her constantly looking over my shoulder offering help and advice. For three years or so I constantly informed her, "You and I are nothing alike." My mother was annoying, worried too much, and wore weird clothes, and I was fun, carefree, and fashionable—it was obvious that we were complete opposites.

What's a Daughter to Do?

Accept That Your Feelings Are Normal

Many girls experience these types of feelings toward their mothers. It's a natural part of growing up. You need to pull away from your mother so you can develop your own personality and figure out what you want for your life. Feeling annoyed and finding faults with your mother is a way to separate yourself from her.

Your relationship with your mother is always evolving. As you grow and become more mature, your relationship will also mature. You may no longer need your mother to do your laundry, make your lunch, or keep you company, but you are still her daughter. You have to work to keep your relationship strong because, as you get older, you don't need your mother less, you simply need her differently.

Many times throughout my teenage years, I felt that I was completely ready for adulthood. I thought the only things I needed my mother for were money, food, and transportation. I didn't realize that I also need my mom for other things, like wisdom, support, love, and understanding. I needed her guidance to help me make decisions I was not yet ready to make on my own. Now that I am at college and no longer have my mother around to do little, everyday things for me, I can see just how important she has been. It would have been very difficult for me to get through my adolescent years without my mother's guidance, assistance, and support.

A study by Teenage Research Unlimited found that 70 percent of teenagers name their mom or dad as the person they most admire.

Sometimes it may seem like your mother is working against you and making your life as difficult as she can. Although there are many times when your mother can be a pain, she is on your side. Your mother was a teenager once too, and she knows how confusing adolescence can be. Your mother has probably experienced similar feelings and has had some of the same problems that you are having right now. Not only can she empathize with what you're going through, she can also offer you tremendous amounts of wisdom from her experiences that will help you through many of your dilemmas. Your mother can show you a side of life that you won't get from your peers.

The hard part is figuring out how to actually get along with your mother. Now that I am no longer living with my mom, it is easy for me to say that getting along with my mother is a piece of cake, but I remember that keeping peace between us was an extremely difficult task that took painstaking effort on both our parts. The best advice that I can give you is to be open to trying new ways of relating to your mother and be willing to work *with* her and not always against her.

Just as being a teenager is new to you, being the mother of a teenager is new for her. Even if you have older sisters, this stage of *your* life is still new for her. Once you accept that you are learning together, it will be much easier to get along. Be open to learning from your mother as well as teaching her. Hear what your mother has to say and help her to understand your point of view. Your mother doesn't know what you want or need from her unless you tell her. You cannot depend entirely on her to make your relationship work; you must put in effort as well.

More than anything, be assured that your feelings of annoyance, frustration, and even hatred do pass. There seems to be a natural progression in our feelings toward our mothers. Strong negative feelings tend to start at twelve or thirteen and peak at fourteen. By sixteen, a lot of it seems to go away, and by eighteen or nineteen, you will have figured out how to get along with your mother. You may even find that you actually enjoy spending time with her.

According to psychologist Terri Apter, who studied sixty-five mother and daughter pairs, girls do not struggle to sever their relationship with their mothers, but to redefine it.

✳ *Daughter's To-Do List*

1. Accept that your feelings toward your mother are normal.
2. Know that your mother has a lot of wisdom that can help you as you grow throughout your teenage years.
3. Be patient with yourself and your mother.
4. Teach your mother how to be the mother of a teenage girl by telling her what you want and need her to do.
5. Be aware that your relationship is changing, not coming to an end.

✳ Mom's To-Do List

1. Tell your daughter that you want to have a good relationship with her.
2. Tell her that you want to work together and that you're on her side.
3. Ask her to be patient with you because you're learning too.
4. Give yourselves plenty of time for practice.
5. Appreciate her struggle and don't take these changes personally.

Responsible Freedom and Positive Limits

Rules for the Weekend

"What's this?" I asked, picking up a yellow legal pad that had "rules for the weekend" written in bold letters across the top.

"The laws I must live by while my parents are gone this weekend," Araya answered. "It's a little ridiculous, huh?"

"A little?" I laughed, "There are three full pages here." I began to read aloud. "Number one, no more than three friends over at a time. Number two, no boys allowed after dark. Number three, your curfew is still midnight. How are they going to know if you stay out past midnight?"

"I don't have a clue," Araya replied. "Read number twelve."

"Number twelve, don't eat dessert before dinner."

"I guess that my mom wanted to make sure that my life doesn't get out of control while she's gone." Araya added with a grin, "You know, eating dessert before dinner can cause serious health problems!"

"This is ridiculous. You're seventeen years old," I remarked. "You think that they'd be able to leave you alone for a weekend without leaving a list of rules." I flipped through to the end of the list. "Here's the last one. 'If you don't abide by these rules, you will be disciplined.' They really didn't leave anything out, did they?"

"Nope, I think they have all the bases covered."

Setting the list of rules back down on the table, I flashed her a grin. "So," I said, "are we gonna have the boys over tonight?"

"You bet!"

Declaration of Independence

Like most teenage girls, I hate being told what to do. Even though I am not a very rebellious person, a defiant feeling starts brewing inside me when I feel like somebody is trying to control me. When a teacher, a coach, or my mom makes a rule that I don't agree with, I want to yell, "You can't tell me what to do," while I run the other way, breaking all the rules and doing exactly what I want.

Think of how you feel when your mother tells you that you're not allowed to have boys over when she is out of town or stay out past midnight. Even if you didn't want to do these things in the first place, suddenly your desire to do them becomes huge. You want to show that you are in control and she can't boss you around, even if she is your mother.

The most frustrating thing for me is when my mom tells me to do something before she has given me a chance to do it on my own. Some Saturday mornings I'll wake up and realize I'm down to my last pair of underwear. Just as I'm getting ready to wash my clothes, my mother will come over and say, "Would you please get your laundry done? I can't even make it to the washing machine because all of your clothes are piled up in there." I clench my fists and tighten my jaw and my first reaction is to say, "I'm not going to do my laundry today and you can't do anything about it." Since I know that wouldn't go over well, I don't. Instead, I walk slowly into the laundry room to get started, but I make a point of saying, "I am going to do my laundry, but not because you told me to. I'm doing it because I want to, and I had already planned on doing it before you said anything about it!" It's my declaration of independence that makes it perfectly clear to my mother that I am in charge of my own life and will do things on my own time.

Nobody likes to have to answer to somebody else or follow rules they don't like. You may wish that your mother would just let you do what you want, but this isn't realistic. Mothers make rules for many reasons, but above all they do it because they care about us. Your mother cares and she is trying to prevent you from making a big mistake or getting hurt. By laying out guidelines for you to follow, she can be better assured that you will be on the right track. But that doesn't mean it's easy to take!

✳ What's a Daughter to Do?

Separate the Ridiculous from the Necessary

It is natural to want to be completely free to decide exactly how you will live your life. You probably don't like it when your mother makes you get off the phone in the middle of a conversation because she thinks it's your bedtime, or tells you to be home at midnight even if you are in the middle of watching a movie at your friend's house. Throughout life there are many rules you'll have to follow, some stupid and some very important and necessary. Your household is no different.

Of course, mothers can make many ridiculous rules. I have friend who, at thirteen, still had a bedtime. "My mother would make me get ready for bed by nine o'clock every night," says Regan, now eighteen. "It used to drive me crazy! I knew that I was old enough to decide when I should go to bed. Maybe my mom was worried that I wouldn't get up for school in the morning or I would be tired and grouchy because I would stay up too late and wouldn't get enough sleep. Whatever her reasoning was, it was pretty ridiculous."

If you really can't stand a rule that your mother has made, sit down and talk about it with her. Try writing a proposal listing why you think the rule should be changed and give suggestions for how you think it should be modified.

Ways to earn brownie points with your mom:

• On occasion, come home before curfew.

• Call your mother to check in and let her know if you and your friends have had a change of plans and will be going someplace different from where you had originally planned.

• Introduce your mother to the friends you like to spend time with.

• Agree to follow some rules that you would normally argue about.

When I was thirteen, I loved to talk on the phone. I would have stayed up all night talking to my best friend or my seventh-grade sweetheart, but my mom always made me get off the phone at 9 P.M. on school nights. This drove me crazy, and I couldn't figure out why she made this rule. I never went to bed at nine, so it wasn't like the phone was keeping me up, and we had call-waiting, so I wasn't tying up the line. Once I asked Mom why she always made me get off the phone at nine. "I just don't want you to be on the phone past nine," she said. This wasn't a sufficient answer for me. "I don't understand why," I argued, and she answered with the old "Because I'm the mother and I say so" line. I let it go for that night, but brought it up a few days later. Instead of whining, yelling, or arguing, I just kept planting seeds of suggestion about changing my "phone curfew." After giving her all the rationale behind letting me stay on the phone longer, she decided to get me my own telephone line. This made things easier for both of us; I got to talk on the phone whenever I wanted and she didn't have to worry about fighting me for the phone.

Keep your requests within reason and don't ask for something you know your mother won't agree to. If you don't want to have a curfew, but you know that your mother won't let you come in at any hour you choose, think of a compromise before you approach her. Instead of trying to get her to drop your curfew completely, ask to extend it an extra hour. When dealing with mothers and rules, sometimes pushing for less will get you more in the long run.

You may also be frustrated because your mother always seems to be making rules for no apparent reason. Talk to her about this. Ask her if she will include you in the rule making and if she would be willing to hear your input. Explain to her that you would feel much better about abiding by the rules if you were able to help make them. Reassure her that you aren't out to eliminate all rules, you just want to have your say.

My mother didn't make a lot of rules, but that didn't mean that I ran wild. We had an unwritten "respect code." When I left the house, I would tell her where I was going, whom I'd be with, and when I'd be home. Sometimes while I was out, I would call and check in just to let her know that I was okay.

This worked great for us because we made a joint effort. I respected my mother and what she expected of me, and she allowed me freedom to do things I wanted without a lot of restrictions. When my mom didn't want me to do something, she would express her objection by telling me why she didn't feel comfortable allowing me to do what I wanted. When I disagreed with her, I would express my feelings about the situation. Sometimes after hearing my side, she would feel better about letting me go and sometimes she wouldn't. We listened to each other and usually came to an agreement that satisfied both of us.

If you talk to your mother and she agrees to loosen her rules, make sure you follow the new ones. This will show her that you are mature and need less supervision. If you show your mom that you can respect her wishes, she will be more likely to give you more freedoms. You cannot control what rules your mother may make, you can only control your actions. You can choose to make living with your mother easy or difficult. If you break a rule, you must accept the consequences. If you

> *I would hate to let my mother down because I respect her so much. Hearing her say, "I'm so disappointed in you" is the worst punishment I could have.*
>
> *—Paige Clark, age sixteen*

want more "adult" privileges, you have to act more like an adult.

When I reached high school and had my own car, I started staying out later with my friends so my mom and I had to figure out a plan that would work for both of us. I told her it wouldn't make me happy to have a midnight curfew. Sometimes my friends and I sat around talking late or watching a movie. My mother told me that she worried when I was out late and couldn't sleep until I was home safely. So, we worked out a plan and decided I would tell her where I was going, what time she could expect me, and that I would call if I were going to be late. My mom always knew where I was and when to expect me home, and because I had a say in it, I never came home after I said I would. I was the only girl in my group of friends without a curfew, but I was usually home and in bed before midnight.

Who's in Charge?

I only remember having to step in and lay down the law to Amanda once during her teen years. She was fourteen years old and we'd been having an awful month. Not only was she talking back, arguing, and not cooperating, she was behaving as if she was the "queen of the castle." She was insulting, demanding, and acting as if I "owed" her. In the throes of "teenage-girl-syndrome," she was definitely getting on my nerves. I didn't like what was going on between us and didn't think she did either, but I wasn't sure how to handle it. My usual lectures, warnings, and attempts at conversation were not working.

I was trying my hardest to take into account raging hormones and the ups and downs of girlhood, but every contact we had was unpleasant. Something between us was off-kilter. Perhaps I'm allowing her to take advantage of my good nature, I thought to myself. I was tired of being tromped on and ignored, but I wasn't sure what action to take. I knew that whatever I did, it would call for all the "mother love" I could muster. She needed an attitude adjustment and I needed creative intervention and spiritual guidance.

I don't remember exactly what pushed me over the edge, but I do remember how I solved it. One day, she was demanding I do this and that for her and I told her that I didn't feel like doing anything for her because of her attitude toward me. She didn't like that and announced, "It's your duty as my mother."

All the saints in heaven must have been watching over me at that moment because I took a deep breath, bowed my head, asked for guidance, and then marched straight into her room. In my best firm and loving voice, without threats or lambasting, I said: "A mother owes a daughter three things: one, a roof over her head; two, food; and three, love. I'm very generous. You have a safe roof over your head and a lovely room of your own. You've never gone without food and even when I'm struggling financially, I willingly stock the kitchen with your favorite food and drink. And you have all of my love. I love you more than I can ever express and I always will. I don't owe you anything else. Everything else you have comes from my good graces. Treat me well and I will give you all I have. Treat me badly and you only get the required three."

For the first time in weeks she was speechless. There was no room for doubt; she knew where I stood. I felt great! Not only was I thinking clearly, I felt like dancing. I was talking in a friendly, warm manner. I wasn't upset or blaming her, I simply made my philosophy of mothering crystal-clear. I could tell by the look on her face that she understood and that she respected me for it. The atmosphere between us shifted immediately and there was no need for further discussion. I smiled at her and went to cook dinner.

In my high school everyone stays out all night for prom. Since I knew my mom would freak out if she knew this, I started talking with her months in advance. Finally, she agreed to let me stay at my date's house with four other couples. I guaranteed her that being at a house was a much safer place than a motel room.

—Katie Anderson, age seventeen

If you bungle raising your children, I don't think whatever else you do well matters very much.

—Jacqueline
Kennedy Onassis

Clearly stating my philosophy has not only helped her, it helps me. Whenever I'm in doubt about how I'm doing as her mother, I refer back to my theory. Since that fateful day, we've laughed together about my pronouncement and, although she's never said so, I think she agrees with my approach to my motherly obligations.

❀ Limits as Road Maps

If you've ever had to set limits for a strong-willed, high-spirited, sensitive teenage girl, you know that discipline is much more than establishing rules and handing out consequences. If it were that easy, mothers would have no hassles at all. You'd make the rules and she'd obey without question. There would be no room for discussion or negotiation. If she broke the rules, she'd be punished. End of story. Maybe in the "olden days" that's how they did it, but since most of us want a more satisfying connection with our daughters, we're willing to work toward a healthier, more inspiring way. Since we want our daughter to discover her inner voice—the true source of self-control and self-respect—we let her have her say. Letting her have her say, however, takes more ingenuity on our part, for it allows her to develop the art of negotiation, which, while it is an interpersonal skill she'll need to navigate all her relationships, can be trying when she practices it on us.

If you've already tried the stern approach, you know that strictness doesn't achieve the self-discipline you hope your daughter will have. If you're overly restrictive, she'll most likely rebel through her words, attitudes, and behavior. However, if you're completely lax and uninvolved, that can have harmful consequences as well. She may do things behind your back and become delinquent or she may become increasingly depressed and socially inadequate, lacking self-confidence because she hasn't had the guidance she needs. Giving her a voice in matters that affect her allows her to become an increasingly competent decision maker. Even though she's likely to make some poor choices as she learns, she will be able to go forward instead of feeling defeated.

Through counseling teenage girls and their mothers, I have discovered a majority of teenagers bristle at the idea of authority figures laying down rules. When I talk with girls about limits, I choose my words very carefully. I have found that they cooperate more willingly when I talk about the responsibilities of freedom. Teenage girls easily understand that with each freedom they gain, they also have added responsibility for taking care of that liberty.

Staying up later than they did last year is a freedom that they can have, as long as they can handle the responsibility that comes with that freedom. I asked a group of thirteen-year-olds what responsibilities went with the "staying up later" freedom. They agreed it was the "get up on time" responsibility. In joint sessions with mothers and daughters, I ask each to write down one freedom and the corresponding responsibilities. Fourteen-year-old Shana wanted the freedom of walking to a friend's house after school, so she and her mother listed the responsibilities that went along with this freedom. Shana listed four: Make sure Mom knows my plans, make sure my homework gets done in study hall before I go, call Mom when I get to my friend's house, and agree on a time I should be home. Her mother agreed that as long as Shana met her four responsibilities, she could have this freedom.

Positive limits are like a road map directing your daughter as she learns to create a wonderful life for herself. Have you ever taken a car trip and gone in the wrong direction even though you had a map? What did you do when you discovered your mistake? Most likely you turned around, read the map again, paid closer attention to the signposts, and found the road you should have taken in the first place. The consequence of taking the wrong turn was automatic: you had to turn around and your trip took more time then you expected. Still, something positive came out of the experience because you probably learned how to read the map more carefully or discovered a scenic, more enjoyable route.

Where do mothers learn
all the things they tell
their daughters not to do?

—Evan Esar

Good limits work the same way. They allow for learning, discovery, and for the mistakes that go along with gaining knowledge, experience, and common sense. Positive limits allow for enjoyment of life. If you punish your daughter for making ordinary mistakes, she will be thwarted in her learning. It's a balancing act. Punishing her too much means she can't enjoy her life; no limits at all means she won't have any direction.

It's not easy to set or enforce limits. No matter how appropriate the limits are, your daughter will test them. When she does, you have to decide how to respond. Are you going to let her learn by suffering the natural consequence or are you going to step in and take control before it gets to that point? When Alice discovered that Jill wasn't turning in her homework, she carefully considered her approach. Should she stand back and watch, knowing that if Jill got a low grade, the school would take her off the basketball team for a semester? Or should she step in and ground Jill until she improved her grade? Would it be better to talk with Jill one more time, or would she learn more by seeing the direct results of not doing her homework? Alice had to make a decision based on the approach that would be most beneficial for Jill's overall learning. Since her nagging wasn't working anyway, she decided to let the chips fall where they would. She backed off for the rest of the semester. Jill came very close to flunking the course, but when she realized the coach was serious about suspending her from the team, she negotiated with the teacher to make up her work and do extra work as well. With considerable effort, she was able to pull her grade up. Jill hasn't had any more trouble with grades since she learned to take this responsibility seriously and Alice says as long as she stays out of it, her daughter does better.

Setting limits requires considerable effort on your part. Some mothers want to have a good relationship so badly that they let their daughters walk all over them; some mothers shrink from their duties because it takes too much effort or they don't know where to begin; and others are overly strict, perhaps out of fear or anger. In my parenting classes, mothers agree that setting limits is uncomfortable because no one else can do it for you, no one can tell you what limits are appropriate or which ones will work best. You have to decide on your own based on your family, your circumstances, and your daughter's needs at the time.

With each limit ask yourself: What am I trying to teach my daughter by establishing this signpost? Does this limit help or hinder her learning?

✳ What about Grounding?

Girls who get grounded all the time become immune to it. "It's no big deal," they say.

If your daughter messes up and you automatically ground her, she never knows exactly why. She thinks you're overreacting or that you don't want to be bothered to understand her situation. If grounding is your only limit-setting tool, you aren't giving her a reason to think about the consequences of her actions.

Instead of grounding her, talk to her about the problem. Let her know that you're interested in her situation. When you explain how her actions are affecting you, she really has to think about her choices and learns to become responsible.

✳ What's a Mother to Do?

Use the Eight Principles of Responsible Freedom

Before you make rules about issues concerning your daughter, talk things over with her. Many mothers avoid talking with their daughters about their expectations, but the time you devote up front will save both of you disappointment and hard feelings in the long run. Knowing what your daughter is thinking about freedoms like curfews, car privileges, drinking, or dating will give you a better understanding of why your daughter insists on having the car every Friday and Saturday night, and will help you to come up with a solution that pleases both of you. When you involve your daughter, you may be surprised by how rational she can be. Tell your daughter she can have plenty of freedom as long as she knows her responsibilities and meets them.

Positive limits work very well with teenage girls when they are based on the following eight principles:

1. Choose your battles carefully. If you want the laundry done at 7 P.M. on Tuesday nights and she refuses again and again, before you make it an issue, ask yourself if this is the battle you want to fight to establish your mothering authority. What point do you want to make? The issue may not be about the undone laundry as much as it's about her lack of cooperation. Be sure you know what you're trying to teach your daughter. With something like chores, the best message you can impart is that cooperation makes life easier for both of you.

2. The most effective limits are delivered in small doses of friendly conversation, not lectures. "Honey, you haven't been meeting your responsibility of getting up in the morning, so I think you might not be ready for this 'staying up later' freedom."

3. Acknowledge her cooperation with plenty of affection, smiles, and praise.

4. Face undesirable behavior with positive conversation. Saying "I'm disappointed you're flunking math, but I know you can turn it around" is more likely to get the problem-solving process started than to scold, "At this rate you'll never graduate." "How can I help you?" is better than "You didn't even try; you're grounded until the end of the semester."

5. Enlist her cooperation in finding a solution. Making rules is simple but enforcing them is not so easy. If your daughter decides not to cooperate with your rules or your punishments, you're in a losing battle. Saying "I

want to let you go to the party, but last time you stayed out past your curfew, so what can we do so we both are comfortable?" includes your daughter in the decision-making process and she'll be more likely to cooperate.

If it isn't illegal or immoral give it your blessing.

—Virginia Satir

6. Don't enforce a consequence that will make you miserable as well. Telling your daughter she can't go to the dance you've both been planning makes no logical sense. Girls respond better to positive conversation and brief explanations of what changes you expect.

7. A good balance for teenage girls is plenty of "Yes" with some "No." As one teenage girl said, "My mom mostly says 'Yes.' If she doesn't agree with me, then we talk it over. Then when she says 'No' I can usually accept it, even if I don't agree."

8. Always keep your eye on the big picture. What are you trying to accomplish?

✳ Questions for Daughters

How do you feel when your mother does the following things? Do these things help you in any way or are they a waste of time? Why?

1. When she tells you you've disappointed her

2. When she grounds you

3. When she ignores you or gives you the cold shoulder

4. When she takes away your car privileges

5. When she won't let you talk on the telephone

6. When she talks to you about the type of behavior she expects

If you have broken a rule, what do you think is the best way to make up for it? Why?

❋ Questions for Mothers

1. What rules and limits did your mother enforce when you were a teenager? What disciplinary measures did your mother use with you? Were they effective? How did these rules affect your relationship with your mother?

2. What do you think is the purpose of making rules? How do you feel about the rules you make? How does your daughter feel?

3. What do you do when your daughter breaks a rule? Has this kept her from breaking the same rule again?

4

Talking about Difficult Subjects

I Can't Tell Her

I can't believe it," I said, amazed at the news my friend had just given me. I'd never faced an issue this big, and I had no idea what I could do to help. "What are you going to do?"

"I don't know," Robin said, her eyes filling with tears. "I don't understand how this happened. We've always been so careful."

Putting my arm around her, I searched for something helpful to say, but couldn't find the right words. "Have you told Andy yet?" I asked.

"No. I know that he'll freak out and I don't know how to bring it up." Robin struggled to fight back her tears. "I can't just come out in the middle of lunch and say, 'Hey Andy, I'm pregnant.'"

"Are you going to tell your mom?"

Robin burst out sobbing. "I don't know if I can. It would just kill her, and she would be so disappointed in me."

I tried to think of a way to help, but I didn't know what to say or whom to turn to.

"I'm only seventeen," Robin managed to get out between her sobs. "I'm not supposed to have to worry about things like this. I'm so scared."

"I'm so sorry," I replied. "I wish that there was something I could do. You've got to talk to somebody. I don't think you can deal with this all on your own."

A study by the Alan Guttmacher Institute suggests that the most effective pregnancy prevention programs are those that include sex education, skills for decision making and communicating with partners, and access to family planning.

✳ Hiding from Mom

One of the biggest issues that girls hide from their mothers is the fact that they are having sex. You probably have had sex education and AIDS awareness at school and know about the many risks and consequences that go along with being sexually active. You may know all about pregnancy and have heard all the statistics about AIDS, but have you ever really stopped to think about what you would do if it ever happened to you? Are you and your partner emotionally ready to handle the pressures that go along with having sex? Have you talked about what would happen if you got pregnant or if one of you got an STD? Although these thoughts may scare you a little, I know they probably will not stop you from having sex.

I am not trying to preach to you or tell you you're too young or that sex is bad. I just want you to really think about it, look into your heart, and ask yourself, "Why am I having sex?" and "Am I really ready to handle all of the consequences that may go along with my actions?" Some teenagers are having sex for the right reasons and are very mature and responsible about it; however, there are a large number of girls who are not. They have sex for the wrong reasons—maybe they feel pressure or having sex makes them feel loved, and they may think, "It won't happen to me."

I know that teenagers aren't always as careful as they think they're being. I have seen girls go crazy with worry when they missed their periods. I've gone with my girlfriends to Planned Parenthood to get the "morning after" pill because they got too caught up in the heat of the moment and didn't use protection. I have comforted girls who were breaking down in tears, desperately wishing that they hadn't had sex so soon.

All of these things happened without their mothers knowing a thing. Ideally, I would tell you to talk to your mother about sex, or any other big issues you're hiding from her, but realistically, I know that many of you won't. However, if you are keeping something big from your mother, like the fact that you are sexually active, there's bound to be a strain on your relationship because when you try to hide something, you are not being honest with your mother or yourself.

Have you noticed how much effort it takes to hide something from your mother? You have to sneak around behind her back and watch what you say. You should ask yourself why you hide these things from your mother. Is it because she isn't easy to talk to and would freak out if she knew what you were doing? Or is it because you feel guilty and are worried that she would be ashamed?

Having sex isn't the only issue that is hard for teenage girls to talk about with their mothers. Maybe you have become heavily involved in drinking, or you've really slacked off in school and are now failing some of your classes. Maybe you have an eating disorder, got caught shoplifting, are extremely depressed, or got a speeding ticket. These issues are not easy to bring up with your mother because they show that you have weaknesses. Yet these are huge issues, and nobody can deal with these things alone.

It's hard to let your mother know that you have made a mistake. I am the type of person who likes to handle everything on my own and I don't want to let my mother down by admitting to her that I have really messed up. However, keeping big secrets from her isn't easy either. One time, when I first got my driver's license, I gave some friends a ride home after school. When I was backing out of their driveway, I hit the gas a little too hard, and ran into the neighbor's fence across the street, knocking it to the ground and denting the back of my car. Not knowing what to do, I sped away. I knew that if I told my mom she would be furious at me, so I told her that somebody hit me in the parking lot while I was in school. She believed me, but I was tormented that she would find out the truth. Lying and keeping this secret from my mother was harder than the punishment that I would have received had I told her the truth.

✹ *What's a Daughter to Do?*

Use Your Good Judgment

If you ever find yourself in serious trouble, you need to go to your mother. I know that telling your mother that you've messed up can be very difficult, but you don't want to get yourself in over your head. Although asking for help may be hard, you will save yourself a lot of grief in the long run.

"One night I was at a party with my friends, and we had all been drinking," recalls Sydney. "After a couple of hours, the guy whose house it was got mad because there were too many people there and he told us that we had to leave. I had driven my car and had planned on sobering up before I drove home. I knew that at that point I couldn't drive home. None of my friends were in any better shape to drive than me. There were some people there who could have taken us home, but in my gut, I felt like I should call my mom. So, even though I knew that she was going to be so mad at me, I called and asked her for a ride. It was really hard to face my mom like that, and even though she was upset with me, she was much happier that I called her instead of trying to drive home."

When you find yourself in a bad situation, use your best judgment.

Don't do something that you know isn't right just because you are scared to talk to your mother. Your mother may be upset and she may get a little angry, but having your mother upset is better than getting yourself into more trouble, getting hurt, or, worst of all, dying. Say to your mother, "Mom, you may be disappointed in me, but I really need your help and understanding right now." Let her know that you know you've made a mistake and realize you can't handle the situation on your own.

If you are too scared to talk to her, try writing her a letter and giving it to her before you leave for school, or ask her to read it while you are at soccer practice or cheerleading. That way she has time alone to think clearly or talk with a friend or your father before you two try to work out the problem. Some problems are too big for you to handle on your own, but nothing is too big for you to work out together.

You may really feel that you are unable to ask your mother for help. If so, try getting help from somebody else. Go to somebody that you trust and think will be able to help. Try using a friend's mother as the go-between for you and your mother. Whatever you do, when you know that you have gotten yourself in over your head, don't try to solve your problem alone. More than anything, you should be safe and do what you know is right.

You Should Have Known Better!

When Amanda was fourteen, she came to me just after I had gotten into bed one night. "Mom, I've done something awful." I knew from the scared look on her face that something was seriously wrong. My heart leaped to my throat and I sat straight up in bed. "Whaaat?" I stuttered, and even before she could say one word, I was already imaging the worst. Trembling and sobbing, she struggled to tell me what had happened.

After she'd started riding the bus on her own to go to the mall, it wasn't long before she and her girlfriend met a boy there. They ate French fries together and walked around the mall. Since he was nineteen, Amanda fibbed a little and told him she was sixteen. She thought he was cute and since he seemed nice, she gave him her phone number.

That was the beginning of her nightmarish experience with a slick-talking stranger. The boy had been calling her for weeks, making lewd comments and demanding that she meet him. She'd been trying to handle it on her own. At first she was friendly, but soon learned that he was much older than he'd originally told her. She told him she wasn't allowed to date, thinking he would stop calling, but he didn't. He called often, demanded to know where she lived, and he was becoming more persistent. She hadn't wanted to tell me about it because she was worried that I'd be mad at her and wouldn't let her go to the mall ever again. Now she realized she was in over her head and needed my assistance.

I admit my first inclination was to say, "You should know better than that." I was tempted to shame her with "See what you've done now," hoping that her embarrassment would somehow prevent her from making the same mistake in the future. I wanted to shake my head in disbelief at her poor judgment. But I didn't do any of those things. Perhaps because I could see that she was so shaken I was able to put my fear and anger aside and really be there for her.

"When was the last time he called?" I asked. "Just a few minutes ago," she replied. As the phone rang again, I asked, "Maybe I should answer it?"

"No!" She was adamant. "What should I do?"

"Tell him in your most powerful voice never to call here again and hang up."

The phone rang, she ran to answer it, and I heard her sternly warn him, "Don't ever call here again!" before hanging up. As she stood by the phone, the color came back to her face. The phone didn't ring again and she looked at me in amazement that she could have handled it so swiftly.

"Are you okay?" I asked. She nodded. "That was scary," I said. "Honey, I'm glad you came to me. No matter what kind of trouble you're in, I want you to know that you can always come to me." She went to bed without saying a word, but it took me much longer to calm down. My mind was racing with all the close calls and dangers I could imagine. I wanted to protect her from her own mistakes and shelter her from any unnecessary pain and suffering. I was angry that she put herself in that position in the first place, and I was afraid to think of what might have happened had she not come to me. I fell asleep reminding myself to have a serious mother-daughter talk with her.

✳ What's a Mother to Do?

You Can Come to Me

The phone call incident made me realize that I had neglected to tell Amanda *directly* that if she were in trouble, she could always come to me. Up until then I'd assumed she knew that she could. As a child she'd come to me with many problems—-a disagreement with a playmate, a difficult teacher, a low grade. But this incident made me recognize that the stakes were now much higher for both of us. With alcohol, drugs, sex, parties, cars, and strangers mixed in, the consequences could be quite serious. Amanda knew my expectations for her behavior and she knew that if she got too far out of line, I could get mad and lower the boom. Until now, that's what I relied on to keep her safe. Was that enough? I thought about it and decided it was not.

I never expected Amanda to get into serious trouble, but I hadn't anticipated that at fourteen, she'd give a strange boy her phone number either. I was glad she finally came to me and I decided to tell her so. I needed to emphasize that I would stand beside her and that she could always count on me to help her. I needed to explain to her that even if I got angry, I would get over it and help her out.

We needed to talk without distractions so I planned to bring up the subject in the car when we were driving into town one afternoon. At home, she might slough me off before I had a chance to say all that I needed to say. In the car, she was a captive audience. I was careful to open the discussion in a non-threatening manner. I told her about a young woman I had once counseled in a hospital who had given birth in the emergency room. Her mother was in the waiting room and didn't even know her daughter was pregnant. The fifteen-year-old girl was giving birth and at the same time begging me not to tell her mother. I also talked about a seventeen-year-old who had gotten into serious legal trouble and hadn't gone to her mother because she was so afraid of her mother's wrath. We talked about several girls Amanda knew who were flunking out of school and how the last ones to know were their mothers. We both knew girls who were having unsafe sex. They never went to their mothers about it because they were so afraid of their mothers' disapproval that they'd do anything to avoid it.

Topics girls have difficulty talking to their mothers about:

1. Sex
2. Bad grades
3. Drugs or alcohol
4. Speeding tickets or any other trouble with the police
5. Fear that their parents might get a divorce and/or remarry
6. Any trouble they've gotten into or big mistakes they've made

Whatever the reason, there are thousands of girls who won't take their troubles to their mothers. Recently, there have been news accounts of young women giving birth, then either purposely or accidentally killing the child. The mother didn't know her daughter was pregnant until she was arrested! I wonder if these girls' mothers ever told them, "Please come to me if you are ever in trouble."

I don't know all the reasons such things happen, but I think we need to let our daughters know that they can always come to us and that we mean it. To me, the most important mother-daughter talk you can have is the one when you let her know that she can count on you—no matter what.

✳ The Beauty of True Communication

My friend Ellen, the mother of two teenage girls, told me once, "I'm not very close to my mother, which is strange because I talk to her just about every day and take her out to lunch, dinner, or shopping at least once a week. But I can't say that I really enjoy her company; I do those things because she's alone and I feel an obligation. She means well, and would be very hurt to discover that I feel this way. I'm wondering if it's a generational thing. Was there something about the way that mothers were encouraged to raise their daughters back when we were teenagers that led to an estrangement? I've never had this with my own daughters and I think our relationship has stayed good because I really listen."

Listen and *silent* have the same letters.

Perhaps that's a clue that when you're silent, you're better able to listen.

A mother–daughter relationship cannot thrive on the mere passing of information between you. It requires genuine, heartfelt, open-minded listening to what your daughter has to say. It's easy to give our kids the feeling we're not listening. Fifteen-year-old Angie said, "I wish my mother would listen more. I know she hears what I'm saying and can repeat it back to me, but she never *hears* me."

A genuine mother-daughter relationship is based on earnest communication. It's pure joy to have a "plugged in" conversation that flows easily and to be appreciated and understood by each other. Even though you've known each other for more than ten years, it's heartening to visit as if you're getting to know each other for the very first time. Now that your daughter is a teenager, in a way that's exactly what you're doing—getting to know her as a young woman. When you also honestly reveal yourself, she's seeing you not as mother but as a person with history.

Remember your teenage days and share your coming-of-age stories with your daughter. You may not think she wants to hear your stories, but she does. Amanda loves hearing stories about my past— the boys I dated, the embarrassing things that happened to me, and the fights I had with my mother. It shows her that I'm a real person. Hearing these stories takes away the harsh viewpoint that girls so often have, and shows a more gentle and more interesting side of their mothers.

Your stories also help her understand that she's having normal feelings. Teenage girls are full of emotions they've never experienced before. They often find themselves depressed for no reason, they doubt themselves, they long for more meaning in their lives. These new thoughts and feelings are scary and hard to handle. It's difficult for a girl to turn to her friends with these big issues because her friends are experiencing similar feelings. Because these feelings and ideas are so new, teenage girls are not yet aware that they are perfectly healthy. Hearing that her mother has gone through many of the same trials helps your daughter know she's not crazy. Sixteen-year-old Alicia said, "One very reassuring thing that my mother said to me was, 'I'd be worried about you if you weren't having these feelings.'"

Don't freak out about the content of your daughter's conversation with you. One way that she matures in her values is by thinking out loud. She might say something that she doesn't really believe as a way of asserting her independence and gaining practice in presenting her point of view. I've known girls to vehemently argue the opposite point of view with their mothers while privately agreeing with them. For example, Janey said to her mother, "I don't think it says anything about a person's character if they smoke." Her mother immediately said, "That's ridiculous! How can you say that? It shows stupidity." Janey told me later, "I don't really think smoking is cool, but my mother is always talking about how awful kids are that smoke. She doesn't know that Grant, whom she thinks is perfect, smokes. She never listens to my opinions. She's worried that I'll start smoking, but just because some of my friends do doesn't mean I will. I was just talking to her."

By not allowing Janey to state her own thoughts, both mother and daughter lost the opportunity to have a friendly disagreement. Insisting that your daughter see it your way does nothing to change her mind or teach her to articulate her point of view. It's better to have her thoughts out in the open than to badger her into acquiescing. It's better to show her that you can disagree and still get along.

✳ How to Have a Mother-Daughter Talk

Tips for Mothers

1. The best place for heart-to-heart talks is often away from the house. Arrange for talks at a quiet restaurant, on a walk, or in the car.

2. Stay centered. Don't let your emotions rule you. You have to be the model for making sound decisions.

3. Be available when she's willing to talk. That might mean midnight powwows. Even if you'd rather be sleeping, it worth it to stay up for a girl-to-girl chat when the stories that she wants to share are fresh in her mind.

4. Let your daughter lead the conversation and don't change the subject. Don't ask too many questions and don't rush in with all the answers.

5. Give your daughter your full attention. Drop what you're doing and concentrate on what she is saying and feeling. Do more listening, less talking.

6. Be lighthearted. In general, girls are more willing to talk with mothers with whom they can laugh and joke.

Reminders for Daughters

1. If you're in trouble, write or tell your mom, "Mom, you may be disappointed in me, but I need your help—I'm in trouble."

2. If you can't confide in your mother alone, ask a trusted adult to help you talk with her.

3. Although it may be hard to get help, you will feel much better once you have. Some issues are too big to handle alone.

4. Remember—everyone messes up. You are not a bad person for making a mistake or getting into trouble. It's all part of growing up, and the key is to learn from your experience.

5

Healing
Your Relationship

No Big Deal

"Shawna! Would you please come here for a minute?" yelled Shawna's mother, Nancy. She dreaded the upcoming conversation but knew she couldn't put it off any longer.

Shawna didn't move. "What do you want? I'm busy doing homework."

"Fine, I'll come up there," her mother said. Turning down her stereo, Shawna quickly jumped up from her bed, hurried to her desk, and opened a book to look like she was studying. Her mother entered the room and Shawna could tell by the look on her face that she was upset.

"What's up?" Shawna asked, pretending to read Biology.

"Can I talk to you for a minute?"

"Talk," Shawna said, keeping her eyes focused on her book.

Nancy sighed, "Could you stop reading for just a minute?"

"I really have a lot to do, Mom. I don't have time for a big talk right now."

"I think you can take a few minutes to talk to me about something important."

With a big sigh, Shawna closed her book and looked up, "Fine! What do you want?"

"Are these yours?" Nancy asked, holding up a pack of cigarettes and wine coolers. "I found them in your car today when I took it in to get the oil changed."

"Why were you snooping through my stuff?" Shawna yelled.

"I wasn't snooping through anything. I was putting groceries in the trunk and I saw these sitting in there. Where do you get cigarettes and empty wine coolers?"

"Around. Why does it matter?'

"It matters because I'm worried about you," her mother said, trying to get Shawna to understand her concern. "Smoking isn't good for you and carrying open bottles of alcohol is illegal. I worry that you're getting too involved in bad things."

"I don't know what you're talking about. A lot of people smoke and they're not mine anyway. It really isn't that big of a deal." Shawna looked back down at her book and said, "I have to finish studying."

Her mother sighed and left the room. Later Nancy told her best friend, "I just don't know what to do, Joyce. Shawna is completely out of control. Just today I found cigarettes and wine coolers in her car and when I asked her about them, she completely clammed up. Her grades are falling at school, she breaks every rule that we make, and she hangs out with a couple of girls that I know are bad influences on her. Whenever I try to talk to her, she pushes me away and won't talk about anything."

"Have you tried getting help from a counselor or something?"

"Yes, I've been working with a counselor, but Shawna refuses to go with me. I just don't know how to handle her any more. I'm at a complete loss."

✳ Out of Control

If you're a mother of a teenage girl who is on the verge or already is out of control, or if your relationship with your daughter is on the rocks, there are steps you can take to bridge the widening gulf between you. However, before you decide what action to take, it helps to understand how you got to this point in the first place. By identifying the reasons for her undesirable behavior, you'll be more apt to find the keys to correcting it. Out-of-control behavior is a symptom of deeper problems. If you treat just the symptoms, the underlying trouble will still be there and will eventually erupt again. By discovering its roots, you can repair the unseen damage and reestablish a healthy and satisfying relationship. Ask yourself what might have caused this rift between you and your daughter and when the trouble began.

I have counseled hundreds of mothers and daughters whose relationships were badly damaged and getting worse. For the healing to begin, it was important for the mother to understand what part she had in fueling the fires of defiance. Ask yourself what you have done to contribute to the mess. If you're willing to take an honest look at yourself, you will find some answers.

Fourteen-year-old Kyla was flunking out of eighth grade, sneaking out at night, smoking, and answering "Whatever" to any of her mother's attempts at conversation.

Her mom, Lois, came to counseling eager to fix her daughter's problems, but did not understand that their relationship also needed healing. Kyla's acting out was a reflection of the breakdown between them. While Lois couldn't stop her daughter's smart comments, bad grades, or smoking, she could take charge of the way she responded to Kyla. Instead of jumping to conclusions and second-guessing, which Lois admitted was her way of staying on top of potential problems, Lois told Kyla, "I'm worried about you and I've been trying to control you. I want to stop our tug-of-war and pull with you, not against you." By acknowledging that she was part of the problem, Lois allowed Kyla to stop pulling so hard in the opposite direction.

Rebellion takes many forms, from harmless talking back to defiant acts of drug and alcohol abuse or sexual activity. As a mother, you have to determine which acts fall under the healthy category and which cross the line into unsafe territory.

Talking back is a clue that your daughter is in the throes of her first teenage rebellion. It signals that, while she's not yet articulate enough to express herself effectively, she's struggling to find ways to assert her autonomy. By thirteen, she's beginning to see the world from a new perspective, and talking back is her unskilled way of presenting her new self to her mother.

According to Philips Consumer Communications, parents think that their teens' top priorities are fun, friends, and appearance. Teens report their top priorities are their future, schoolwork, and family.

Navigating your way through the minefields of the talking-back stage is one of many skills you'll need to parent your adolescent. In order to reconnect with an out-of-control daughter, you'll have to deal effectively with the talking-back issue.

Linda brought her fourteen-year-old daughter Drew to counseling. Drew was flunking eighth grade and talking back to teachers. She was lying, shoplifting, and had already had sex with at least two different boys. Linda was at the end of her rope and joined a support group of other parents who were struggling with the same issues. But the standard "Get tougher" advice was not working.

I have always grown from my problems and challenges; from the things that don't work out, that's when I've really learned.

—Carol Burnett

When they came to counseling, Drew was so antagonistic toward her mother that she refused to talk in front of her. No matter what Linda said, Drew either gave her a mother a dirty look, snapped a smart remark, or talked back. Linda handled Drew's talking back by giving her daughter a stern look, delivering a lecture, and threatening, "Don't talk to me in that tone of voice." It was nothing new for Linda to deliver an ultimatum that she couldn't enforce, and it was typical for Drew to retort, "I'd like to see you try." They were on a merry-go-round of destruction, getting nowhere fast. For things to improve, both mother and daughter had to change how they talked with one another.

✳ What's a Mother to Do?

Let the Healing Begin

While some people claim that when a daughter is rebellious her mother is to blame, this usually is not true. Blaming the daughter for the difficulties does nothing to resolve the situation either. There are many forces at play, and many circumstances contribute to the predicament. When a relationship is shaky or strained, there's bound to be something in both mother and daughter that desperately needs healing. As the mother and the adult, you have to make the overture toward this end. If you've done it before, you must do it again, for there might be another angle.

I can't tell you how often mothers attending my parenting workshops complain about their daughters' attitudes. The mothers are out of ideas on how to turn their relationship around, and they ask for other mothers' input. However, as soon as a suggestion is made, the upset mother begins voicing objections. She admits that what she's doing isn't working, yet she's already decided that the suggestion being made won't work either. She's certain that she's tried everything, and usually appears as rebellious and uncooperative as her daughter.

These negative stances won't get you out of the rut. Even if you've tried everything you can think of, that doesn't mean there isn't a solution. Often we are so close to our own problems that we can't find the obvious answers. But if you're willing to stay open-minded and seek help, the answer will come.

Healing messages daughters need to hear:

- You've made a mistake. You can fix it.
- I will help you.
- What can we do?
- It's over now. We can start fresh.
- I know you are sorry. I forgive you.
- I made a mistake. I'm sorry. Will you forgive me?
- What can we learn?

❊ What You Can Do to Start Repairing a Damaged Relationship

1. Let your daughter know she has a right to be upset and that she has a right to express her opinions. Tell her that you need her help to understand. Ask her to tell you what is troubling her.

2. Say to her, "I can listen better when you talk to me respectfully. I will also speak respectfully to you."

3. Consider the big picture. Don't make a big deal out of her tone of voice. Focus on what she's trying to explain, not how she is saying it.

4. Get outside opinions, but be sure they apply to your situation. Following the advice of friends who don't understand the subtleties of your situation can get you into more trouble. A mother whose daughter was out of control came for counseling and said, "I read lots of parenting books and tried to do what they suggested. When that didn't work, I talked to friends and followed their advice. Unfortunately, I didn't listen to my own

common sense. I threw my own intuition aside and now things are worse. If I had listened to myself and my daughter in the first place we might not be in this mess."

5. The "fix my daughter" approach won't work. Both parties have to be willing to negotiate and find solutions they both can live with. There are times when there's nothing you can do to get your daughter to cooperate except wait until she's ready. If your daughter obstinately refuses to work with you, realize that you can't control her behavior, but you can control your own. As the mother, you can make the changes you feel are necessary, but you may have to wait for your daughter to come around on her own.

How Did This Happen?

Have you ever thought about how your life turned out the way it has? Did you ever notice how from kindergarten through junior high everybody was pretty much on an equal level? You all wore the same type of clothes and enjoyed doing the same types of things. Then, somewhere along the line, either late middle school or early high school, people start to develop their own personalities. That's when you begin to notice two very distinct groups: the "good" crowd and the "bad" crowd. At one point, almost everybody was considered to be a "good" kid, but now people have strayed away from that label. Your peers start breaking rules, lying to their parents, smoking, or drinking, and some have become completely out of control. Perhaps you have.

I am not saying that if you smoke, drink, and have sex then you are a bad person. Practically every teenage girl has broken a rule or experimented with smoking or alcohol and lied to her parents about it. I have occasionally gone behind my mother's back and done things she wouldn't have liked, I have lied to her and snuck out of the house at night, but mostly out of curiosity and the excitement of experimentation and not anything more serious. Yet some girls take this experimenting and rebelling to a more risky level. They lie to their parents and teachers and rarely abide by *any* rules. Their attitude is one of complete rebellion, and they have lost control with their mothers and themselves.

If you realize that you are in a state of complete rebellion, you may want to ask yourself what has caused you to get there and why you feel the need to lie and break your mother's rules.

Maybe it started as innocent experimentation when you were younger. Maybe you started by smoking one cigarette, drinking one beer, or lying to your mother about where you were going and whom you'd be with. Eventually you became so caught up in it that you're not even sure how you got yourself here. Or maybe you made a conscious decision to rebel; maybe you deliberately chose to go against your mother and do things that you know would make her worried and angry.

"My mother always wants things her way," says seventeen-year-old Stacy. "I don't always want to live my life the way that my mom thinks I should. She makes all kinds of rules and threatens to punish me if I don't do what she says. What she doesn't understand is that she can't control my life, and I'm going to do what I want regardless of the rules she makes."

Fourteen-year-old Brooke says, "My sister is perfect. She gets straight A's, she is involved with everything at school, she's beautiful and has a boyfriend. I'm nothing like her, and my mom can't accept the fact that my interests are different from my sister's. I guess I feel like I have to rebel to make my mom understand that I am my own person."

✳ What's a Daughter to Do?

Look Inside Yourself

Why do you feel the need to rebel against your mother? Has she hurt you in some way? Are you angry about something? Maybe your mother is forcing you to be someone you aren't. Maybe your mother doesn't allow you to express feelings and thoughts that are different from hers, and rebelling is the only way that you know how to show you are different. Maybe your rebellion is a cry for help, for attention, or for love. Most of the girls I have known who are completely rebellious had something missing in their relationship with their mothers. Perhaps your feelings have been deeply hurt in some way, a way that you might not even understand.

William Frey, research director of Health Partner's Research Center in St. Paul, Minnesota, believes that shedding tears may help the body flush out some harmful chemicals produced under stress. Frey, who's been studying crying since 1979, says it's healthy to cry.

Not only is rebellion hard for your mother to handle, it isn't healthy for you. It probably doesn't make you happy to have such a broken relationship with your mother, and probably you wish things could be different. Trying to understand your feelings and learning to communicate them are the first steps in creating a better relationship with your mother. To understand your own actions, you must be completely honest with yourself. Step back for a minute and look at the things you do. Has your rebellion gotten you the things you want in life? What satisfaction do you get from breaking rules and rebelling against your mother? Are you happy with the way you live your life? Is there anything you'd like to change?

Changing your life and your relationship with your mother is possible. However, the most important thing is that you and your mother should *both* be willing to change directions and keep your hearts and minds open. You must listen and try to understand one another. Simply saying "I want things to be different" is not enough. You need to be ready to work together and be willing to forgive not only your mother

Be open to wisdom wher-
ever it appears—even if it
comes from your mother.

—*anonymous*

but yourself as well. Change is not easy. You have to work at it every day and realize it could take months or even years before you are able to have a good relationship with your mother.

A friend of mine used to complain that her mother was too controlling. She rebelled against everything her mother said, and the two of them fought constantly. When my friend asked me for advice, I told her that maybe she should stop fighting with her mother. Her response was "I'm not changing until my mother does." This stubborn attitude will not help anything.

Do whatever you can to clear up any hurt feelings between you and your mother. Maybe you should go to family therapy together. If you find your mother isn't willing to change, you should get help on your own. You need to talk with somebody about your behavior. Try talking to an adult whom you trust and who cares about you. It could be a teacher, a coach, a school counselor, a youth group leader—these are all people who are there to help you. Talking about your feelings will help you a lot, and it is okay to ask for help if you don't think that you can work things out alone.

❀ A Five-Day Healing Process for Mothers and Daughters

A relationship that has been broken for years will not heal in a mere five days, but following these steps will get you headed in a positive direction. For this process to work, both of you must participate. If your intention is to get the process over as quickly as possible, you will not succeed in healing. If your intention is to heal the misunderstandings and problems between you, this process will be very effective.

Day 1

Ask yourself if you are ready to heal your relationship with your mother/daughter. If you answer "Yes," you are ready to continue. If you answer "No," or are not quite sure, reread this chapter and chapter 2, on your evolving relationship. Focus your attention on your desire to heal your relationship for the entire day. Say a prayer asking for guidance and healing.

Day 2

Complete this questionnaire and write down your answers.

1. Briefly describe your relationship with one another.
2. What have *you* done to contribute to the mess you're in?
3. What would make your relationship more satisfying for you?
4. What do *you* want your mother/daughter to do differently?
5. What does your mother/daughter want you to do differently?
6. What prevents you from having your desired relationship now?
7. What are you willing to do to make your relationship better?
8. What other things might *you* do to improve your relationship?

Day 3

Set aside an uninterrupted hour to go over your questionnaire together. (It may not take that long, but set aside that time anyway.) Flip a coin to determine who goes first. The first person reads each question out loud and gives her answers slowly. The second person listens without interrupting or asking questions, and no rebuttals or comments are allowed.

When the first person has completed answering the questions, the second person does the same. The first person now listens without talking or asking questions. When the second person has completed answering the questions, thank each other for participating in the process.

Day 4

Begin doing one thing differently to make your relationship better. Keep in mind the things your mother/daughter has asked you to do differently. Perhaps your mother has asked you not to swear or play your music so loud. Perhaps your daughter has asked you not to listen into her phone calls or wants you to knock before entering her room. Making a small change goes a long way in showing the other person you are sincere in your desire to heal your relationship.

Amanda hated it when I asked her questions about her day immediately when she arrived home from school. I knew this bothered her, but I kept doing it until she blew up at me. Since I wanted our relationship to improve, I knew I needed to change. From that day on, I didn't ask her questions when she walked in the door. Instead I let her come to me. After that, instead of going immediately to her room, she started hanging out in the kitchen and chatting with me.

Day 5

1. Do something special for your mother/daughter, but don't tell her about it. Perhaps you can volunteer to do the dishes after dinner. One mother removed the time restriction she had placed on telephone use.

2. Say something kind to each other.

3. Appreciate yourself for all that you are doing and for being a loving person.

Repeat this healing process until you can honestly say to yourself that healing has taken place.

6

Trust Is Where It's At!

What about This, What about That?

"Can I spend the night at Andrea's house?" asked Erica. She took a deep breath. Everytime she asked her mom to do something, Erica had to go through the third degree before she could get an answer from her mother.

Her mother looked up from the book she was reading. "Have you finished your homework?" she asked.

"I've done some," Erica answered. "But it's Friday. I still have the rest of the weekend to do it."

"You shouldn't put it all off to the last minute," her mother sighed. "You won't get it all done if you wait until Sunday night."

"Yes I will," Erica pleaded. "I don't have that much. Please just let me stay the night over there."

"Why don't you girls stay over here?" her mother asked. "We can go rent a movie, and there's all that leftover pizza in the fridge that you can eat."

Erica was getting frustrated with her mother. "We stayed here last time and we want to go in her hot tub tonight."

"Are her parents going to be home? I want to call and talk with her parents."

"They're home, Mom. I promise. You don't need to call."

Her mother insisted, "I won't let you stay over there unless you let me talk to her parents."

Although she was embarrassed, Erica agreed and dialed the number for her mother. After talking to Andrea's parents for five minutes and making sure the girls would not leave the house and would be in bed at a reasonable hour, Erica's mother agreed to let her stay the night.

As she was packing her things, Erica's mother stood in the doorway of her room and asked, "You aren't going to have boys over, are you?"

"No, mother," Erica said, wishing her mother would be satisfied. "We're not having boys over, but I don't see why it would matter if we did. We're fourteen; I think that's old enough to hang out with boys."

"I mean it, Erica. I don't want you in that hot tub late at night with a bunch of boys. If I find out that you two were up with boys until all hours of the night, I'm going to be very angry."

Trying to remain calm, Erica said, "Mom, we won't have boys over. How come every time I want to go some place with a friend, you have list of things that I can't do? It's like you don't trust me or something."

"I trust you," her mother said. "I just want to make sure that you don't give me a reason not to trust you."

Erica sighed. "There's Andrea," she said, hearing a knock at the door. "I gotta go."

Grabbing her overnight bag and pillow, Erica ran to meet her friend at the door. Her mother followed close behind, reminding her daughter, "You call me when you get over there and remember to thank her parents for coming and picking you up."

"Okay," Erica said and opened the door to leave with her friend. As the girls walked down the driveway, Erica's mother yelled after her, "I'm coming to pick you up at 10 A.M. tomorrow morning to go shopping, so make sure you get enough sleep!"

※ *Are You Trustworthy?*

Have you ever noticed how the girls with the strictest mothers are the ones who are the most rebellious? The mothers who don't trust their daughters have the wildest, most untrustworthy daughters. It seems logical that the girls who don't behave in a trustworthy manner shouldn't be trusted. However, I think it happens the other way around: a mother doesn't trust her daughter first, so her daughter doesn't act trustworthy. From what I've noticed, the daughter becomes what the mother expects her to be.

My mother has always trusted me. At fourteen, she allowed me to have friends over to our house even if she wasn't home. When I was sixteen, she allowed me to stay home alone when she went on a book tour for five days. My mother always made it perfectly clear that she trusted me, so I never gave her a reason not to trust me. When my mom would leave me home alone, other mothers would tell me, "If you were my daughter, I would never trust you to stay home alone." This always made me laugh inside because when my mother left town, I never once had a party, while their daughters, forced to stay with relatives, figured out how to sneak back into the house and had parties behind their parents' backs.

Mothers show their trust in different ways. Some mothers give their daughters large amounts of freedom from the beginning, until they do something to make their mothers lose that trust. Other mothers make their daughters earn trust by passing "tests" that show they can be trusted.

If you want your mother to trust you, you must be trustworthy. Showing your mother that she can trust you means respecting the rules you have made together, telling her the truth, and not doing things behind her back.

Krista often sneaks around behind her mother's back and lies to her. Telling her mother she's going to stay at a friend's house, she actually stays at her boyfriend's house when his parents are gone. Krista hasn't given her mother a reason to trust her, yet she still complains about her lack of freedom. She says, "My mom has never caught me lying, so she has no reason to believe that I'm not telling the truth." Although Krista's mother has never caught her in the act of cheating, she probably senses that her daughter is untrustworthy. Many mothers have an excellent sense of when their daughter is lying.

Many girls sneak behind their mothers' backs because they want to do something that their mothers won't let them do. They feel their mothers are being unreasonable when they won't allow them to take the bus to the mall with a friend, go to the movies alone with a boy, or drive to the mountains with a group of friends to go camping. It can be frustrating when it seems like all of your friends are allowed more freedom than you. Before you lie and sneak around, try to understand why she doesn't want you to do what you want to do. Maybe you will learn that she is scared or uncomfortable about certain situations.

Your mother may give you trust in small amounts. When she gives you a little bit of freedom, show that you are able to handle it, and soon she will give you more. If your mother finds out that you have lied to her, she will take back her trust and trust you even less than she did in the first place.

Honestly, I don't know of any teenage girl who tells her mother everything about what she is doing. There have been many times when I have fudged the truth about what I was doing, not to hide from my mother, but to protect her from unnecessary upset. Sometimes I would go to parties where friends were drinking. I knew that if my mother knew about it, she might get upset even though I wasn't drinking. I knew that I was okay at these parties and that I could handle myself well, but I choose not to tell my mother because I didn't want to create an unnecessary conflict.

You walk a fine line when dealing with the issue of trust with your mother. You should know the difference between slightly altering the truth by leaving out a little detail and completely lying to cover up what you really did. There are many things that it's best for a mother not to know; however, if you want to be trusted by your mother, you must learn when to use the "what she doesn't know won't hurt her" policy appropriately.

If your mother just doesn't trust you and you feel like you haven't done anything to deserve this, talk with her. Ask her why she doesn't trust you. Find out if there is something that you have done to make her lose her trust in you. Maybe your mother isn't a trusting person or has convinced herself that she cannot trust you. Work with her to create guidelines that will allow you more freedom,

> *Few things help an individual more than to place responsibility upon him and to let him know that you trust him.*
>
> —*Booker T. Washington*

then show her that you can be trusted by living up to what you've agreed upon.

What's a Daughter to Do?

Build on Trust

Here are some things I've found that help to build a trusting relationship:

1. Let your mother know your plans.

   Tell your mother where you are going and who you'll be with. Don't make your mother drag your plans out of you. If she knows what is going on, she will feel much more comfortable and better able to trust you.

2. Give her the number where you will be.

   If you are going to be staying the night some place, give her a way to reach you. Offer the information before she has to ask you for it. Allowing her to get hold of you if necessary shows her you have nothing to hide and aren't sneaking around behind her back.

3. Follow the rules you have agreed upon.

   This is a big one. If your mother is allowing you to do something new, you must do what you agree upon. If you say that you'll be home from camping at noon on the following day and don't show up until 5 P.M., she probably won't let you go camping the next time that you ask.

4. Accept when she says "No."

If your mother isn't comfortable allowing you to do something, accept it. It may take a little while before she feels
comfortable letting you do certain things. If you are understanding, next time you ask, she may give you the freedom
that you want.

Many people believe that teenagers are wild and untrustworthy, but this isn't necessarily true. By the time you are a
teenager, you are smart enough to know what is right and
wrong. Be honest, not only with your mother, but with
yourself. Use your best judgment and know when you have
gone too far. If you want your mother to trust you, you must
be mature and act like a young adult.

The Realm of Trust

Consider for a moment how you might feel if, upon turning
thirty-three, suddenly everyone looked for ulterior motives
behind your every thought and action. Wouldn't it seem as
if you were living in a land of strangers instead of friendly protec-
tors? Wouldn't you want to distance yourself from people who were
suspicious of you just because of your age?

The widespread "dissing" of today's teenagers tempts parents to
assume the worst about their daughters and become suspicious,
overly protective, and controlling. This creates an even greater distance between them. Adolescent girls are all too often typecast as
moody, rude, temperamental, sexually promiscuous, irresponsible,
pouty, sulky, sneaky, and unreasonable. Classifying a girl this way
tears her down and doesn't help advance the healthy self-image you
want her to have. These stereotypes pit mother against daughter as
if they were rivals competing on opposite teams. While some
teenage girls act out their frustrations in negative ways, most do not.
As your daughter begins to experience the ups and downs of her
emotional life, these behaviors *will* pop up; however, they do not

define her. Assuming the worst about her will only make matters worse.

Worrying that your daughter will someday run wild creates fear in you and breeds rebellion in her. If your daughter has never done anything wrong, but is continually treated as if she can't be trusted, she will begin to act that way. Why should she do the right thing if she's always treated like she has done something wrong anyway? When you convince yourself that your daughter is going to misbehave, you also convince her.

If we treat people as they are, we make them worse. If we treat people as they ought to be, we help them become what they are capable of becoming.

—Goethe

Lowering your expectations of your daughter and watching her every move produces mistrust. "Mom, why don't you trust me any longer?" thirteen-year-old Carrie asked. "I'm your mother and I'm not suppose to trust you," was her mother's bad response. If you believe that your daughter will act like a monster, she probably will.

Trust doesn't mean blind faith, closing your eyes, or looking the other way. It does not mean shirking your parenting responsibilities, overlooking the obvious, or being gullible. Trusting involves being attentive, observant, and wide awake. It means placing your trust skillfully and sensibly by being a caring, hands-on parent. I trusted Amanda with everything, from homework and that she would not throw parties when she was home alone to keeping me informed of her comings and goings and properly entertaining boys in her bedroom. I didn't just close my eyes, though. I knew she was doing her homework because her grades were good; I knew that she wasn't giving parties when I was gone because our friends and neighbors looked out for her; and I knew that she wasn't behaving inappropriately in her bedroom because the door was open and I frequently delivered pizza and Cokes.

Trusting her has provided additional bonuses. On the few occasions when I've said "No" to something she wanted to do—like staying in a hotel room with a older date on the night of the prom when she was a sophomore—she knew it wasn't because I didn't trust her, but because I didn't approve of the plans. Because I trusted her implicitly, she was able to trust my judgment on these decisions and didn't give me a hard time.

✳ What's a Mother to Do?

Trust Skillfully and Sensibly

Skillfully trusting your daughter comes from trusting yourself and your instincts. It comes from knowing that you are raising your daughter so that she is competent to make the right decisions. It's recognizing the level of privilege and responsibility she's ready to handle. Your trust is the core ingredient that allows your daughter to rise to the occasion.

Don't let other people—in the media, or friends, family, and acquaintances—influence you on whether or not you can trust your daughter. Teenagers are not all the same. What may be true for your neighbor's daughter will not be true for your daughter. Your daughter will become what you believe she is.

Set high moral standards and believe that she will live up to them. Don't use a guilt trip to pressure her into doing the right thing. Instead, tell her, "I know you'll do the right thing." Show her that you trust her to follow through because she is a good person, not because you're forcing her to do it. Show her that you have faith in her because you know she's a smart girl who can make good decisions.

Girls don't want to let their mothers down. The more trust you put in her, the more she will want to live up to that trust. You want to create a relationship where she behaves properly because she doesn't want to let you down, not because she is afraid of punishment.

Every day, your daughter has plenty of opportunities to get away with something. She makes many decisions about how she will behave. When you think about it this way, you can see how much she really can be trusted. Give your daughter the chance to spread her wings *and* do the right thing. Honor her for all the wonderful choices she is making. Tell her how great you feel knowing she's responsible.

If she does make a mistake, show your concern and disappointment, but don't withdraw all of your trust. Talk over what happened and say, "Yes, you made a mistake, now let's learn from it and start over." Share a similar mistake you made and tell her how you benefited from the experience. Talk about how she might handle the same situation differently the next time. Give her another chance to show you both that she is trustworthy. If she lets you down again, continue to keep your standards high while believing in her goodness. Don't rant and rave as if all hope is lost.

Sixteen-year-old Claire was supposed to be spending the night at Jaimie's but left without telling her mother and went to a teen dance club with her boyfriend. When her mother called Jaimie's house to talk with Claire, she found out Claire wasn't there. The next morning, instead of lowering the boom, she talked over her feelings of disappointment with Claire and decided to continue trusting her. Claire's pattern of skipping out with her boyfriend when she was supposed to be someplace else continued for almost a year. Each time mother and daughter talked it over, and even though Claire lost a privilege, and learned there were consequences for lying, her mother never stopped trusting her. By the time Claire turned seventeen, she stopped sneaking out with her boyfriend and was always where she said she would be.

Unwavering trust will pay off. A girl who is trusted, even if she repeatedly lets you down, will eventually become dependable. If your daughter messes up, explain to her that you're starting over. Talk about what actions she can take so you can wipe the slate clean and move on. Face cracks in trust by talking about what happened so you both can understand what needs to be done to prevent trust from completely shattering.

Placing your trust skillfully involves recognizing the level of privilege and responsibility your daughter is ready to handle. By meeting her responsibilities—whether it's schoolwork, staying out later, dating, or driving—she demonstrates that she's ready to take on the added responsibility that comes with the new privilege.

One mother told me, after her seventeen-year-old daughter didn't come home until 4 A.M., "We're figuring out the steps my daughter needs to take to reinstate her privileges. I know she's trustworthy. She doesn't have to earn my trust; she always has that. She just made a mistake; we all do. I'm wondering if she was ready for the added responsibility that comes with going to parties. We're talking about it and I need her to show me through her actions that she can handle the responsibility that comes with having more freedom."

A daughter who knows that she's got the unwavering trust of her mother develops lasting self-confidence. Pour all your energy into trusting her and don't waste your time on doubt.

❋ Three Ways Moms Demonstrate Trust

1. Accept her choice in friends.
2. Put her in charge of the homework.
3. Let her stay home alone.

Can you think of others?

❋ Three Ways Daughters Show That They Are Trustworthy

1. Call home if your plans change.
2. Complete your homework.
3. Do well in your daytime job, i.e. school.

Can you think of others?

7

Courage, Brains, and Heart

The Essence of Self-Esteem

"Vote for Amanda!" Those three words had been consuming me night and day. With the elections coming soon, I hoped those words would stick with others as much as they had with me.

The past few weeks had been crazy. Putting my schoolwork and other obligations on the back burner, I had been totally focused on my campaign. I devoted hours to painting huge posters and designing flyers. I spent many sleepless nights working to develop the perfect speech, then reciting it over and over in my head. Now it was finally coming to an end. The outcome of all my hard work came down to these next few crucial moments.

I sat out in the hallway with the other students, anxiously awaiting the election results. I looked around me, predicting who the winners would be: hilarious, fun, crazy Seth, who had been my friend since elementary school, would be president; Jocelyn, one of my best friends and a natural-born leader, no doubt would win for vice president; and Dave, who was outgoing and friendly and always made very intelligent comments in Leadership class, would be secretary. Rachel, who had convinced all the hottest guys in school to take off their shirts and paint "Vote Rachel For Treasurer" across their chests before walking around during the election assembly, was a shoe-in for her office; and I, Amanda Ford, cute, enthusiastic, hard-working, spirited, and fun-loving, would be elected Juanita High School's public relations officer. I just knew we would make a perfect team.

We all sat waiting as the current officers called us in one at a time to look at the election results which had been painted on a huge poster. This was to avoid hurt feelings and awkwardness among the winners and the losers, but I knew I didn't have anything to worry about. Throughout the campaign, people would tell me things like, "There is no way that you are going to lose," or, "I have never even heard the name of the guy who is running against you. You'll definitely win!" I just hoped that all my friends would win too. It would be terrible if one of us didn't get elected to office.

"Amanda, you can come in now." Feeling a little nervous and anxious as I walked back into the room, I took a deep breath and closed my eyes as I turned the corner to where I knew that the poster would be hung.

I opened my eyes and quickly read over the poster. President: Seth; Vice President: Jocelyn; Secretary: Dave; Treasurer: Rachel; and Public Relations: Kevin.

I couldn't believe it. I stared at that last name and blinked my eyes hoping that it would change, but it didn't.

"There must have been a mistake counting the votes," I said. "I'm positive that's what happened. They must have got my votes mixed up with Kevin's."

The current president came and put his arm around me. "I'm sorry," he said, "You had a good campaign. It was a tough election."

"Are you sure this is right?" I asked, "Are you sure there wasn't any mix up or something?"

Nodding, he said, "I'm positive."

I turned and went out the back door of the building. I wandered around outside almost in a dream. How could I have lost the election when everyone around me was so sure that I would win? Were they all just trying to humor me by saying I would be elected even though they knew there was no chance?

Eventually I found myself in the gym. Heading for the girls' locker room, I thought to myself, "I'm such an idiot! How could I have possibly believed that I would win? Obviously nobody likes me; what was I thinking?" The locker room was empty and I sat down on a bench and began to cry while every possible reason for my losing the election ran through my head.

"I'm not funny," I thought. "Nobody thinks that I would do a good job. I'm stupid and ugly and I might as well drop out of school. What am I supposed to say to people when they ask me about it, 'Yeah, I'm an idiot whom nobody likes and I lost to Kevin?' What is wrong with me? I'm so embarrassed. I'm not going to be able to show my face 'cause everyone will know I'm the girl who lost the election. I'm worthless and I can't do anything right."

I'm Proud of You for Trying

I hated seeing Amanda's disappointment when she lost the student body election. If she wanted to be public relations officer, I wanted it for her also. Besides, I knew she was just right for the job. She had drive and enthusiasm and would go out of her way to do a great job. I don't know why she lost, but she did, and for a couple of days she was devastated. Worse than seeing her disappointment over losing, however, was hearing her beat herself up. Hearing her call herself "stupid" and saying that she couldn't do anything right made my heart break. There was nothing I could do about the election results, but I could do something about her self-doubt. I decided right then and there that I'd continue doing everything I could to build her up. I wasn't going to let one little high school election spark a downward spiral in her self-confidence.

Sugar and spice and everything fun and intelligent and passionate and creative and strong and tender and firm and soft and wild and wonderful... that's what little girls are made of.

—anonymous

"It took a lot of courage to give a speech in front of the entire student body," I told her. "There're plenty of kids who would have liked to run for office, but who are too afraid to even try." Later, I said, "I was so proud of the way you congratulated Kevin. Offering your support to him the way you did shows you've got a big heart."

"The people who succeed in life aren't afraid of failure," I reminded her. "Losing the election doesn't mean you're stupid, but calling yourself names isn't using your brains," I told her in my best lighthearted manner. "Instead of wasting your time beating yourself up, think about what you've learned by running for office and you'll be able to use those lessons someday. I'm proud of you for going for it."

✳ The Minefield of Imperfection

Whether it's losing an election, striking out at the baseball game, not understanding the physics equation, getting pimples, or being ignored by classmates, what often seems inconsequential to us is monumental to our teenage daughter. Going through seven years of adolescence is like walking through a minefield of "shoulds." Suddenly girls are told they're not okay and images of how they "should" act, look, feel, and think pop up everywhere, reminding them that they don't measure up. Their self-perception is blurred as they compare themselves to others. Girls are especially susceptible to depression; they also tend internalize their problems and are highly sensitive about relationships.

If you've ever suffered from wobbly self-esteem or been plagued by lingering insecurities, you know what a daunting task it is to overcome the residue of self-doubt. No mother wants to pass on that burden, but, unfortunately, we can create insecurities in our daughters without even realizing it.

The best legacy that a mother can give her daughter is strong self-esteem. When they are young, children are showered with praise by mothers, fathers, teachers, friends, and family. Remember how much you cheered when your daughter first learned to ride her bike and how you used to post her spelling tests and art projects on the refrigerator for all to admire? As a girl gets older, the rarer it is for her to hear parents cheering her on and the less she sees her school-work posted around the house. "Once I reached twelve, my mother's praise stopped altogether," said Jade.

A girl begins to doubt herself as she reaches adolescence. Faced with new pressures and expectations, she is experiencing self-doubt in a way that she never has before. Her teachers no longer gush over her and her friends have quit giving her compliments when she does something good. At thirteen, she is more unsure of herself than she was at ten. These new insecurities are scary and can lead to signifi-cant depression. Your daughter needs your support and reassurance that she is a wonderful person. Without it, her self-esteem will grow even more shaky and possibly be lost.

An adolescent girl's world is one in which she is never good enough. A reasonably happy childhood can turn into a nightmarish existence as she copes with all the complicated life choices. Even a girl with high self-esteem is looking for the thing that's wrong with her. Feeling that she is lacking in some way, she begins to think, "Boys would like me if I had Stephanie's body," or, "I would have more friends if I could be as nice as Jane." This is a downward cycle that can lead to problems with alcohol, drugs, grades, depression, friends, and boys.

According to the U.S. Center for Mental Health Services, as many as one in eight teenagers suffers from depression at any given time.

When you shoot for the moon, even when you miss you're among the stars.

—anonymous

As a mother, you have the job of building your daughter's self-esteem. It's easier than you think: simply praise her. Telling your daughter that she is beautiful, smart, and can accomplish whatever she wants will go a long way toward shoring up her self-esteem. She wants to know that she is making a positive difference in your life. Confident that you approve of her, she's better equipped to withstand the outside blows she'll face.

A self-confident girl knows that people will like her for who she is and she respects herself too much to hurt herself. She won't purposely get into harmful situations and she can stand up for herself and do what she knows is best. With your constant praise and support, there's no need for her to follow the crowd because her confidence is being built at home.

Teach your daughter to love herself. Don't overly praise her in one area and leave out others. Teach her to love her whole self— mind, body, and spirit. If a girl feels unsure about herself in one area, it will show through in all areas of life. A girl who thinks she is too fat will hold back from trying out for cheerleading or taking the lead role in a school play, just as a girl who believes that she is stupid will stop trying to get good grades and lose her dream of becoming a doctor. These insecurities are completely in her head and can be remedied through your continual praise and love.

❄ What's a Mother to Do?

Believe in Her and in Yourself

I have many faults and I am not a perfect mother. There are some areas of mothering that I don't particularly enjoy, like playing nurse when Amanda is sick, being a homeroom mother, or helping with homework. However, as I look back on our relationship, I can proudly say there was one area where I excelled. I believed completely in Amanda's abilities and told her so every day: "You're smart," "You're attractive," "You are kind," "You're amazing," "You can handle whatever life brings your way," "You're creative." Knowing I believe in her has served her well. To me, she is a fantastic person full of light and love who can make a meaningful contribution to the world. "You have so much to offer your friends," I tell her. "Any guy would be lucky to have you for a girlfriend." I write "I love you" on notes and I tell her in person, "There is nothing that will make me stop loving you."

Perhaps there are areas of mothering you don't enjoy or aren't skilled at. Like me, you may have doubted yourself as a mother. Perhaps your own self-esteem is shaky, and even though you know your daughter needs as many positive deposits in her self-esteem bank as she can get, you wonder if you have any reserve to spare to help build hers. Perhaps you doubt your ability to support your daughter because no one ever supported you.

It's a big task to be a mother of a teenage girl. It's difficult to manage it all. Keeping our own lives running smoothly while watching out for our daughters requires great effort on our part. We take care of so many things. We work, clean bathrooms, juggle bills, take phone messages, volunteer, sew hems, and bake birthday cakes. So much of what we do takes place behind the scenes and goes unnoticed, yet without us, our daughters' lives would be much harder. We know we're doing a great deal for our families, but we don't give ourselves enough credit. While we give our daughters slack, we expect the impossible from ourselves.

Since Freud began blaming mothers for every trouble in the psyche, mother-bashing has become a popular activity. If we don't do something perfectly, we give ourselves a tongue-lashing. We believe we are responsible for our daughters' complete happiness, and we forget about the outside forces we can't control. We beat ourselves up and put ourselves down. While we see the strengths and beauty in our daughters, we overlook our own.

Our daughters wither under criticism and so

If I have a daughter someday, I will tell her every day how beautiful she is and I will hug her, so that she knows what it's like to be held.

—Leigh, age fifteen

do we. Our daughters thrive with emotional support and so do we. If we want to make our daughters strong, we have to believe in ourselves too. Every time we say a loving, positive word to our daughter or give her credit for an accomplishment, we need to give ourselves acknowledgment as well. After all, she is who she is because of you. She's becoming her best because you've given your best.

As a little girl, Amanda loved *The Wizard of Oz,* and even as a teenager, she watched the movie dozens of times. In the eighth grade, while campaigning for student body office, she fretted, "I'm probably not good enough." I suggested she watch *The Wizard of Oz* again and pay attention to the lessons. The Cowardly Lion, the Scarecrow, and the Tin Man each thought that they were lacking something but on the Yellow Brick Road they discovered they each had exactly what they needed to have a wonderful life. All of us have times when we can't see ourselves clearly and think that we are lacking. If we look closely, though, we will discover that we all have courage, brains, and heart.

MOTHER-DAUGHTER HOMEWORK ASSIGNMENT

Watch *The Wizard of Oz* together. Praise yourselves for your courage, brains, and heart.

❖◈❖◈❖◈❖◈❖◈❖◈❖◈❖◈❖◈❖

Aren't I Good Enough?

There are many things in junior high and high school that can make you feel worthless. As a young girl in elementary school, I didn't experience these things and I believed in myself. I thought I could be and do anything I set my mind to. At ten, I felt ready to conquer the world. Never doubting myself for a second, I knew I would live up to my dreams. My family and teachers told me that I was a beautiful and valuable girl, and I believed in myself 100 percent. Yet somewhere along the road of my life, things began to change. I stopped believing I was the best and started to experience self-doubt.

Once you reach adolescence, the lessons that you were taught in elementary school about loving yourself and being valuable stop. Finding fault in yourself, you never quite feel like you are good enough. Supportive attitudes from your family and teachers turn into disapproval. Instead of loving you with your faults, they attempt to fix your imperfections.

Throughout my adolescence, I always felt like I wasn't good enough. I never got straight A's, I wasn't the best artist or exceptionally good at sports, I didn't get voted to be on the Homecoming Court, I couldn't tell funny stories. I felt like I had nothing, no shining qualities that made me extraordinary. I looked at my closest girlfriends and saw amazing attributes in all of them—they were pretty, fun, smart, athletic, and everyone liked them. I was the one in the background, and I felt ugly, boring, stupid, and clumsy in comparison.

My mother would always tell me, "You are so talented. You can do anything that you want. You are amazing." These comments kept me going, even though I usually didn't believe her. I didn't feel talented and I knew nobody except my mother saw my incredible potential.

Doesn't it always seem like everyone around you has it better than you? You notice great things in everyone else, but can't seem to find them in yourself. The insecurity girls experience during their teenage years brings out a lot of negativity. We can be judgmental, quick to criticize others and put people down behind their backs. All of this negativity and focus on others' flaws makes it hard to see the positive in yourself.

Your mother is supposed to be a source of infinite love and support, the one person who will love you no matter what. But instead of putting an end to our insecurities, our mothers often aggravate them by trying to improve us. Instead of accepting us the way we are, they try to make us better, which can make us feel hurt, angry, and more insecure.

Your mother can put you down in many different ways. She may say, "You could have gotten better grades," or, "I wish that you would keep your room cleaner," or, "You should be better at soccer." Maybe your mother puts down your friends, saying, "I don't really like those girls that you hang out with." She's probably not aware that your self-esteem is taking huge blows from her disapproving comments.

✳ What's a Daughter to Do?

Ask for Your Mother's Help

It has been awhile since your mother was a teenager, and she may be out of touch with how many insecurities you have as a teenage girl. If you feel your mother isn't sensitive to your feelings and is being detrimental to your self-esteem, let her know. All your mother may need is for you to tell her the best way to help you. Try talking to your mother or writing her a letter expressing how you feel. Tell her you understand that she is trying to help you, but she is not doing it in the best way. Give your mother specific examples of the comments and actions that make you feel inadequate. Tell her how you feel about yourself and that her reassurance and compliments are much more helpful to you than her attempts to help you fix your imperfections. If you bring your mother's actions to her attention, she will be better able to help you build your self-esteem.

If your mother doesn't seem to understand where you are coming from and continues to make comments that hurt your self-esteem, let me reassure you that something within your mother, not within you, is

---

A REMINDER FOR MOM

It is extremely hard for a teenage girl to come to her mother for help, so when she does, consider it a huge compliment. It shows that she trusts you and respects your opinion. If you freak out, you could damage that trust and you could ruin any chance of her coming to you for help again.

causing her to act the way she does. Maybe she is dealing with her own insecurities. Mothers want their daughters to be better than themselves, and they don't want their daughters to suffer the same pains that they did when they were young. They try to make up for their own faults and insecurities by attempting to improve you. Maybe she was raised in a critical home and she doesn't know how to relate to you any other way. Maybe your mother is a perfectionist, always worrying about what others will think, and feels she is never good enough. Whatever your mother's problem, you need to know that it is simply her own insecurities coming through.

If you have tried to get support from your mother and it's not working, it is okay to get that support elsewhere. Go to somebody whom you trust and who will listen to you, like your father, a teacher you admire, a coach who cares about you, or even the school counselor. Tell them how you feel about yourself and how you don't feel like you are getting the support you need from your mother. Not only will you feel better talking about your feelings with somebody, but you will learn that there are people who believe in you. This person may become a new source of support and encouragement. He or she can help you build up your-self-esteem and will believe in you when you feel that nobody else does. Don't feel guilty for talking to another person. We all need to be able to share our problems and we deserve to have somebody who can help build us up.

Talking about your low self-esteem can seem hard and it may seem easier to turn to other things to make you feel better. Many girls with low self-esteem will become sexually active to feel like they are loved and wanted, or start drinking or using other drugs. Although these things will let you forget about your worries temporarily, they are not permanent solutions. Eventually the boy will dump you or the "high" from the drugs will wear off, and you will feel much worse than you did before. You will look for something else to fill your empty feeling, and again it will fail you. Unless you deal with your feelings of self-doubt in a healthy way, you will put yourself on never-ending cycle of self-destructon.

According to the 1997 President's Council on Physical Fitness and Sports, regular physical activity helps girls feel better about themselves; female athletes do better academically and have lower school drop-out rates than their non-athletic counterparts; and regular physical activity can enhance girls' mental health, reducing symptoms of stress and depression and improving self-esteem.

Surround yourself with only people who are going to lift you higher and think like a queen. A queen is not afraid to fail. Failure is another stepping-stone to greatness.

—Oprah Winfrey

It is normal for your self-esteem to drop once you have reached adolescence, but fortunately this is temporary if you deal with it in healthy ways. Don't put pressure on yourself to be perfect in every way. Just because you don't get straight A's doesn't mean that you are a slacker, and having a messy room doesn't make you a slob. Everyone has strengths, and the key to good self-esteem is recognizing your strong points and building on them. The sooner you do this, the sooner you will be on the road to a better, more positive self-image.

✳ Good Messages Mothers Can Send

1. I love you! There is nothing that will make me stop loving you.
2. You are remarkable! You can do anything.
3. You have courage, brains, and heart. I believe in you.

✷ Getting to Know All of You

Write your name at the top of a sheet of paper.

Draw a line in the middle of the paper.

Number 1 to 5 above and below the line.

Above the line, list five positive words that describe you.

Below the line, list five negative words that describe you.

Read your name and all the words out loud.

Put your thumbs in the air

and say, "Yes! Yes! Yes!"

We all have positive traits,

we all have negative traits.

You have nothing to be ashamed of.

Accept and love all of yourself,

as you are.

8

Avoiding Guilt Trips

If You Loved Me

"Mom!" Kristen yelled, as she ran downstairs to find her mother.

"I'm in here," her mother called from her bedroom.

Kristen entered her mother's room. "Can I go with the Stuarts out on their boat tomorrow?" she asked.

"Tomorrow's Sunday," her mother said, giving her daughter a stern look. "You know that Sunday is always family day."

"I know, but you said that we don't have any specific plans and we're probably just going to stay around the house anyway."

"It doesn't matter what we're doing. What's important is that we spend time together."

"I know, but it isn't very often that they invite me to go out on their boat with them. I'll be home for dinner." Then she added, "Besides, Parker missed the last family Sunday for his baseball game."

"Fine. If you want to spend family day with the neighbors, go ahead," her mother sighed. "You know, someday you'll realize how much you take your family for granted. The neighbors won't always be there for you, but your family will."

❊ Why Can't You Do This for Me?

I have friends whose mothers are experts at using guilt to control their daughters. These mothers' tactics are carefully crafted. They make sad faces, use hurt voices, sigh helplessly, and say things like, "Nobody cares about me," or, "I do so much for you, I don't understand why you can't do this for me," or, "I hope that you can find some time in your busy life for me." They tug at their daughters' consciences and manipulate them into doing what they want. These tactics make their daughters feel terrible; even I would feel guilty just witnessing one of these guilt trips.

Guilt is an awful feeling, but there's an upside to it. A guilty conscience keeps us in check and makes us accountable for our actions. If we didn't have a conscience, we would have no reason for behaving morally. Good guilt is knowing the difference between right and wrong, and feeling guilty when you know that you've messed up is okay.

Unhealthy guilt is when somebody makes you feel bad for something that clearly isn't your fault. Trying to have a relationship with a mother who uses guilt as a controlling tool can be extremely frustrating. These mothers seem to take everything personally and their feelings are hurt if you look at them the wrong way. You are unable to communicate your thoughts directly and you must tiptoe around your mother's feelings so that she isn't thrown into a state of upset.

"My mother always wants to be completely involved in my life," says Shannon, seventeen. "I tell her a lot of stuff, but if I refuse to tell her every last detail, she walks away hurt and says that I don't love her. I wish that she wouldn't equate my love for her with how much I tell her." Fourteen-year-old Michelle adds, "I wish that my mom would just ask me directly when she wants something from me instead of laying guilt trips on me."

If your mother is using guilt trips on you, it is likely that her mother raised her using guilt and that's the only way she knows how to communicate her feelings, needs, and wants. Maybe your mother has a lot of hurt and guilt inside herself, and the only way she knows to ease her guilty feelings is by finding something to blame you for. Your mother may not even be aware of what she is doing and may not know that she is giving you unhealthy feelings.

☀ What's a Daughter to Do?

Right Your Wrong, but Don't Wear a Guilt Hat

The key to dealing with a mother like this is learning how not to wear the guilt hat your mother places on you. Don't accept blame for her unhappiness, and don't put guilt trips on other people. Using guilt is not a productive way to express your feelings.

If you realize that you have done something that has genuinely hurt your mother's feelings, do whatever is necessary to right your wrong. Clear the air by admitting what you did or said was wrong, and apologize. Not only will you feel better, but your mother will too.

If your mother tries to make you feel guilty for things that you know are not your fault, call her on it. Guilt trips are a sneaky, manipulative way of gaining control. If you are up-front with your mother, it forces her to be direct as well. Explain to her how this negative way of communicating makes you feel, then ask her to be direct and up-front with you. You shouldn't feel guilty for things that you know you haven't done wrong.

Once my mother was trying to make me feel guilty about wanting to go to the movies alone with my friends, so I said, "I've been going to the movies with you for thirteen years, now I want to go with my friends once in awhile. Don't take it so personally, Mom. It doesn't mean that I don't like you, I just want to do something new." By being direct, I forced my mom to be aware of the guilt that she was using to make me hang out with her.

According to Teenage Research Unlimited, most teens enjoy being with their families; however, when asked, "If you could have a guaranteed great time, whom would you rather have it with, your family or your friends?" sixty-three percent choose friends.

Using guilt to get what you want from your mother or make her feel bad because you're upset is an unhealthy communication style as well. I've used guilt on my mom by saying, "All my friends' moms are letting them go," or, "I'm the only girl at school who doesn't have a jacket like that," hoping that by making her feel bad, I would get my way. Try not to play these types of games. Be direct with your mother and let her know exactly what you want from her. If she has done something that upsets you, let her know.

Maybe your mom forgot to leave you money so you could order pizza for dinner since she was going to be at a meeting when you got home. Even though you were annoyed that you had to make your own dinner, tell her how she has upset you instead of saying, "I sat around starving all night since you didn't leave me money." Make her aware of what she can do so that the same thing doesn't happen in the future. If you communicate directly, your mother will learn from you that guilt trips are not a healthy way for her to express her feelings or to get what she wants.

❋ Know That You Are Important

My artist friend Surya teaches a painting class for women entitled "Painting Your Mother." Grown women have been thrown into a tizzy at the mere thought of this assignment. Women drop the class because the agony of recalling the feelings that they harbor toward their mothers is too overwhelming. Some women paint their mothers beautifully, while others' images of their mothers are horribly distorted.

You have more influence on your daughter's life than you might think. I have known women who spent their entire lives trying to shake off the residue of guilt tied up with their mothers. Even when they describe themselves as "ideal daughters," the guilt still exists, and it becomes a negative ingredient in their adult relationship. Guilt saps the joy they could share and keeps both of them from feeling good.

My mother won't admit it, but I've always been a disappointment to her. Deep down inside, she'll never forgive herself for giving birth to a daughter who refuses to launder aluminum foil and use it over again.

—Erma Bombeck

Guilt trips start in the teen years when mothers imply, "If you really loved me, you would do such and such." There are thousands of guilt-producing messages: "If you loved me, you'd stay home once in a while," or "If you loved me, you'd do what I want you to do," or "How could you do that to me?" Like chains, these comments may keep your daughter close but eventually she'll break away and move as far away from you as fast as she can.

Guilt trips wear many disguises, and it's not always easy to recognize when we're using guilt. As a single mother, I often felt guilty that I had to work late, that I couldn't always cook healthy dinners, and that I didn't have all the time, energy, or money that I wanted to give to Amanda. Instead of telling her directly how I felt, I'd unconsciously dump guilt on her. I'd sigh and buy her the expensive shoes instead of saying, "I can't afford those now." I'd snap and pick her up from a party instead of telling her that I was too tired and needed to go to bed early.

I often felt that I was going out of my way to make her life comfortable. I'd drop what I was doing to deliver the lunch she left on the counter or I'd put aside a project I was working on to drive her to the store at the last minute to get the poster board she insisted she needed right then. After months of putting aside my own needs, I'd feel taken for granted and,

Of all the haunting moments of motherhood, few rank with hearing your own words come out of your daughter's mouth.

—Victoria Secunda

instead of taking care of my own needs directly, I'd send her a guilt message like, "You don't appreciate how much I do for you."

It's not that Amanda didn't see or appreciate what I was doing, it's just that she wasn't able really to understand. A person who has never been to the moon has no concept of what it's like to live there. You can tell her stories and show her pictures, but she will never fully understand until she's lived on the moon herself. Your daughter cannot be expected to fully understand all that you have done for her until she has children of her own. So, when you do things for your daughter, don't expect huge applause. Although she appreciates you immensely, she doesn't understand exactly how much you put yourself out for her.

I have heard mothers say, "I'm doing this for you" and then get hurt or mad when their daughters don't appreciate it. Before you volunteer to be the advisor for the school play, chaperone the dance, or sew emblems on the shirts, know who you're really doing it for. If you enjoy these activities and your daughter doesn't object, then go right ahead, but don't expect or demand adulation from her. If you're taking tickets at the ball game because you think she wants you to, check it out with her in advance to make sure. If you're really doing it for her, do it as a gift with no strings attached.

Lynne said, "When Chloe's room is piled so high that she can't close the door, instead of automatically cleaning it for her and then feeling resentful if she doesn't say anything, I ask her in advance, 'Would you like me to clean your room and change your sheets?' At least that way I know she's noticed. When I'm finished, I say, 'Honey, I made your bed.' She usually says 'Thanks, Mom,' as she's running out the door."

✳ What's a Mother to Do?

Tell Her Directly What You Want

It's not pleasant to be raised by a martyr mother. Martyr mothers sacrifice their own lives and then use guilt to keep their daughters close. They operate under the umbrella of "If you really loved me, you would do such and such." They ask, "How could you, after all that I've done for you?" They use a hurt tone to show their displeasure.

Controlling your daughter with guilt trips will backfire. She'll be riddled with guilt, which has long-term consequences. As a freshman in college, eighteen-year-old Jill came to counseling because she had difficulty getting out of bed in the morning, was missing classes, drinking more than she wanted to, and suffering from bulimia. She had difficulty make decisions.

Another way to get your teen to be more responsible about chores is to provide something to look forward to—a vacation from chores. After all, even adults look forward to vacations.

—Joyce L. Vedral, Ph.D.

When I asked her what she wanted for herself, she answered, "My mother says a dental hygienist is a good career." When I ask her what she liked to do for fun, she shrugged and said, "My mom and I go out to dinner." Every answer she gave referred to her mother. Jill actually knew more about her mother than she did about herself. She tried very hard to please her mother and felt guilty not taking her wishes into account. The mere thought of choosing something her mother might not approve of filled her with self-condemnation. She wanted her mother's love and affection, yet she was overwhelmed and crippled by it.

MOTHERISMS

- "You know I don't sleep until you get home!"
- "Money doesn't grow on trees."
- "This hurts me more than it hurts you."
- "I hate having you drive alone at night."
- "Do as I say, not as I do."
- "Act your age."
- "Better watch out or your face will freeze like that."
- "I would never have talked to my mother like that."
- "Never say 'Shut up,' say 'Be quiet.'"

Guilt is a big motivation killer. If a girl feels guilty because her mother is unhappy with her own life, she'll eventually throw her hands in the air and give up because no matter what she does she can't fix it.

If you suspect that you may be laying guilt trips on your daughter, ask yourself these questions: "What am I trying to achieve?" "What do I need from her that I'm not getting?"

As mothers, we want our daughters lives to extend beyond our home *and* we want her to stay connected and involved with her family. Finding a balance between the two is impossible unless you know yourself and can communicate directly to your daughter. Telling her what you want works better than saying, "You never spend time with me." Beating around the bush only keeps her guessing at what you really want. Telling her directly how you feel is healthier than hinting.

Martyr mothers count on their daughters to fill up the emptiness in their own lives. While it's natural to put your daughter's needs before your own, especially when she is young and more dependent, now that she's in her teens and is branching out, so can you. What would you like to do that you haven't done recently? Is there something you wanted to do when you were her age that you didn't, but could do now?

Your daughter is sensitive to you and feels guilty for having a fuller life. She feels sad about your suffering. Unconsciously, she's afraid that by carving out a life different from yours, she will lose your love. She may not allow herself to be successful or happy if she feels that you aren't. The very best gift you can give your daughter is living a life that makes *your* heart sing. Mothers with full, rich lives are a pleasure to be around.

Separating to develop yourselves will give you more to share when you do come back together. Your daughter will be pleased that you're enjoying yourself. While she's going to school and making new friends, she can be at ease knowing you're doing the same. When you come back together, your new experiences enrich both your lives. By taking responsibility for your own happiness, you're teaching her that's she's responsible for hers.

One last word about guilt. You are not responsible for everything; neither is your daughter. There are many outside circumstances beyond your control. By taking responsibility for things truly in your sphere of influence, you'll create a good relationship with your daughter and enjoy your life more.

✳ Guilt Tips for Mothers

Guilt is like quicksand—you can get stuck in it. If you find yourself laying guilt trips on your daughter, it's likely that you were controlled by guilt when you were a teenager. To get out of the quicksand, try this. On a strip of paper, write one item you feel guilty about. Continue listing as many guilty feelings as you can. Separate the guilt strips into two piles: "Things I can do something about" and "Things I can't do anything about." Discard the second pile and say, "Good-bye to useless guilt." Now read over the first pile and prioritize your guilts. Take action against each guilt. For example, you may need to tell your daughter that you are sorry for laying guilt trips on her. Apologizing will release you from guilt as long as you follow up with a change in your behavior.

✳ Give Yourself Time to Think

Daughters use guilt trips on us too. Avoid being talked into something you don't want to go along with by giving yourself time to think before you answer. I learned this from experience. When Amanda was fifteen, she asked me—while I was on the phone—if I would drive her to Bend, Oregon, for the weekend so she could attend the homecoming dance with her good friend who had moved there. I thought it sounded like fun to get away so I nodded "Yes" without thinking it through. By the time I'd gotten off the phone, she'd already told Zack and his mother we were coming. Later in the evening, when I finally had a chance to check my schedule, I realized I'd said "Yes" too quickly. When I told her that I didn't

Every time I give my daughter a piece of advice, I learn plenty.

—anonymous

think it would work out since I had a speaking engagement that weekend and she was scheduled to take her SATs, she pulled out all the guilt trips she could muster. "But you promised." "They are already counting on it." "This is *sooo* important to me." My head was swirling with all of her arguments, and I couldn't think straight. I was feeling "guilty" and all I'd done was answer too soon.

Well, I moved heaven and earth so she could go, but it was a good lesson for me. When I'm in doubt, I say, "I'd like to think that over and get back to you." It works like a charm every time.

✾ Reminders for Moms

1. If you don't want to buy your daughter something, tell her why directly.

2. Ask for the appreciation you want. For example, "I went out of my way to drive you to that party, and I was disappointed that you didn't say a word."

3. Give yourself a break. Just because you can't do everything doesn't mean that your aren't a good mother.

4. Give yourself thinking time before you answer.

✾ *Reminders for Daughters*

1. You are compassionate person, but you are not responsible for your mother's happiness.

2. Let her know directly what you want. For example, "I would like you to buy me a leather jacket" is better than "Everybody has a leather jacket but me."

9

Escaping Humdrum

Mother and Daughter Bonding

On a separate piece of paper, each of you fill in the blanks in the following, then compare your answers:

The last time we (mother and daughter) had fun together was when we _____. I had a good time because _____. My (mother/daughter) would (agree/disagree) that this was a fun time. My (mother/daughter) and I spend time together doing fun things (how often?). Other mothers and daughters probably spend (more/less) time having fun together than we do. I think that my (mother/daughter) spends too much time _____, and not enough time _____. I have the most fun with my (mother/daughter) when she _____. One thing that my (mother/daughter) enjoys doing is _____. Two things that I like to do with my (mother/daughter) that takes thirty minutes is _____. I would like to spend half a day doing _____ with my (mother/daughter).

✳ I Have To Do Something with My Mom

What do you picture when you think of spending time alone with your mother? Do you imagine a night full of excitement, laughter, and tons of "girl bonding," or does the mere thought of spending time with your mother bore you to tears? For many girls, the words *fun* and *mother* are never found in the same sentence. When I complain to my mom about having nothing to do, she says, "Why don't we go to the movies?" "With you?" I ask. Going out with Mother seldom qualifies as fun. It seems more like required work, or an obligation—something you feel that you have to do. My idea of "living it up" usually does not mean spending time with Mom. I've seen her every single day of my entire life. That's a lot of time to put into one person. So when I have free time, I choose to spend it with my friends.

> According to Teenage Research Unlimited, African American teens are more likely than Hispanic or white teens to describe their family as "fun." Younger teens, who are less involved in dating than older teens, are more likely to enjoy family outings and activities than teens age sixteen or older.

I'm not alone. "I like hanging out with my friends better than my mom because I can be myself around them," says sixteen-year-old Bria. "I can say anything I want to them, and they understand what's going on in my life because they are with me every day at school."

However, there are occasions when spending time with my mother *isn't* last on my list of things I want to do. As I got older and had more responsibilities, I also had more pressures, and I began to find out that spending time with my mother was actually a nice change of pace. It wasn't upbeat, fast-paced, or exciting like going to a party with my friends, but it was pleasant; time with her was calm and relaxing. When I'm overworked by school and overwhelmed by friends, it's nice to spend a night or two with Mom. If my friends are pressuring me to go out, and I really don't feel up to it, the old "I've gotta do something with my mom" excuse comes in handy.

Don't be so quick to dismiss your mother as a source of relaxation. By using your imagination you can think of something new to do, and you might even have fun together. Don't get caught up in the idea that "Mom is too old" to be adventuresome or that it's impossible to have fun with her. Moms aren't always boring. My mom and I have gone whale-watching, kayaking, and horseback riding. We go to art shows, plays, craft fairs, and antique stores. We've gone out to get our hair and make-up done, gone on picnics and to concerts in the park, and sometimes we just sit on a bench together people-watching and commenting on what we see.

"Bonding" with your mom allows the two of you to be together in an atmosphere away from the ordinary routine. You're so familiar being together at home, where she's so busy making rules, taking care of the family, and working, that you might have overlooked another side of her. Getting out of the house puts you on a level more like friends. Doing new things together takes you out of the mother-daughter world. Your mother will probably never be like one of your girlfriends, but bonding with her as a friend puts your relationship on a new footing.

✳ What's a Daughter to Do?

Half an Hour for Mom

Between both your busy schedules, it may seem impossible to find even half an hour when you're both free to take off together. "Together time" does have advantages, and even though it takes effort on your part, it pays off in little ways. Getting to know your mother as a person rather than just the woman who takes care of you helps you gain insight into what makes her tick. That has definite benefits because, when you have inside clues about her temperament, you have an advantage when you need to convince her to go along with you. When you're able to relax and hang out with your mother, you may find it's easier to talk to her about issues that have been sore points between you. She'll feel that she's important to you and included in your life. If she feels like she gets time with you, she may be more likely to cooperate when you want to spend extra time with your friends.

Before you decided that "quality time with Mom" is completely out of the question, unrealistic, or pure torture, I suggest you give it a try. Ask her to take a five-minute walk around the block, move up to a thirty-minute activity, and eventually make plans for a half-day outing. Take the initiative and plan an outing. Tell her you're doing it because quality bonding time is good for your relationship. (When she faints, be sure to pick her up off the floor.)

"I always felt like my mom didn't want to spend time with me outside of our normal day," said my sixteen-year-old friend, Heather. "So, one Friday night I asked her if she wanted to go to a movie and then out to dinner together. She was so excited. She told me that she had never really asked if I wanted to hang out with her because she thought that I always wanted to be with my friends and never with her. She didn't want me to feel pressured to spend time with her if I would rather be doing other things."

Devoting a couple hours every other week to doing something that you both will enjoy is reasonable. I'm sure you can think of something to do. My mother always wants me to go to the movies with her, but the thought of sitting in a movie with my mother bores me to tears, so I suggest we go out to dinner instead because we both enjoy that. If you aren't both excited about what you're doing, you aren't going to have any fun.

Sometimes my mother and I will go into the city (which is only about twenty minutes away) and stay in a hotel for the night. We pretend to be tourists and we go shopping, sightseeing, ride the ferry, sit at a sidewalk café, and order room service. By the end of the weekend we both feel rejuvenated and ready to head back to our busy lives. After a day of hanging out, my mother has had enough of me too, and she is eager to be left on her own for awhile. If you make a pact with your mother to go away together for a night once a year, perhaps she won't bug you so much in the meantime because she'll have this special outing to look forward to.

What do girls do, who haven't any mothers to help them through their troubles?

—Louisa May Alcott

During junior high and high school the good times go unnoticed because the fights get overemphasized. Think about the good times you've had with your mom. Were they planned in advance or did they arise spontaneously? Bonding with your mother can be as simple as laughing at a funny TV commercial, running errands with each other, or riding the bus to a new part of town. Recognize the good times you have with your mother every day. Point out the good times to her so that she recognizes how much time you really are devoting to building a strong relationship with her.

According to Teenage Research Unlimited, swimming is the most popular sport for teenage girls.

Quality Minutes

I've never quite understood the purpose of perpetuating the myth that teenage girls are impossible on every level. First of all, it's not accurate. Relationships of any kind have their difficult stages and those between mothers and daughters certainly have their challenges, but what about the other side of the coin? You never hear much about the joyful connections or the silliness you share. What about those delicious, heart-melting moments when you're in tune with each another? Those lovely seconds when you're reading and she flops down beside you, or those minutes when

I have a surprise for you. It's not your birthday. It's for no reason at all. Just a surprise, a little one, but a surprise.

—China Deaton

you're singing the oldies, or the hectic hours watching her get ready for the prom? Those are the moments that add up to years worth remembering.

I like hanging out with my daughter. I treasure the moments when we can run away from the flurry of daily demands. In fact I like it so much that I've been known to bribe her by saying, "Honey, I'm going to the mall, do you want to come along?" I know she can't resist the high probability that I will buy her some clothing or those shoes she's been hinting about. I've been known to rearrange my schedule at a moment's notice just because she's in the mood for a visit. I've even spent more money than I probably should have to eat at our favorite Italian restaurant for no reason other than we like to dine in style.

Mothers always complain, "As long as she gets her way, she's happy." While it's true that teens are absorbed in their own little worlds, I don't hold that against Amanda. I've had the same tendency myself. It's true that girls are dramatic and often exaggerate everyday events, but so what? A little spice and drama never hurts.

Although I don't take all of my daughter's advice, I do appreciate it when she gives me her opinions. Amanda bugged me for two years to update my sunglasses, insisting that the ones I wore were out of style, too big, and made me look like a bullfrog. I told her that I liked them, so she put up with me and them for another year. Then one day while we were looking at cosmetics in the department store, I suddenly was trying on sunglasses. Using a little psychology, she seized the opportunity, and said, "I know you like your bullfrog glasses, but these small ones are stylish and flatter your face." The sales clerk nodded in agreement and, before I knew what happened, I was wearing the new ones and receiving compliments from my friends. Now I regularly take Amanda shopping and she updates me.

❋ What's a Mother to Do?

Plan "Girl Time"

I often felt neglected because fourteen-year-old Amanda would rather "bond" with friends than with me. In desperation I tried a more creative approach: I thought of things we could do together that would be fun. After vetoing dozens of suggestions, she was finally willing to try one. We enrolled in an eight-hour beading workshop and made necklaces together. It was fun, and this training still comes in handy. When the clasp broke on my necklace recently, I'd forgotten the proper restringing technique, but she remembered and did it for me. I like it when she takes care of me and tell her so, which is also good bonding.

Every once in awhile I have bright idea for another "mother-teenage daughter bonding activity." We've gone horseback riding up Cougar Mountain and have taken kayaking lessons on Lake Washington. She likes kayaking so much that she'll even get out of bed to go with me at 6 A.M., my favorite morning hour. I like her willingness to compromise and tell her she's a good sport. My appreciation brings us together in another way.

Bonding during the teenage years paves the way for a close adult relationship. Instead of wasting precious time mourning the lose of the sweet, innocent child you once had, put your energy into building on the relationship you've got. Time spent with your teenager will be in shorter spurts, but it's just as meaningful as the time you spent with her when she was a toddler. Put effort into finding sophisticated activities to spark her interest. On your way home from an errand, surprise her by turning into a music store and picking out a CD. Sneak away for an hour and browse through vintage clothing stores, or go on a hike. Develop your sense of humor and find things to laugh about. If you can't laugh together then your bonding activities will fall flat. Laughing with your daughter puts you two in tune, and that's the warm feeling you want her to remember.

It's easier to get along with each other when you're laughing.

Your daughter will not remember details of her infancy or how you got up in the middle of the night to comfort her when she had a nightmare. She might vaguely remember the hours you played Barbies with her during her childhood. Looking back, she'll easily remember her teenage years and what you did or didn't do or what you said and the way that you said it. Be sure you have some positive, upbeat experiences to fill her memory bank.

"My mother started a tradition with me and my sister that we've continued with our own daughters," Tracey told me. "Since teenagers are interested in looks and being 'pretty' we take each of our daughters to the make-up counter on their thirteenth birthday and let each of them each have a free beauty consultation. We call these outings our 'girl hour.'"

With ingenuity you can find hundreds of ways to stay connected. As you both move through the adolescent phase, remember that these tiny moments add up to wonderful times. Talking about how special these activities are to you is a good way to keep the positive feelings fresh. Taking pictures and recording the spontaneous happenings around the house are just as meaningful as photographing the planned events. A picture of her on the phone will tell an important story when she's looking back ten years from now.

Coming-of-age rituals create memories while validating the fact that your daughter is growing up and you're proud of her. A "sweet sixteen" birthday party can be a glorious occasion with which to honor the young woman your daughter has become. Toasts and celebrations of all the "firsts" during these years are ways to stay strongly connected.

The sixteenth birthday is a big milestone and is often elaborately celebrated with a party. Sugar is the traditional symbol of turning "sweet sixteen" and, according to tradition, the birthday girl wears a corsage of sugar cubes and ribbons.

✳ Guidelines for Girl Time

1. Do something new and exciting you both can enjoy.
2. Don't force each other, and work around your schedules.
3. If you're out of practice having fun, start small.
4. Spontaneous spurts of fun are often the best!
5. Show appreciation for those moments when you're laughing and horsing around.
6. Take pictures of your outings.

PART 2

Rolling with the Punches

10

Quarreling

Pick It Up!

Rushing past me, Mom threw the bags of groceries on the counter as I sat at the kitchen table working on my Physics project and eating cookies I had just made.

"You need to clean up your mess," she said.

"You could at least ask," I replied, annoyed by her demand.

"Amanda, I really don't have time for this. Please clean up your mess."

"I'll do it in a bit. Would you chill out? I'm in the middle of this right now."

"I have a meeting here shortly and I can't have the house looking like a pigsty! You need to move your stuff out of the kitchen!"

"Dude, you don't have to yell about it! Just ask nicely and I'll do it!"

❋ Military Secrets

We all know that mothers and daughters have fights, but we never really know for sure what starts them. Nobody ever *really* talks about them. The subject is a closely guarded secret—almost as closely guarded as Pentagon secrets! In case you thought you were the only ones who got into ugly spats, I have news for you: you're not!

Quarrels begin so unexpectedly. One moment all is rosy and then you are suddenly cast into hell. It is so unexpected, shocking, and upsetting. One moment everything is fine, the next moment your stomach turns inside out, your heart seems to have collapsed, and you're either flushed with anger or crying. You try to express what you're feeling and talk sensibly about it but you keep making a mess of it. They are "only mother–daughter quarrels" but they feel like sheer agony.

According to researchers, college girls recall fighting with their mothers about sixteen times per month.

*—Holmeck and Hill,
Journal of Youth
and Adolescence*

There are all kinds of quarrels, about anything—from phone use, chores, going to bed too late, and privacy to family obligations, curfews, and boys. You try to convince her that the generic hairspray is just as good as the expensive brand name, and she tries to convince you that "everyone's doing it."

Quarrels express themselves in different ways, through hot anger, cold withdrawal, tears, and even violence. One thing characterizes all quarrels: the "Blame Game." We mothers are as guilty as our daughters in maneuvering and finger-pointing. She blames us and we bounce the blame right back at her. We've convinced ourselves she's wrong because she's the teenager, and she's convinced you couldn't possibly understand, because you're from an older generation.

Giving advice comes naturally to mothers. Advice is in the genes, along with blue eyes and red hair.

— Lois Wyse

Blaming isn't pleasant, but most of us find it preferable to feeling hurt and easier than taking responsibility for our own behavior. It's not sufficient to simply wait for this stage to pass; we must learn better ways to negotiate through the turbulence.

Mother-daughter quarrels can be quite educational. They teach you to consider the other person, that it's better to take responsibility for your own words and actions, and to forgive. Every fight and misunderstanding I had with Amanda was an opportunity to learn something about myself and a chance to practice a more joyful way of relating.

You've probably also said horrible things to your daughter. I once told Amanda she was behaving like a "spoiled, ungrateful little brat." The moment I said it, I felt she was behaving poorly, but the way I said it and the force behind my anger left me feeling horrid. From that, I discovered the benefits of keeping my mouth shut until after the heat of the moment had passed.

I've learned plenty of other lessons as well. By the time Amanda was sixteen, I learned to my pick my battles carefully. What difference does it really make if the bathroom isn't kept up to my standards or if she leaves her dishes in the sink? Someone once said real mothers often have sticky floors, filthy ovens, and happy kids. I realized that mothers who have good relationships with their teenage daughters don't fight about wet towels on the bathroom floor, how much she's talking on the phone, or whether she empties the garbage immediately. They don't nag about homework or demand to know all the details of her social life.

By the time Amanda was seventeen, I learned that having the last word is not the best way to get my point across. Now when I feel the urge to give advice, I try to choose the right moment and use my best lighthearted manner. If I'm concerned that she's lounging when she should be doing her homework, I'll say in an upbeat voice, "Honey, I know you are in charge of your homework, but I feel like I'm shirking my duty if I don't remind you about getting started." If I scold or harp, yell or shriek, she shrugs off what I'm saying, but if I deliver my message as a suggestion instead of order, she's more likely to hear what I am saying. I've learned to lighten up, see the humor in our situation, and laugh at myself. By the time Amanda was eighteen, we could laugh about what she calls my "mega-overprotectiveness." I can even agree with her that my warnings about avalanche dangers every time she goes skiing is probably overdoing it.

WHAT ARE YOUR TOP TEN QUARRELS?

Number in order from one to ten and share your answers.

Allowance	Homework
Chores	Talking back
Talking on the phone	Dating
Friends	Smoking, alcohol, and
Curfew	drug usage
Driving the car	Cleaning your room
Bedtime	Other

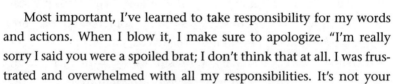

Most important, I've learned to take responsibility for my words and actions. When I blow it, I make sure to apologize. "I'm really sorry I said you were a spoiled brat; I don't think that at all. I was frustrated and overwhelmed with all my responsibilities. It's not your fault." When I swallow my pride, her attitude toward me changes and she becomes cooperative. Being able to 'fess up when I've been out of line has resulted in sensitive, healing conversations between us and prevented resentments from souring our connection.

We've learned that quarreling isn't the end of our relationship; we can disagree and still get along. I've learned that apologizing is better than letting poisonous remarks stand in the way of loving one another. When you apologize, you show it is not a weakness to admit being wrong. By apologizing to your daughter, you demonstrate real strength of character.

❋ What's a Mother to Do?

Say to Her, "Help Me Understand"

Mother-daughter quarrels teach you to avoid pitfalls by recognizing strategies of domination and manipulation, whether they are your own or someone else's. Perhaps you've used rage or physical violence to control your daughter. One mother I know has used her psychosomatic illness as a way of manipulating her daughter. It requires considerable skill to see the patterns leading to conflict and to avoid those patterns.

Uncovering the patterns is important because how you deal with conflict is the most important factor in the lasting success of your relationship. Learning to deal with conflict means understanding that a quarrel doesn't have to be the end of the world. Closeness sometimes requires fighting, and there's nothing wrong with it as long as it results in growth and realization. You can disagree, argue, and get mad, but the love between you will still be there.

When your daughter is in a negative mood, don't respond in the same manner. When you do, I'm sure you notice a negative chain reaction. Her negativity sparks negativity in you, which provokes more antagonism, tension, and hostility. Before you know it, you're entangled in a web of tears, cross words, slammed doors, and tension. To top it off, you can't put your finger on what started the commotion in the first place.

If you find yourself yelling and on the verge of strangling her, it's best to take time out. Let her go for a walk or call a friend, and then you do the same. Have a cry, or talk it over with someone you trust. If she says she can't talk about it any longer, respect her wishes. If either one of you is so upset that you can't think straight, drop it for at least an hour. Nothing has to be settled immediately.

Are there solutions to all these quarrels? Yes and no. There will always be differences between you. Sooner or later you will quarrel. The only lasting solution is unconditional love and simply appreciating your adolescent daughter without qualifications.

Loving without conditions does not mean without demands. Sometimes we need to make demands on our daughters. We may get angry with them, but we should never close our hearts to them. We can clash with them on many issues as long as our love for them is not an issue.

You arrive at unconditional love by recognizing that you are capable of it. Both you and your daughter have pure love at your core, and you should ask her, "Help me understand" and mean it.

Your daughter craves your understanding. I've learned from my counseling work that both mothers and daughters feel devastated by their fights. One mother pointed to her fourteen-year-old daughter and said, "Look at her face, she's a smart aleck, she isn't even listening to me. I slapped her to get her attention. If she keeps this up, I'll send her to live with her father." As she went on listing her grievances and hurling insults, the young girl sat stone-faced.

I spoke to the daughter alone later, and discovered her mask of coldness was hiding the deep hurt she was feeling. She sobbed and talked about the guilt she felt because her mother was so unhappy since her divorce. She was depressed and trying not to show it because she didn't want to add to her mother's worries.

Several sessions later, the mother again began blaming her daughter. When her daughter started crying as if her heart would break, the mother stopped in her tracks. Until that moment, she had assumed her daughter didn't care, but the tears led to much-needed understanding and conversation. The mother discovered that her daughter had learned to hide her emotions, and the daughter learned that presenting a withdrawn face actually led to more arguments. With this new awareness, they were able to slowly reestablish trust and kindness. The mother became more sensitive to her daughter's feelings, and the daughter became more cooperative.

As mothers, it is our responsibility to make the first move toward making amends. Your daughter may never show you how hurt she really is. She might be afraid that if she approaches you, it would open the whole mess up again.

Over the years, I have written Amanda many notes apologizing for my words or actions. I've gone to her room and told her that I was sorry. Even when I felt that I was right, I made the first move toward reconciliation. Sometimes she forgave me right away; other times the wound was too deep for her to accept my apology at once. Because I followed my apology with a change in my behavior, she ultimately forgave me. These apologies were important because neither one of us can remember what most of our quarreling was about. We do remember, however, that we forgave each other.

One of the reasons people quarrel is that we're so serious. We seem to relish agreement and being right more than playfulness. To open your heart and forgive is much more fruitful provided we're willing to do it. Mother-daughter struggles are perennial dramas, but the ending is up to you.

Better to apologize a thousand times than let one poisonous remark remain without an antidote. Your apology means everything.

—Joyce Vedral, Ph.D.

Win-Win Arguments

When I lived at home, I disagreed with my mother on a regular basis. The fights that we had rarely started over big, controversial issues, but were usually about something small, like who last used the scissors and didn't put them back. Before we knew what was going on, my mom and I would be involved in a screaming war over something completely trivial.

By age fourteen, I'd perfected my arguing technique. I knew that leaving my dirty dishes in the sink or sighing and rolling my eyes when my mom asked me to take out the garbage ticked her off. I was perfectly aware that declaring myself "right" and my mother "wrong" would keep an argument going for days. I even knew that saying, "You're right, Mom. I'll do what you want," would put an end to any fight we were having, no matter how blown-up it was.

Have you ever found yourself caught in the middle of an argument with your mother and, even though you know you're being ridiculous, you keep fighting anyway? I have, and I can never figure out why I do this. For all my arguing skills, ending arguments seems to be what I do the least. Even though I really hate bickering with my mother, my pride gets in the way and I would rather win the fight than put a stop to it by admitting I may be wrong.

A daughter and her mother are never free of one another—no matter how they disagree. For they are so entwined in heart and mind that, gladly or unwillingly, they share each love, each joy, each sorrow, and each bitter wrong life long.

—Pam Brown

Eventually, I learned that having the last word was just the opposite of winning. Although it was difficult to swallow my pride and say, "You're right, I'm wrong," it was worth it. The more I took the initiative to end the disagreements, the less we fought. By allowing myself to lose a few arguments, I won.

Teenagers often have a reputation for being completely irrational. I used to always say, "I am not acting like a child!" but sometimes when I looked at my behavior, I thought, "Wow, I *am* acting like a child." It was humbling to see I was being reduced to a child when things didn't go exactly my way, and I realized that if I acted like a mature person, arguments with my mother would turn out much better.

You may feel that it is not your responsibility to end a fight with your mother. Sara says, "My mom is the adult. She's the one who is supposed to be mature and end the fights. If she doesn't want to fight, then she needs to lead by her example." You may agree with this argument, but you need to remember that your mother is still learning too. Quarreling this way is just as new to your mother, and you may need to take the lead and teach your mother how to stop fighting. If you want to have a win-win relationship with your mother, you need to take on some of the responsibility as well.

Arguments between you and your mother are inevitable. Having a healthy relationship doesn't mean that you are free from argument, but that you understand what things are worth arguing about. The sooner you learn this lesson, the sooner you two will be on the road to fewer arguments. Fighting takes two people, and if one person drops out, then the fight stops.

What's a Daughter to Do?

Use "Fight Enders"

Here are some "fight enders" that you might want to try to help avoid a lot of fighting and bad feelings.

- Do it now.

   It took me until seventeen to learn that 90 percent of our arguments could be avoided if I would just empty the trash when it got full, or pick up my wet towel off the floor right when my mother asked me. I know it's annoying to get up in the middle of watching television or to cut short a phone conversation with your best friend, but if you do what your mother wants you to do right away it will save you unnecessary arguing. Even if you don't feel like the chore is urgent, your mother probably has reasons for needing it done right away. (If she doesn't, humor her anyway.) Not only will your mother appreciate that you've done what she asked, she'll also be greatly impressed by your maturity.

- Be wrong once in awhile.

   Don't get so caught up in winning all the time. Not everything is worth being right about, so pick your battles carefully. Even if your mother is being completely irrational and you know you are right, it doesn't always pay to prove her wrong. Look at the big picture and let go of things that really aren't important. You can end a lot of arguments and save yourself a lot of grief simply by saying, "You're right." If you withdraw from the fight, your mother will have nobody left to argue with.

- Laugh it off.

   Not everything needs to be taken seriously, and even fights have a bit of humor in them. Mothers and daughters have a tendency to be too serious and intense with each other. Learn to see the humor in your quarrels and you will put a quick end to many of your fights.

❀ Tips for Mothers for Win-Win Quarrels

1. Apologize when you have gone over the line.

2. Notice how she's cooperating with you. Tell her how much you appreciate her efforts.

3. Let her be right! Say to her, "I think you might be right," or, "I see what you mean."

4. When you don't understand why she's so upset, say to her, "Help me understand."

5. Allow time for both of you to cool down if things get too heated.

6. Be willing to forgive, forget, laugh about it, and move on.

7. Compromise and find a solution you both can live with.

11

Driving and Other Rites of Passage

Driving Lesson

'll drive!" I said, flashing my mother a smile. I just got my driver's permit and jumped at any chance to sharpen my skills. I loved being behind the wheel, it made me feel grown-up and independent.

"No, honey. I think I'll drive this time," she said impatiently. Her tone of voice made it obvious that she wasn't in the mood to play driving instructor.

"Mom," I said, irritated at her lack of enthusiasm. "I have to learn! How do you expect me to become a good driver if you don't let me practice? You never let me drive. Don't you want me to get my license when I turn sixteen?"

"It's not that I don't want you to get your license," Mom said, trying to show that she did sympathize with my plight. "Don't you just think it would be easier if I drove this time?"

"No." Giving my mother a hard glare, I whined, "I don't understand why it would be any easier. You aren't going to get us to the store any faster because we would both be driving at the same speed limit."

Sighing, she gave in and handed me the keys. "Fine," she said.

I smiled. "Thanks, Mom."

As we climbed into the car, she said, "Now I want you to pay attention. Driving is a big responsibility and you must always concentrate on what you are doing. Do you hear me?"

"No I can't hear you," I replied sarcastically. "Why don't you talk a little bit louder."

"I mean it, Amanda! If you aren't going to be serious, I'm not going to let you drive. Don't test me."

"I'm only joking, Mother," I said, fastening my seat belt and adjusting the rearview mirror. "I'll be serious. I promise."

I put the car into reverse and backed out into the residential street rather quickly. As I put the car into drive, my mother grabbed the handrest and clutched it as hard as she could. Out of the corner of my eye, I could see her shoulders get tense and felt her nervousness fill the car.

"You have to be very careful here," she said, as we neared a crosswalk.

"I know." I drove safely through the crosswalk, but my mother, with her hand grasping the door and her tense shoulders, was making me nervous.

"Can't you just relax, Mom?"

"No, I can't. Now watch what you are doing. There's a stop sign coming up."

"Thanks, I can see," I said as I looked down to turn on the radio.

"You can't see because you're looking down at the radio! You may think that you are paying attention, but you aren't. You always have to watch the road!" My mother braced herself, pressing her legs firmly into the floor of the car, and said, "Start slowing down."

"Mom, would you let me drive?" I yelled. "I know when to start slowing down for the stop sign!"

"Don't yell at me! You need to listen to what I tell you to do!"

"I would be able to pay better attention if you weren't always telling me what to do and grabbing onto the doors to brace yourself!" I argued as I came to a sudden stop at the stop sign.

When I am reincarnated, I want to come back in this world as a mother who doesn't drive.

—Erma Bombeck

Irritated, my mother said, "I've been driving for longer than you've been alive. If you want to learn, you have to listen to what I say. And if I feel like I need to grab onto something for safety, then I'm going to do it!"

"That's it! You drive! I'll never drive with you in the car again." I said, unbuckling my seatbelt and opening the car door. "All of my friends are much better at this than you are!"

✷ Firsts

I don't think that anything in our relationship was as stressful as when my mother tried to teach me to drive. She would grab the handle on the side of the door, press her feet into the floor as hard as she could, and yell, "STOP!" at every stop sign, crosswalk, and intersection. She got angry and would say that I wasn't paying enough attention to the road. If we both could have chosen, she wouldn't have been the one to teach me to drive, but since she's the only active parent in my life, she was the one who gave me driving lessons.

Learning to drive was exciting and meant new independence. I pictured myself cruising to the mall with my friends with the windows wide open and our favorite song playing on the radio. Having a set of car keys in my hand made me feel on top of the world. Getting my license was something I had eagerly anticipated. I wanted the freedom to run errands by myself or go to a football game without being dropped off. I could hardly wait for my sixteenth birthday, but my mother wasn't filled with this same excitement. Seeing me behind the wheel brought out her nervous side.

Maybe she realized I was growing up, or maybe she didn't want me to be driving around the streets with all those other crazy drivers, or maybe she just thought I was a terrible driver. Whatever the reason,

Everybody told my dad that as soon as I put on heels, I'd quit baseball. But I started wearing heels at fourteen and kept right on playing.

—Ila Borders, who at twenty-three became the first female to pitch in a pro baseball game

teaching me how to drive filled her with tremendous trepidation.

Getting my driver's license at sixteen was not the only thing that thrilled me and made me feel grown up. Through junior high and high school, my life was full of many growing-up passages. My first boy-girl party at thirteen, my first bus trip across town to go to the movies with friends, my first formal dance, my first high heels, and, following my high school graduation, my first parent-less summer vacation with my girlfriends at the beach.

It's amazing how many emotions all these "firsts" stirred in me—they filled me with joy, nervousness, exhilaration, anxiety, happiness, and sadness all at once. As I look back, I see my life will never again be exciting in the same way it was in high school.

All of these things, while wonderful for me, seemed to make my mom tense and touchy. She liked me being her little girl and now I was growing up. You may find that while you are looking forward to staying out past midnight, your mother is becoming unstrung. Seeing you riding in a car with your friends or pinning a boutonniere on your date remind your mother that, although you're not completely an adult, you are already making decisions on your own.

Some mothers show their uneasiness by becoming overprotective and making ridiculous rules. Others, like my mom, constantly remind their daughters to be careful. Others stay awake at night until their daughters arrive home safely. Others seem not to notice or care about these big moments.

✳ What's a Daughter to Do?

Reassure Her and Listen—She May be Right

When I was younger, I often dreamed of the day I would turn sixteen. I imagined coming home from school to find a cherry-red convertible sitting in the driveway with a big white bow tied around the front. I'm not the only person who's hoped to get a fancy new car for her sixteenth birthday, and I'm not the last one to be a little disappointed when all I received was the old family car.

Don't get me wrong, I *was* thankful to get a car, but I secretly envied my friends who drove cute little sports cars and I longed for something more racy. I was forced to drive what quickly was dubbed "The White Egg." It never broke down or needed any major repairs, it was clean and got great gas mileage, but I didn't care for it very much. I often drove it around recklessly, running stop signs, not using the "one car length for every ten miles per hour" rule, and occasionally backing thoughtlessly into a mailbox or trash can. One devastating event made me realize how much I had taken that little car for granted and how I hadn't heeded my mom's advice.

It was a typical Friday night as I headed for the basketball game. I drove through an intersection with the radio playing, munching on a piece of pizza, when suddenly the bright red of brake lights flashed in my face. At that moment I knew I would hit the car in front of me. I slammed on my brakes, hoping that the damage to the cars wouldn't be too bad, but my prayers were unanswered. I watched as the hood of my poor little egg got crushed under the bumper of the Bronco in front of me.

As the cops wrote out the report I stood in the road next to my car and sobbed. I cried for my car, for my foolishness, and for my spoiled attitude and selfishness. They say that just before you die your life flashes before your eyes. As I stood there watching my car get towed away, *its* life flashed before my eyes. I remembered my first flat tire, my trips to the Oregon coast, and the simple rides to school. I guess the saying, "You never miss a good thing until it's gone" really does apply.

After the accident, I figured I would get money from insurance and just get a new car. Unfortunately, things weren't that easy. I had to file a police report, call the insurance companies, talk to the witnesses, and go to court. It took a long time to get another car.

Now that I'm back in the driver's seat, my crazy ways have changed. I now understand and practice the art of safe driving. I've stopped fixing my hair and looking for CDs in the back seat while I drive, and most important, I do not tailgate!

Losing my car was a rite of passage I could have avoided had I listened to my mother's good advice about being a responsible driver. She generously reassures me that being able to admit my mistake is another rite of passage that shows I've matured.

I learned the hard way that a mother's advice can be helpful. When Mom saw me venturing out as a teenager, she got nervous and would sometimes go way overboard in reminding me to be careful and pay attention. When I rode the bus to the mall, she told me not to talk to any strangers; when I went to the ocean with my girlfriends, she warned me that if I swam too far out, the undertow would pull me out to sea. My mother gave me these reminders every time I did something new and it drove me crazy. Did she think that as soon as I left her sight, I would lose every piece of good judgment that I had? It made me feel like she didn't have faith in me anymore or thought I was an idiot.

Usually when she gave me unsolicited advice, I'd ignore it. I decided she really didn't know what she was talking about. With my driving, I felt she was overreacting by telling me to drive carefully. I thought I was a "number one" driver. Once I got my license, her reminders to drive safely didn't stop, and I continued to ignore her warnings. When I got both a speeding ticket and was involved in a car accident within two years of getting my license, I was forced to stop and listened to my mom's concerns. I could have saved both of us a lot of grief and stress if I'd followed her advice and paid attention, but instead I had to learn a very expensive and painful lesson.

At nineteen, after surviving many rites of passages, I've discovered that Mom really does give sound advice and her warnings are appropriate. She doesn't think I'm a bad decision maker, she just knows things that I don't. Since she has lived longer than I have, she's more aware of the consequences and possible dangers of my actions.

Although her nervousness still drives me crazy, I've learned how to deal with her. Instead of interrupting her, rolling my eyes, and saying, "I know, Mom," I listen to her. Then I reassure her I will be careful and promise her I'll use my best judgment. When I respond like this, Mom finishes warning me in about five minutes and I've avoided a big argument.

When your mother gets nervous, makes rules, or tries to hold you back from experiencing some of things that you are excited about, try to understand that she's not trying to ruin your life or spoil your fun. Accept that your mother will always be concerned. She acts this way because she loves you and wants to protect you. Do whatever you can to ease your mother's nervousness. Be responsible and reassure her that you won't do anything crazy. Ask yourself: Does my mother have a point? Should I be paying attention?

Terrified of Autonomy

I was tired of being a chauffeur but giving my daughter the car keys completely terrified me. I've been fearful many times but seeing my sweet one behind the wheel reminded me that she was entering another stage of her life that was out my control and had higher stakes than ever before.

Any mother who has turned the keys over to her daughter knows that this is truly a heart-stopping moment. Now our "baby" has wheels to drive away from our "nest." Amanda and I had some upsetting trips in our car until I recognized that driving lessons were not my area of expertise and turned the teaching over to our neighbor Rodney, Aunt Kathy, and the driving school.

Turning sixteen and getting a license is big event. Loaning your daughter the car, even if only for a quick trip to the grocery store, gets you worried. Even if she makes it home without a scratch, you realize that you have added worries now, from the cost of insurance to drunk drivers. You hope and pray that nothing disastrous happens to your precious daughter.

There are plenty of other issues to tackle as well, some realistic, some not. A teenager

To grown people, a girl of fifteen-and-a-half is a child still; to herself she is very old and very real....

—Margaret Widdemer

without wheels is still dependent for rides; once she has transportation, she's eager to go even more places. And go she does. Once Amanda was driving, I was left behind with a wild imagination. What was she doing? I realized how much I gleaned about her life simply by listening to her chat with her friends in the back seat. Now that she was catching rides or driving herself, I missed overhearing their informative, gossipy conversations. Not only was I dealing with my terror of the potential dangers of her less-than-adequate driving skills, I was also grieving the loss of one more conduit to her life.

There were other concerns, too. Cars, staying out late, boys, and curfews come as a package. My client Karen naively thought she still had a modicum of control over her fifteen-year-old daughter who didn't have any interest in learning to drive and relied on public transportation. Then she brought home her first boyfriend, who was nineteen, had a car, facial hair, and no curfew. "Looking back I can laugh, but at the time it wasn't funny. I had a lot of things to get used to. When she stayed out late, I couldn't sleep. I tried to use logic and explain that her curfew was for me because I was old and needed my sleep, but she didn't accept my reasoning. Fortunately after five months of torture and worry, nothing bad happened, and she broke up with him."

Each new passage brings tremendous grief. When Amanda was seven, she said to me, "I'm so happy today that even if a bee stung me I would still be happy." When she was thirteen, I asked her about her day and she glared at me and barked, "Just once I wish I could come home to a little peace and quiet!" It's a mixed bag. You appreciate the new freedoms her independence gives you, you enjoy watching her direct the school play, yet you still have to navigate your way through her back talk while grieving the loss of your "baby."

Not all passages are pleasant, but one thing remains constant—she will always need you. You are her strongest ally, biggest supporter, and loving guardian. If she has you on her side, she'll have someone to turn to throughout her life. She'll be able to handle the setbacks with the same courage you've shown sitting in the passenger seat with her behind the wheel. Even if you can't stay calm when you're teaching her to drive, at least laugh about it and know that there are plenty of opportunities when you can demonstrate once again how truly brave and brilliant you are.

❋ What's a Mother to Do?

Go for a Walk, Cry, and Pray

As a mother of a teenager on the verge of being on her own, I often ask myself things like: Have I taught her *all* she needs to know about *everything* she needs to know? Did I set a good example? Does she know about the benefits of eating fruits and vegetables? Did I warn her about the dangers of traveling through Europe on her own? Have I taught her about money management? Will she remember to take her vitamins? Have I encouraged her to follow her own heart and reminded her to take time to smell the roses? Have I given her good values and good self-esteem?

These questions make me realize my fears have gotten the best of me. Ruminating over what could or might happen does absolutely nothing. When I'm overwrought and tangled in my own fears, I call my friends who have teenage girls, and we empathize and comfort one another.

Being a mother means sometimes aching for our daughters. We've lived long enough to know that life takes unexpected turns. We may never say anything, but since infancy we've suffered when she's suffered. When she fell and hurt her knee, when her best friend moved away, when she lost the election or didn't get invited to the dance, we cried too.

When Amanda rear-ended that car, she was so upset she couldn't stop crying or catch her breath. I was so mad that I couldn't comfort her as I'd done a thousand times before. My neighbor said things like, "Thank heavens no one was hurt," and, "It's only a car." I was truly grateful Amanda was okay, but I still plunged into a state of

My mother raised me, and then freed me.

—Maya Angelou

grief. I'd been a single mother for sixteen years, carrying the full weight of financial and emotional responsibilities, and I'd always held her best interest first, but at that moment, I felt depleted. This rite of passage not only meant I'd be chauffeuring again, it heaped a mound of pressure onto an already a full plate. I was face to face with the fact that there were forces in my daughter's life that I couldn't control. I cried for several days and couldn't talk about it.

Not all rites of passages are pleasant. When things go wrong, we feel it's our fault and think of all the warnings we should have delivered. We relive our mistakes and wonder what we could have done differently.

At times like this, Amanda usually says to me, "Get a grip, chill. I can handle it; everything will be all right."

So I "get grip and chill." Tormenting myself by thinking of all the things that might go wrong is exercise I don't need. She's right, and she's bounced back from all her disappointments (and car wrecks). She's demonstrated to me hundreds of times that she can make good decisions and is handling her life very well.

You love your daughter so much that it's impossible not to worry now and then. Mothers with daughters much older than mine tell me that fretting accompanies each new thing she tries: mountain climbing, marriage, motherhood. As she grows up, she practices gaining skills while you practice loving her enough to give her room to forge her own destiny. When you're overwrought and anxious about what she's doing, give her your best advice, then go for a walk, have a good cry, call a friend, and pray that she'll be taken care of when she is beyond the sphere of your immediate influence.

✳ *Tips for Daughters*

1. Focus on one helpful tidbit in your mother's warnings.
2. Reassure your mother that you will use your good judgment.
3. Remember that both of you are going through these passages.

✳ Tips for Moms

1. Turn driving lessons over to someone who is good at it.
2. Talk about your expectations before you get in the car.
3. Know that with each passage there will be celebration and grief.
4. Remember that talking back is another rite of passage you have to get through.

12

Clothes and Costumes

Are You Wearing That?

Christine stood in front of her closet trying to decide what to wear as I sat on the bed flipping through her photo album. Our ride would be arriving any minute to pick us up. She chose a short, denim skirt that hung in the back of the closet and quickly pulled it on.

"Does this look okay?" she asked.

"Yeah, I like it," I replied.

As she sat down on the bed to put on her sandals, Christine said, "Now I remember why I don't ever wear this skirt; it's so uncomfortable." She stood up, tossed her skirt to the ground and grabbed her favorite pair of jeans. She threw them on, quickly pulled her old black T-shirt over her head and exchanged her sandals for a pair of tennis shoes. Christine sighed with relief, "Much better. I don't know why I even try to dress up because I always end up wanting to wear my jeans."

I laughed. "No kidding!"

After she finished getting ready, the two of us ran downstairs to the chen to wait for our friend. Christine's mother, Karen was standing over the sink washing dishes. When we came into the room, her mother looked up from the sink, carefully examining her daughter from head to toe and said, "I thought you girls were going out tonight."

"We are," Christine replied. "Amy will be here in a few minutes to pick us up."

Raising her right eyebrow in disapproval, Karen asked, "Are you wearing that?"

Christine gave me a look that said, "I should have known this was coming," and sighed. Her mother was constantly complaining about her clothes. "Mom, we're just going over to Kevin's house to hang out. There's no reason for me to dress up. Besides, this is the most comfortable thing that I have."

Karen threw her towel onto the counter, looked Christine in the eye, and said, "I'm not saying you should dress up, but it would be nice to see you in something other than those old jeans every once in awhile. What happened to those nice black pants we bought a few weeks ago, or that cute little jeans skirt? Both of those look so cute on you."

"Nothing happened to them, Mother. I just don't feel like wearing them. I want to be comfortable."

"I don't know why I spend money on new clothes when all you ever want to wear are jeans." Looking at me, she added, "Amanda's not wearing jeans."

Their argument was cut short by a knock at the front door.

"That must be Amy," Christine said. We were both relieved that this conversation had finally come to an end.

Christine and I went quickly to the front door, but her mother followed close behind. Before we even had a chance to greet Amy, Karen was talking. "Hello Amy. You look so cute tonight. Doesn't Amy look nice, Christine?"

"Good-bye, Mother," Christine said, hoping Karen would get the hint that she had finished talking about clothes. But before we could leave the house, Karen looked at her and said, "Honey, will you at least wear your hair down? It looks so pretty when you don't put it up in a ponytail."

This was the last straw for Christine. Ripping the ponytail holder from her wrist, she looked her mother straight in the eye as she tossed her hair into a ponytail. "Good-bye, Mother," she said, and quickly shut the door behind her.

✺ *"Is* That *What You're Wearing?"*

Another one of those timeless mother-daughter trials is the clothing disagreement. This has been happening since our mothers were young and will continue when our daughters have girls of their own. Teenagers are notorious for doing outrageous things with clothing, and mothers are infamous for disapproving of their clothing styles. It seems ridiculous for you two to be fighting over something as petty as clothing, but mothers and daughters argue about it regularly. Practically every girl has heard her mother ask the question, "Is *that* what you're wearing?" Whether your skirt is too short or your pants are too baggy, your mother always has something to say about your outfit.

You should know what outfits your mother hates and what type of clothes she wishes you would wear everyday. I could easily go through my closet and put together an outfit that would make my mother applaud with joy, just as I could pick something out that would make her scowl with disapproval.

There would be nights when, after I had gotten ready to go out, my mother would give me her "I don't like what you're wearing" look. When she would do this, I would either go to my room and put on something I knew she liked better, or I would keep the outfit I was wearing to prove I was perfectly capable of picking out my own clothes. During my nights of independence, I would feel uncomfortable and self-conscious about the way I looked. I would try to convince myself that I looked fine, but I could never quite shake my mother's disapproving look from my mind.

What makes clothes such a big deal? Why do our mothers get worked up when we want to wear jeans and a T-shirt when we go out with our friends? If my mother had it her way, I would wear knee socks

Typical underwear we wore on a date: girdle, garter belt, and stockings with seams. If we had our periods, we also wore a sanitary belt and a Kotex or Modess pad. We wore underpants over everything, then a half-slip, then a crinoline.

—Ilene Beckerman

and penny loafers every day. Often it is simply a matter of the generation gap. We feel most comfortable in the clothing that represents our generation. Think of your grandmother in her polyester pants, orthopedic shoes, and her short, permed hairdo. She feels comfortable with her style because it is represents people of her generation in the same way that your style represents your generation.

The clothes you wear most likely reflect some aspect of your personality and your friends. "My mom says, 'I wish that you would dress more like a girl,'" says fifteen-year-old Carmon. "She doesn't think that it's right for a girl to wear jeans and tennis shoes. What she doesn't understand is that all of my friends dress this way. If I dressed the way that she wanted me to, I'd be completely out of place."

HOT TIP FOR DAUGHTERS

Save your clothes. Twenty years from now they will be stylish again or valuable as vintage clothing. Perhaps your own daughter may one day wear your shoes to a theme dance or your prom dress to a Halloween party.

❀ *What's a Daughter to Do?*

Compromise Once in a While

Because normal teenage clothing today was not normal when your mother was a teenager, she probably does not understand your choice of clothing. My mom use to tell me about how she wasn't allowed to wear pants on campus when she was in college in the '60s. They wore skirts, even in the snow. Maybe this is why my mom doesn't completely understand why I wear jeans most of the time.

Your mother may feel that you are a reflection of her, and you will make her look bad if you wear clothes that make her uncomfortable. Maybe she finds your choice of clothing sloppy or thinks that you dress too old for your age. Sixteen-year-old Leah says, "I like to wear black skirts and high shoes. I think it makes a statement, but my mom thinks it makes me look like a twenty-year-old."

While your mother may never understand your type of clothing, you two can work together to eliminate unnecessary arguments. The next time that your mother gets upset about what you're wearing, try to figure out what exactly she doesn't like. Learn to work with her so that the clothing battle can be put to an end.

The main time my mother and I would argue about clothing was when we were going to be spending time with extended family or *her* friends. I would be ready to go, wearing something that I felt like wearing, yet my mother would complain. "What's wrong with this?" I would ask.

"It just doesn't look good," she would say, a bit flustered. "I wish that you would wear something a little nicer."

Annoyed, I would look in the mirror and examine myself closely to understand why my mother disliked my outfit. Turning to her, I would say, "I thought you liked this outfit. When I wore this to school last week, you said it looked cute."

"You look too sloppy for going out to a nice dinner."

"Gosh, you make me mad! I do not look sloppy!"

Whether I changed or not, it would be a frustrating battle and leave us both irritated for the rest of the night. I began to get tired of these fights and devised a strategy to avoid them. I realized that when we were doing things with my mom's friends or family, she really wanted me to look nice. So I began to check with her before I would decide what to wear. I asked questions like, "What are you going to wear tonight?" or, "Do you think it'd be okay if I wore my khaki skirt and a sweater over to Grandma's?" These simple questions helped us avoid extensive arguments.

There are certain times when your mother has a right to dictate what you should wear, like a family function or meeting her coworkers. Your mother feels uncomfortable when you dress sloppily around her friends, just as you would be embarrassed if she came to school wearing a tight black miniskirt and high heels. When you are on your mother's turf, you should be respectful and dress in clothing that makes her feel good about both of you.

Once you have agreed to these things, it's okay to ask her to agree to your clothing terms as well. Ask your mother to let you to wear what you want to without giving you disapproving looks and comments. Explain to her why you choose your clothing, and let her know that when you are with your friends, it isn't inappropriate. Tell your mother that every girl is different, and ask her to respect your choice of clothing.

It's Okay to Let Her Be Herself

It sounds so petty, and as a mother I'm supposed to be more mature, but I have given my daughter disapproving glances and asked, "Are you wearing *that*?" I was never embarrassed by how she looked, I just liked her to look "sweet" on certain occasions. Maybe I remember how adorable she looked in that blue velvet dress or those overalls when she was little. Maybe I balked at her wearing comfy jeans for family dinners because I hated the fact that she was no longer my "baby," but a young women with her own mind. Maybe I wanted her to look sharp for my friends and family so they could see what a fine job I'd done raising her.

Ultimately, I had to let go of my ego and remember that my relationship with her was more important than what other people thought. When it came to clothing, it was much better to have peace between us then tension over what she wore.

Adolescence is a time to experiment and try new styles, and we've all been through it ourselves. From saddle shoes to platforms, from poodle skirts to baggy jeans, teenage girls throughout the decades want to fit in and be stylish. The clothes that teens wear are fads that go in and out of style quickly. These fads are important to your daughter because her clothes reflect the developmental stage she's going through and are outward symbols of her internal quest to find her place in life. Adolescent preferences remind everyone that, while they're shedding the cloak of childhood, they're not yet ready to wear adult garb.

Accepting your daughter's choice in clothing sends her the important psychological message that "It's okay to be you—no longer a child, not yet an adult, but a glorious, incredible, magnificent teen." Her choice in clothing is an emblem of the "never-a-dull-moment in-between" years. Your acceptance of her taste in clothing tells her that the teenage years are as important as any other stage in life. Your daughter needs acceptance so she can successfully shape an autonomy separate from you. By disapproving of what she's wearing, you may be giving her the subtle impression that you also disapprove of her, or your protests may lead her to annoy you with even more extreme choices. If you accept these fads as normal and interesting, you're giving her permission to break out of your mold and embark on the journey of being independent from you without being completely alienated.

Whether it's a beehive or spiked hair, baggy jeans or miniskirts, let her know it's okay for her to develop her own opinions, styles, and tastes. Tell her it's perfectly normal to explore her options and, even though you may not always like her choices, she still has the right to do it her way. She won't stay in the "I've got to be me" phase forever and, most likely, she won't wear ripped jeans and T-shirts for the rest of her life. While she is wearing clothes you don't appreciate, though, it's best if you can understand them as simply an outward symbol of the teenage years.

According to a 1997 annual consumer survey conducted by Kurt Salmon Associates, 88 percent of girls between the ages of 13 and 17 say they "love to shop."

❀ What's a Mother to Do?

Use Your Power Constructively

As a mother, you have tremendous power over your daughter. If you doubt this, think about your own mother and the ways she still affects you. Even as an adult, there are probably times when you're reduced to a sulking teenager in her presence. A hint of disapproval from a mother can devastate a daughter and turn a simple disagreement into a defiant act of rebellion.

What you say about her clothes and how you say it does matter. You have a staggering amount of influence, so use it wisely to keep her enthusiasm high for exploring her creativity and self-expression. If you don't like the clothes she's wearing, it's better to hold your tongue. If it's really inappropriate for her to wear sloppy, holey jeans to hang out with her friends, they'll set her straight. If the other kids find it acceptable, your insistence that she change will mostly breed exasperation but can also evoke resentment toward you and more doubt about herself.

Look at the deeper reasons for your desire to control her wardrobe. Martha wears clothes to enhance her femininity and tries to convince her fourteen year-old daughter, Allison, to wear "something pretty." Allison prefers clothes that are comfortable. Their fights over how Allison dresses might be avoided if Martha looked for the deeper meaning in her messages. Is she trying to make her daughter more attractive to guys? Others mothers are fearful about their daughters' emerging sexuality and prefer that they camouflage their bodies.

For my Hunter College senior photograph in the 1953 yearbook, I wore a white dotted-Swiss blouse with large, bouffant sleeves. I wore it backward because I thought the neck looked more attractive on me that way.

—Ilene Beckerman

Don't generalize or put a negative label on your daughter. Get to know her as a person. When fifteen-year-old Stephanie started dressing all in black, her mother hated it so much that she poked fun of Stephanie by calling her a "misfit." Labels and put-downs won't bring understanding between you. If your daughter is dressing in ways that worry you, it's best to communicate with her instead of dismissing her preferences altogether.

You can sidestep many disagreements if you concentrate more on who she is than what she's wearing. Try not to criticize, and give her genuine, uplifting, empowering words of appreciation. "You look lovely in that shade of blue." Don't use your positives to manipulate her into doing what you want, however, because that will backfire. Don't let criticism or sarcasm creep in either. Saying "It's about time you wore that cute skirt I bought you" is not constructive.

Any talk about fashion and beauty is best done in a supportive way. Ask her, "What style of clothes do you like?" or, "What colors are your favorite?" Find out if your tastes are similar or different. Tell her about the styles you wore when you were her age, and what your mother thought about your clothes. Your daughter needs kindness, acceptance, and positive encouragement to blossom. Fifteen-year-old Kelly chose a very provocative slinky black dress to wear to her first high school dance. Her mother knew that girls often want to dress older than they are, but since she didn't want her daughter to feel ashamed of her body, she carefully chose her words and said, "You do look good in that dress, but I wonder if it's really you? Maybe it's a little too sexy for this dance? Let's put it on hold and look around." Her mother didn't say she couldn't have it, so there was no need for Kelly to get defensive. Kelly ended up choosing a purple velvet dress that they both really liked. "You've got great style," her mother told her.

FASHION AND TRAVEL QUIZ

Write your answers on a sheet of paper and share them with each other.

Q. If you could only pack five pieces of clothing to take on your next vacation, what would you take and where would you go?

No matter how perfect
your mother thinks you
are, she will always
want to fix your hair.

—Suzanne Beilenson

Reprimanding your daughter for what she's wearing chips away at her burgeoning self-respect and has its consequences, from your daughter feeling uncomfortable with her body to not knowing what she wants or needs. Accepting her where she is—not where you think she should be or where you want her to be—allows her to change her mind, which she probably will do many times in the coming years. Showering her with acceptance gives her the go-ahead to find her own sense of style and allows her to trust her choices. You can have fun together by reminding yourselves that developing flair and style is one of the perks of being a young woman.

When she's wearing spiked hair, greet your daughter with appreciation for her struggles, patience for her attitude, and lighthearted good humor. Show a sense of wonder for the costumes that she's sporting and for the young woman she's becoming, and greet her with gladness for arriving at another magnificent stage of her life.

❋ Tips for Moms

1. Let your daughter modernize you—pick out something she thinks you'd look good wearing.

2. Share your stories of your "teenage costumes." What styles did you wear at her age, and what reaction did your parents have?

3. Honor her requests for how she wants you to dress around her friends or when attending her school functions.

4. Avoid sprucing her up. Don't tell her to get her hair out of her eyes or make negative comments about her clothes. Don't straighten her blouse or brush the lint off her sweater. She will feel you are invading her physical space.

13

Body Piercing, Tattoos, and Other Desires for Adventure

Belly Button Piercing

"Are you sure you that you really want to do this?" my mother asked, hoping that I would decide to change my mind at the last minute.

"Yes, I'm positive," I said, even though my stomach was swarming with butterflies. I couldn't back out now. I had already told everyone at school that I was going to get my belly button pierced and they would think I was a liar if I didn't go through with it.

"Maybe you should think about it a little more," my mother said. You could almost see, "What's happening to my little girl?" and "What are the other parents going to think of me if I let her do this?" going through her head. When my mother agreed to let me get my belly button pierced for my fifteenth birthday, I knew she thought I wasn't serious about it. Now, as we walked down the city street looking for the tattoo and body piercing shop, my mother began to realize that I was serious.

"I'm not sure this is such a good idea after all," she said.

"Mom, we've already discussed this. It's not that big of a deal. Nobody's going to see it. Besides, you promised I could do it."

As we walked down the dark staircase and into the tattoo parlor, the people inside gave us strange looks. My mom in her black pantsuit and me in my penny loafers didn't quite fit in among the people with numerous body piercings and multicolored hair. The atmosphere made my mother a bit nervous, but I was excited. I was taking a risk and trying something new.

"Can I help you?" asked a man whose arms, hands, and neck were covered in tattoos.

"I want to get my belly button pierced," I said enthusiastically.

"How old are you?" he asked. "If you're under eighteen, you have to have your parent's permission."

Pointing to my mother, I said, "That's my mom. She says it's okay." My mother smiled to show she had consented to this crazy plan of mine.

After deciding on a small, silver ring with a purple bead on it, I followed the man back to the piercing room, with Mom trailing behind.

"Will this hurt?" I asked as I climbed up onto a white padded table like you would find in a doctor's office.

"No," he said.

I didn't believe him.

Mom looked anxiously around the room. "Is everything clean?" she asked. "You do sterilize, don't you? Are you sure that she won't get an infection? You've done this before, haven't you?"

"It's going to be fine. We've never had any problems," the man answered.

"You know, honey, you don't have to do this if you don't want to," my mom said, her final desperate attempt to change my mind.

"I want to," I said, grabbing her hand tightly for support as I anticipated the pain.

About sixty seconds later, the man said, "You're all done."

I sat up and looked down at my newly pierced belly button.

"Does it hurt?" my mom asked.

"No," I said. "It's not too bad. Do you like it?" I waited to see her reaction.

My mother smiled. "I think it's kind of fun. In fact, it looks cute."

"I guess it wasn't as bad as you expected, huh, Mom?"

She laughed and said, "I guess not."

"You Let Her Do What?"

I wasn't totally comfortable with my decision to let Amanda get her belly button pierced. I'm sure you understand how a mother can be talked into something without being sure of how it happened. You know how your daughter begs, pleads, reasons, and talks circles around you until you finally give in? It was like that with the belly button piercing.

Maybe it was because I never did anything "wild" when I was a girl. I grew up in Nampa, Idaho, in the '50s, and by the time I'd graduated from high school in '62, the only impetuous thing I'd ever done was write "Elvis" in red lipstick on the wallpaper at the only movie theater in town. After the owner called my mother, she cried for days about how I had ruined my dad's reputation as the town banker. I begged her not to tell him and she promised she wouldn't if I "acted like a lady" from then on.

We are all filled with a longing for the wild.

—Clarissa Pinkola Estés

Growing up, I dreamed of running off to San Francisco and becoming a beatnik or a hippie. When I asked my mom if I could get my ears pierced, she said, "Ask your dad." Dad said, "If God wanted you to wear earrings, you would have been born with holes in your ears." Thirty years later, with my mother's "You're giving her *what* for her birthday?" ringing in my ears, I drove Amanda to the "iffy" side of town to get her belly button pierced. Maybe it was because I felt stifled as a teenager that I didn't want my daughter to reach adulthood frustrated by unfulfilled longings. All I know for certain

Every daughter must have an adventure; she needs to create her own story to become her own person.

No matter how much mothers, anxious for their daughter's safety or success, insist that they "go straight" to their destination, daughters must always take their own circuitous route, and mothers can only watch and suffer, or watch and rejoice.

—Josephine Evetts-Secker

was that seeing the satisfaction on her face made me feel better.

I continued to feel fine throughout the parental cross-examination I had at the high school football game that night. When Megan's mother asked me in an accusing tone, "Why did you let her do that?" I couldn't muster up a sound explanation so I shrugged my shoulders. But deep inside I felt confident that I'd done the right thing.

✳ What's a Mother to Do?

Know Yourself

Please don't think for a minute that I'm telling you to let your daughter get her belly button pierced. I'm not. Every mother–daughter relationship is different, and what's acceptable to me may not be acceptable to you. Permitting your daughter to spread her wings, however, can be fun for both of you. When you know your own needs, you're not as frightened by your daughter's longings, and you can be open to your daughter's explorations. This helps you decide the best way to add excitement and you can try something new together.

✳ When Appropriate, Indulge Her Desire for Adventure

Teens like excitement, and your daughter is no exception. She will take chances and look for thrills. She'll probably do things that you don't understand and your worrying goes with the territory. Your daughter wants adventures that don't include you. If you're willing to spice up your relationship, her urge to *always* look elsewhere will

According to *The Information Please Girls' Almanac*, there were 77,735 women competitors at the Women's International Bowling Congress championship tournament in Reno, Nevada, in 1988.

lessen. With some creative planning and a little ingenuity, you can turn a potential battleground into an adventure.

Like you, she has her longings. When you explore them together, you add sparkle to your relationship. By knowing your longings and sharing some of them with her, she'll begin to see "the girl" in you, not just "the mother."

Gail takes her daughter on a whitewater rafting trip each summer. Sandy and Meg go on a "girls only" hiking and camping trip each summer with their daughters. "We get to know each other as 'wild women,'" they say.

Mothers who were restricted as teenagers often worry that if their daughters are having too much fun, they will become uncontrollable and irresponsible. Mothers who ran wild as teens worry that their daughters might make the same mistakes. Wanting to avert heartaches and catastrophes, they pull the reins tighter. Other mothers live with their heads in the sand, oblivious to what's going on.

Despite your concerns, it's always better to stay current with your daughter's thoughts and dreams. Put effort into creating an environment where she feels comfortable sharing her dreams with you. Many mothers pooh-pooh their daughter's plans by saying "That's ridiculous" or "Why do you want to do that?" without even listening to the answer. Pushing her excitement underground keeps you in the dark and in a constant state of worry. If you listen, you'll be better able to steer her in a positive direction. When I agreed with thirteen-year-old Amanda and said, "You're right, it would be fun to drop out of school and travel the world; why don't we?" she replied,

"I'm not dropping out of school and you can't make me."

I'm not saying you can't put your foot down and say "No." After Amanda got her belly button pierced, she started hinting about a little tattoo on her ankle. I said, "Absolutely not." I knew she wasn't serious because she dropped it right away. Then she mentioned piercing another hole in her ear and I pulled out the standard, "Not while living under my roof." She laughed and I knew that she was teasing. We like joking with each other in this way. It proves to me that just because she tries something "far out" doesn't mean she's going off the deep end. Two years later, she took out her belly button ring and that was the end of it. Because I didn't balk at what she wanted, the belly button ring didn't become a symbol of rebellion.

There is a difference between healthy risk-taking and dangerous risk-taking. Unhealthy risks such as drinking and driving or unprotected sex have dire consequences. Positive risks boost confidence and reduce anxieties; they allow your daughter to grow emotionally, physically, and mentally. Seventeen-year-old Andriene took a summer job in a state park a thousand miles away from home. Fifteen-year-old Jolee rode her bike across the state with four friends and one adult guide. Sixteen-year-old Amber is a proficient mountain climber, thanks to her dad's encouragement. Positive risks translate into gaining life skills, courage, and resilience. Girls who've never taken a chance are more afraid of failure and hold themselves back from positive experiences like trying out for the school play or running for student office.

According to *The Information Please Girls' Almanac,* Tania Aebi was the first American woman and the youngest person ever to sail alone around the world. In 1985, at the age of nineteen, she undertook the 27,000-mile adventure on her twenty-six-foot sloop, the *Varuna.* She returned to New York in 1987.

According to *The Information Please Girls' Almanac*, the first all-women auto race took place in 1909. It was a round-trip race from New York City to Philadelphia. There were twelve competitors. The Woman's Motoring Club cup went to Alice DiHeyes of New Jersey; she drove a Cadillac with four female passengers.

Overprotective mothers may think that they're keeping their daughters safe by sheltering them; however, reining them in too tightly can backfire since their daughters don't get the chance to sharpen their risk-assessment skills. Teenage girls need to become independent and develop good judgment. When your daughter has opportunities to take healthy risks, she develops a strong sense of self and is less prone to gravitate toward dangerous risks or negative peer pressures.

For your daughter to spread her wings safely, you'll have to stretch with her. You're both likely to have a good time if you do, and she'll gain the skills that will lead to success as an adult.

It's So Exciting!

When I asked my mother if I could get my belly button pierced, I didn't think that she'd actually say "Yes." It was spur-of-the-moment idea inspired by an MTV video. Maybe it was because piercing my belly button would be completely out of character. Perhaps I was tired of being predictable or maybe I just thought it looked cool, but I felt a strong desire inside me and knew I had to do it.

I presented the idea to my mother and, to my shock, she agreed. Although my peers were able to understand this impulse, their mothers weren't. My friends thought the small ring in my stomach looked cool and could empathize with my desire to do something different. Yet, to many mothers, the fact that I had got my belly button pierced was a sign I had gone bad.

Teenagers usually start new trends, so while you may understand that getting a tattoo doesn't mean you've turned into a rebellious hellion, your mother doesn't. It's normal for us to want to try new things and express ourselves in new ways.

As a teenager, your mother probably didn't know anyone with a body piercing or tattoos, while you probably know at least a dozen people who have them. So what is normal and commonplace to you may seem unusual and a little scary to your mother. Maybe she thinks it is a sign you are hanging out with a "bad crowd," or maybe she has no reason at all and just says "No." Whatever her logic, when you want to do something a bit out of the ordinary, you need to approach your mother with the right tactics.

✳ What's a Daughter to Do?

Use Good Timing and Be Mature

If there's something that you want to do, like dye your hair platinum blonde or get another ear piercing, figure out the best way to approach your mother. Don't announce in the middle of dinner that you've decided to get a tattoo. Pick an appropriate time to ask her what she thinks about your getting a tattoo. Try to explain why you want to do it and give her good reasons for why she should give you the go-ahead. Usually the standard "All my friends are doing it" doesn't work with mothers. If you want your mother to give her blessing, you must think through your approach and present yourself maturely.

Temper tantrums are not classy. Give your mother the positive benefits of trying something new. If she sees you have really thought about it and can present your desires in a mature way, she will be more willing to listen to your arguments. Listen to what she has to say in return. The best way to keep your mother from freaking out is to approach her in a level-headed, easygoing manner.

Unfortunately, because you are not yet an adult and are still being supported by your mother, she has the right to put her foot down. I know how frustrating it can be when she uses her authority and doesn't let you do something that may seem perfectly harmless. Many of us feel a strong desire to rebel when our mothers pull out their famous "Not while you're living in this house" line. Despite your desire to take charge of your own life, you must stop and think whether getting a tattoo to spite your mother is really worth all the trouble it will cause. Is it worth being grounded for a week or losing your car?

If your mother doesn't agree with your plan, the best thing to do is keep cool. Even though your initial reaction may be to argue until she gives in or go behind her back, maturity will get you much farther. If you keep your cool, the next time you want to do something that seems a little off the edge, your mother might be more willing to give in.

If your mother consistently refuses to let you try your new ideas, you can bask in the satisfaction of knowing that once you are on your own, you can do whatever your heart desires.

> Healthy excitement, like all good play, serves a purpose. It allows us to let off steam and know ourselves from a different angle. It energizes us and gives us new enthusiasm with which to face our regular routine.

Mom's Guidelines for Challenging Adventures

1. Pick three things that you wanted to do as a teenager but didn't get to try. Choose one and invite your daughter to do it with you. If she doesn't accept the invitation right off the bat, do it with a friend or by yourself. By

the time you're ready to do the second thing on your list, she might be ready to join you.

2. Steer her toward excitement and challenging adventures. What after-school activities can she particiate in? Check out the local YWCA or consider taking a class together.

3. Enlist her good judgment by thinking through the pros and cons of risk-taking behavior with her.

4. Share your own risk-taking behavior with your daughter and tell her what you've learned.

5. Celebrate the risks that pay off for her. Commend her for her good judgment and courage.

✳ Daughter's Plan for Adventure

Write down three wishes. Think about how you can begin to make your wishes come true and ask your mother for backing. Design an action plan and set a timetable. What do you need to do today, tomorrow, and the next week to keep you on your wishing course?

14

I've Got Legs!

Body Image and Eating Disorders

Just Five Pounds

"Do you like this one?" Lindsay asked, holding up a long red dress to show her mother.

"That's nice," her mother answered. "Let's go try these on."

Lindsay and her mother walked to the dressing room with dresses piled in their arms. The prom was still six weeks away, but it's never too early to start looking for dresses. The two entered the dressing room to begin the rigorous and nearly impossible task of finding the perfect dress.

"Crystal bought her dress last weekend," Lindsay said as she slipped the first dress over her head. "It's long and white and looks so cute on her."

"I'll bet it does," her mother responded. "Crystal is so slim, she looks great in everything. Some people are just blessed with perfect bodies."

"I kind of like this one," Lindsay said, looking at herself in the mirror.

Her mother, examining her daughter carefully, said, "Turn around. I don't know, I think it makes your hips look too wide."

"Yeah, I guess you're right," Lindsay agreed with a frown. She pulled off the dress and reached for the next one. As she slipped it over her head, her mother said, "You know, honey, I've been meaning to tell you I don't think you should keep making those fruit-and-yogurt smoothies every morning for breakfast. I know they're nonfat, but they still have a lot of calories in them." As Lindsay finished putting on the second dress, her mother said, "Let me see."

"Wow," said her mom. "That one would be great if you lost just five pounds. It looks good now, but if you lost some weight, it would be fabulous." Then her mother's eyes got big as she had an idea. "I have a great idea. Why don't we go on a diet together? I need to lose a few pounds, too. If we both do it, we can keep each other going. I'll even buy you that dress as motivation to lose the weight."

The average American woman weighs 144 pounds and wears between a size 12 and size 14.

❊ I Wish I Were Pretty

Every girl knows how it feels to hate something about the way she looks. As a culture, we place a high value on looks and, whether you are directly aware of it or not, there is immense pressure for girls to be slender, with flawless skin and long, shiny hair. Your teenage years strongly influence your body image.

They certainly did for me. When I was thirteen, a guy pointed to me and I overheard him say, "She's ugly," as I walked by. In the ninth grade, I got all dressed up to go to a dance with a guy from another school

If shop mannequins were real women, they'd be too thin to menstruate.

only to have him spend the entire night talking about how gorgeous all the other girls in our group looked. In high school, when my friends and I would go out, my girlfriends always looked better than I did, and they would meet the guys while I stood unnoticed in the background. All these humiliating experiences made me feel bad about my looks. I've talked to my friends about these things, and all of them, even the ones I believe are the most beautiful, have had similar experiences and feelings. You are not alone in thinking you don't measure up. We all have negative feelings and thoughts about ourselves, but those put-downs don't have to ruin our lives. What matters is what we do with those negative thoughts and feelings.

The way you feel about your looks completely influences your life. Having a negative idea of your body is all-consuming and often holds you back from doing things you want to do. You may think your thighs are too fat to try out for the dance team or that you're too ugly to run for school secretary. In junior high and high school I told myself that if I were prettier, I would have a boyfriend.

We girls are incredibly critical of our looks and are always comparing ourselves to others. We look at our friends or models in magazines and think, "If only I looked like her, my life would be better." We watch our guy friends drool over beautiful, older girls and we listen to them talk about breasts, butts, and legs so often that we find ourselves to be inadequate in comparison.

All this takes a toll on your self-image and confidence. Luckily for me, my mother was always telling me things like, "You are so beautiful," and "You have the cutest little body." I didn't usually believe her and thought she was just saying those things because she was my mother, but it helped to hear that somebody thought I was pretty. By reassuring

One out of every four college-aged women has an eating disorder.

me, she helped me build a positive self-image and not let negative thoughts about my looks take over my life.

I was appalled at the way some of my friends' moms talked about their daughters' looks and weight, making comments like "Don't eat that, you need to lose weight" or "You're getting fat." I couldn't believe that mothers actually said such mean things. If your mother is like that, you will have a much harder time discovering what is lovely about you. You will have to work hard to love yourself as you are.

Your mother may try to help you feel better about your looks by saying things like, "I don't think that outfit is very flattering on you," or she may buy you make-up saying, "If you wear this, you will be beautiful." She thinks she is helping you, but all you want to hear from her is that you are already beautiful and wonderful. If you say, "I think my legs are fat," she will want to help you. She may say something like "I'll help you go on a diet" or "Why don't you go running?" showing that she is trying to help you, but she's really only confirming your insecurity. She doesn't realize that by trying to improve your imperfections, she is hurting you much more than she is helping.

A negative body image can be as simple as thinking that your nose is too big, but it can lead to serious problems like eating disorders or severe depression. I have known girls with serious eating disorders and the main thing I wonder is, "How could her mother let her get that way?" Not all mothers are supportive, and not all mothers know what to do.

Are you at risk of an eating disorder?

If you answer "Yes" to five of the following statements, you are at high risk for having an eating disorder.

1. I cringe when I look at myself in the mirror.

2. I weigh myself several times every day.

3. I obsess about eating, weight, and my body size all the time.

4. I feel guilty or mad at myself after I eat.

5. I have a rigid exercise plan.

6. I vomit or take laxatives if I eat too much.

7. I eat when I am lonely, anxious, or depressed.

8. Food and weight control my life.

9. I go on fattening food binges.

10. Occasionally I starve myself.

11. My mom tells me that I am too fat or too thin.

✳ What's a Daughter to Do?

Get Help If Necessary

If you find you have a problem with eating or have a friend who does, get help. If you can't talk to your mother about it, go to your best friend, a teacher, a coach, a youth-group leader, or anyone that you trust. Having eating problems doesn't always mean having anorexia or bulimia; it can also mean eating only fruit for lunch or rice for dinner. When you find that you would rather be skinny than healthy, you have a problem.

✿ *Write a Letter*

It 's hard to talk about how you feel about your body, but if you feel like you need help from your mother, tell her. It isn't easy to say, "Mom, I hate the way I look," so you may want to write your mother a letter expressing your negative self-image. My friend Rebecca gave this letter to her mother:

> *Dear Mom,*
>
> *I am writing you this letter because I need your help. I am beginning to feel that I am losing my self-confidence. More and more I feel that it's hard for me to believe in myself and it seems like my self-esteem is at an all-time low. I'm not sure exactly why I have been feeling this way and I need your help.*
>
> *The other day when I went to go get ice cream with my friends and you said, "Try to get sorbet instead of ice cream because it's less fattening," my feelings were hurt. It seems like you think I'm fat and you want me to lose weight. It's hard for me to feel good about myself when you make comments like these and I am feeling self-conscious about my body more than I ever have before.*
>
> *Right now I need your reassurance more than anything. I know that you are trying to help and aren't trying to hurt me. Please be aware of the things that you say to me. I wish that you would encourage me when I say bad things about myself instead of trying to give me advice on how to fix myself.*
>
> *Love, your daughter,*
> *Rebecca*

Reading this letter helped her mother understand what Rebecca was experiencing and made her aware of the destructive things she was saying to her daughter. The letter also helped her mother realize how to support Rebecca's self-confidence.

✻ Strengthen Your Body Image on Your Own

Putting so much importance on looks is stupid, but we do it anyway. We shouldn't worry about wearing the perfect outfit or having perfect hair. Looks are only one small part of who you are, and they don't show your personality or what you are like as a person. Teenage girls are their own worst critics. Ask any girl if she thinks that she is pretty and she will probably say "No." There have been many times when I have agonized over a zit on my face that nobody else even noticed or looked at myself in the mirror, hating my clothes, only to have my outfit complimented by my friends at school.

No one's looks are perfect. Even the models in the magazines are airbrushed!

Remember, body image really means what you think of your looks and your body. You can think whatever you want if you stop comparing yourself to others. Here are steps I have taken to help myself regain confidence when I am feeling down about my body and the way that I look.

1. Don't point out your faults.

   We all do this. You and your girlfriends are standing in front of the mirror in the bathroom between classes when you say, "Look at this ugly zit on my forehead!" Then your friend joins in and says, "At least you have pretty hair. I hate my hair!" The conversation continues this way until you have all pointed out every flaw on your bodies.

   You may not realize it, but this type of talk is very detrimental to your body image. Always talking about things you don't like about yourself puts negative feelings in your head. Don't draw attention to your "faults," and next time a conversation like this comes up, try not to join in. Look at yourself in the mirror and find something you like about yourself. Think to yourself, "My hair looks nice today," or "I've got nice, bright green eyes," or "I have been blessed with nice legs!" Thinking about the positive things and will have a good influence on how you view your looks.

2. Pamper yourself.

I love the way I feel when my nails are done and I have taken the time to curl my hair. When I put time into pampering myself, I feel good about myself and the way that I look. Obviously I don't have the time or the desire to put such an effort into my looks every day, but doing it every so often gives me a stronger self-image.

Do whatever makes you feel good about yourself. Paint your nails, give yourself a facial, or wear something that makes you look and feel good. Carry yourself like a supermodel and believe that you are gorgeous.

3. Be good to your body.

When my body image is low, nothing helps me better than going for a run, hitting the weights at the gym, or going to yoga class. Being active and eating healthy boosts my energy level and makes me feel like I'm doing something good for myself. Don't take your workouts to extremes. If you find that you are working out solely to lose weight and feel depressed when you don't see the results you want, you are being unhealthy. Try to keep your workout focused on feeling good rather than losing weight. The key is to do something you enjoy that makes you feel good. Go horseback riding, run, play tennis, swim, or skate; all these activities will get you moving and help you feel great in the body you've got.

According to the President's Council on Physical Fitness and Sports, girls who participate in sports and exercise have positive feelings about their bodies, improved self-esteem, tangible experiences of competency and success, and increased self-confidence.

4. Focus on something besides looks.

Don't base your self-worth on your looks. Think about the other qualities that you like about yourself. Kindness to others, your skill at the piano, or your ability to make people laugh are all attributes that make up your personality and are much more important than looks. Focus on these things and you won't feel the way you look is the only thing that matters.

Don't judge others by the way they look. Don't say things like "She always wears the ugliest shirts" or "Why doesn't she get a new hairstyle?" Sometimes I would find myself looking at another girl and wondering, "Am I prettier than she is?" Being prettier than the girl I was comparing myself to was like being better than her in some way. To get away from putting looks at the center of your world, you must stop judging others by their looks.

Do My Legs Look Fat?

When Amanda was in the seventh grade she complained for the first time, "I'm *sooo* fat and ugly. I need to go on a diet." Her comment got my immediate attention and scared me because her self-perception did not match with reality. She wasn't fat or ugly. I knew that thinking such negative thoughts about herself could become a self-fulfilling prophecy. It certainly had for me. "Honey," I said, "It hurts me to hear you talk to yourself like that. Please don't call yourself names." Then I told her the story of my continuous struggle. "When I was your age, I thought I was fat and ugly too. For years, I called myself names, thinking that if I were mean enough to myself I would find the willpower necessary to stick to a rigid diet. It didn't work and I called myself so many nasty names that I actually started believing what I was saying."

She listened carefully to my story. She had seen me struggle to feel good about my body and she knew I felt embarrassed about being overweight. "If you call yourself horrid names, you will turn into exactly what you are calling yourself." I told her. "That's how it happened to me. I wasn't fat or ugly when I was a teenager, but I called myself so many horrid names that it affected my self-image. It wasn't until I was in my forties that I realized I was an attractive woman. I've had to work very hard to get out of the habit of being mean to myself.

"Take my advice," I added. "If you want to be healthy, in good shape, and pretty, give yourself compliments, call yourself love names, and say positive things about your body. If you say positive things every day, you will start believing in yourself and then you will become exactly that."

Instead of saying, "My legs are too fat," I suggested she say, "I've got legs!" That's right! "You've got legs, honey! It isn't the size, the length, or the shape that matters. What matters is that you've got legs and they can take you places you've never been before and bring you back again."

Your adolescent daughter is her own worst critic. (I certainly was when I was that age, weren't you?) In her mind, she is never good enough. She doesn't need her mother pointing out her flaws because she already knows them and has mentally blown each one way out of proportion. If her mother, the person who is supposed to love and accept her unconditionally, finds her flawed, why should she, or

"I'VE GOT LEGS!" MEDITATION

Put on your favorite music, turn the lights down low, and light several candles to create a pleasant, comfy atmosphere. Look at yourself in the mirror. Say three positive things about your body; for example, "My skin is soft." "My hair is shinning." "I've got legs!" If you find criticism creeping in, turn your attention away from the negative and focus on what you can appreciate. Whenever you pass a mirror at the mall, be sure to appreciate your image by giving yourself a compliment and saying, "I've got legs!"

anyone else, accept her as she is? The cycle of self-loathing and improvement is born.

Thinking we are helping by encouraging her to stand up straight or saying "You look better with bangs," we often don't realize the negative impact of our good intentions. Statements like "If you just wore a little bit of make-up, you'd be beautiful" or "Don't eat butter on your popcorn—it's full of fat" are harmful. While our intent is to encourage our daughter to become the best that she can be, these messages are doing the opposite. One statement is not enough to damage her, but weeks and months of "improvement messages" pile up. You help your daughter more if you affirm that she's lovable as she is. When you teach her to love what she already has, you give her the gift of feeling good about herself.

Everyone's body is different. Teach your daughter to love and take care of hers the way that it is. Tell her she's beautiful. Frequently I ask girls what they will do differently when they are mothers. Fifteen-year-old Jade said, "I will tell her every day how beautiful she is. I will respect her and who she is."

Twenty years ago, a model generally weighed 8 percent less than the average woman; today she weighs 23 percent less.

A psychological study in 1995 found that spending three minutes looking at models in a fashion magazine caused 70 percent of the women who did so to feel depressed, guilty, and shameful.

✳ Build Her Up

Nowhere is the "If you can't say anything nice, don't say anything" policy more appropriate then in the area of your daughter's body, looks, and weight. Popular culture places so many unrealistic standards on young women about their looks that by the time your daughter reaches her teens, she's been inundated with thousands of messages about how she must improve her body and lose weight to be attractive. These are unrealistic and discouraging ideals—nobody can ever measure up to the models and actresses she watches. She can't possible look like the sixteen-year-old idol she sees in the magazines or on the screen because that model doesn't even look like her own pictures—the photos have been airbrushed.

In an attempt to look acceptable, teenage girls easily become preoccupied with appearance and weight. Bulimia and anorexia occur during adolescence and are serious illnesses with long-term consequences. Girls with anorexia are obsessed with thoughts of food and eating as they starve themselves. They often have an overachiever mentality and suffer from compulsive exercise, fatigue, cessation of menstrual periods, and low self-esteem. Girls who suffer from bulimia tend to maintain a normal weight; they use food for comfort and overeat, then vomit to avoid gaining weight.

Many mothers have a "fear of fat" which they project onto their

According to *Mademoiselle*, the average percentage of adolescent girls who believe they are overweight is 55 percent; the percentage of girls who really are overweight is 13 percent.

daughters. Let your daughter know that while you appreciate her physical attributes, what you really admire is her spirit, good humor, brains, and enthusiasm. Tell her that what makes a young women attractive is an "air of aplomb" that comes from liking who you are. Tell her that lasting beauty shines from within.

When she complains "My butt's too big" or "I hate my nose," "My stomach bulges" or "I'm ugly," don't laugh and tell her she's ridiculous. Don't attempt to cheer her up either. Listen to the frustration she's sharing; even though you see the situation differently, her feelings are real to her. If you ignore them or ridicule her, they will intensify. It's painful to feel that you are lacking the one perfect trait that would make your life better. Tell her you understand and share a story from your own teen years when you were feeling the same.

When thirteen-year-old Rachel cried about the shape of her ears because a boy had called her Dumbo, her mother Maggie listened carefully. After Rachel had finished pouring out her embarrassment, Maggie shared a painful teenage memory of being teased about her "horse smile." By sharing a similar frustration, she let Rachel know that we all have physical quirks. "Maybe I have a horse smile," said Maggie, "but I like horses, so what's wrong with that? Besides I have beautiful horse eyes." They sympathized with each other's suffering until the pain had lessened. Rachel was able to be more objective as well and said, "So what, big ears like Dumbo mean I'm going places."

Your daughter will get over her hurt and find inner strength to conquer her demons if she knows you are standing with her and that together you can cry over it, laugh, and move on.

Do whatever you can to build her up. Give her a beautifully bound edition of *The Ugly Duckling*. Write her a letter in the front of the book telling her that you can see she's getting lovelier every day. Look at her with admiration. Make food a non-issue. Have plenty of healthy, good-tasting snacks available. Don't talk about dieting— yours or hers. Focus on making mealtimes happy. Encourage her interests in sports because of the joys of teamwork and the positive highs that come from moving your body. You want your daughter to feel good from the inside out so that she can enjoy her own vitality and all that it means to be a woman.

More girls than ever participate in sports. According to a survey conducted by the National Sporting Goods Association, girls comprise about 37 percent of all high school athletes. Women comprise 33 percent of all college athletes and approximately 39 percent of United States Olympic team members.

15

Bring on the Boys

Where's Your Boyfriend?

"Aren't you going out tonight?" Darcy's mom asked, seeing her daughter reading at the kitchen table.

"No, not tonight," answered sixteen-year-old Darcy.

"Why not?" asked Darcy's Aunt Sally, who was visiting for the evening. "It's Friday night. Where are your friends?"

"Kelly and Jen are both out with their boyfriends and Melanie is on a date with some guy from another school. Besides, I'm not really in the mood to go out."

"That's neat that Melanie is going out with a boy from another school," said Darcy's mother. "Is he cute? Maybe she could have him fix you up with one of his friends."

"Yeah, maybe." Darcy was obviously uninterested.

"I never hear about you going out on dates or having a steady boyfriend, Darcy," said her aunt.

Before Darcy even had a chance to answer, her mother was speaking for her. "Darcy says that she just isn't interested in any of the boys at school. She says that they aren't worth dating. I don't understand it because she has so many guy friends. I try to get her to date a couple of them, but she won't."

"They're my friends, Mom." Darcy and her mother had been through this nearly a dozen times. "I'm not interested in them like that."

"You know, Darcy, you can't always be so picky," her aunt advised.

"She's right," added her mother. "You have to be willing to give guys a chance. Wouldn't you like to have a boyfriend during high school? You would have fun if you had a boyfriend."

"Mom, I can have fun without a boyfriend too. What's the point in dating somebody if you don't like them?"

"I know you can have fun, dear. But it's just a different kind of fun with a boyfriend. I just don't want you to miss out on all the excitement of having a boyfriend."

Don't Call Boys!

Peeking out of her bedroom door, fourteen-year-old Jessie surveyed the hallway. Seeing no sign of her mother, she slipped back into her room, picked up the phone, and quickly dialed the number.

When the person on the other line answered, she asked quietly, "Is Burke there?"

"This is Burke."

"Hi, it's Jessie," she kept her eyes fixed on the doorway so she could see if anyone came in. "I got a message that you called."

"Yeah. Jordan, Kirsten, and I are going to the movies tonight. I was wondering if you wanted to come with us."

"I'd love to, but I have to ask my mom first," Jessie said. "How are we going to get there?"

"Kirsten's parents are going out to dinner and they said that they'd take us and pick us up when they are done with dinner."

"That sounds great, Burke! I'll...." Jessie stopped as her mother entered the room. "Umm, I'll go ask my mom. Call me back in ten minutes, okay?"

As Jessie hung up the phone, her mother asked, "Who were you just talking to?"

"Burke Kennedy. He wanted to know if I could go to a movie tonight with him and Kirsten and Jordan."

Crossing her arms and shaking her head disapprovingly, her mother said, "I didn't hear the phone ring. Did he call you?"

"He called earlier today," Jessie said. "Dad gave me the message, so I just called him back."

With a sigh, her mother said, "You know I don't want you to do that. It isn't right for girls to be calling boys!"

"Was I supposed to not call him back? I'm thirteen, mom, and this isn't the '50s. Girls call boys all the time. It isn't that big of a deal. Now, can I please go to the movies tonight?"

"Just the four of you?" her mother asked. "It sounds like a double date. You know you aren't allowed to date until you are sixteen."

"We're just friends," Jessie tried to explain to her mother. "Going to the movies with Burke and Jordan is like going with my girlfriends. I don't like them like *that*."

"It is nothing like going with your girlfriends. They're boys!"

"Mom, what are you worried about? We're just friends!" Jessie insisted. "It's not like we're going to have sex in the middle of the movie!"

Taking a deep breath, her mother said, "I don't like you hanging out alone with boys," as she left the room.

✳ Boys! Yikes!

Boys! A complicated matter for mothers for reasons that aren't always clear. Peggy came to counseling to talk about her fourteen-year-old daughter whom she described as "boy crazy."

"I'm worried that she'll be consider a slut."

"Why would you think that?" I asked. "Were you a slut?"

The rules for girls were more complicated. We were told that sex would ruin our lives and our reputations. We were encouraged to be sexy, but not sexual. Great scorn was reserved for "cockteasers" and "cold fish." It was tough to find the right balance between seductive and prim.

—Mary Pipher, Ph.D.

"No, she confessed, slightly embarrassed, "but I wanted to be."

As a teenager Peggy was not allowed to date. If Peggy mentioned a boy, she was scolded for her impure thoughts. If she was caught wearing lipstick or fingernail polish, she was forced to wipe it off. Peggy had numerous crushes and felt ashamed about her feelings. She wrote dozens of letters to teen idols and hid them from her mother. The more she tried to avoid thinking about parties, boys, sex, or being pretty, the bigger the desire became. She was riddled with guilt and wondered if she was "oversexed" in some way. When her own teenage daughter showed interest in boys or wanted to wear lipstick, it triggered Peggy's old confusion. She wasn't able to sort out what constituted appropriate behavior so she came to counseling.

As Peggy's story points out, one thing that makes the boy issue so complicated for mothers is that their own unresolved sexual fears and fantasies can be projected onto their daughters. But unresolved fears and fantasies are not the only issue to face; there are countless others.

When my friend Abby learned that her fifteen-year-old daughter had a date to the school dance with a boy who had a questionable reputation she tried to stay calm, but when she met the boy's parents two hours before the dance, she was even more concerned.

According to researchers at the University of Minnesota, teenage girls who feel understood by their mothers have their first sexual experience later than teen girls who are not connected to their mothers.

What could she do? The dress was bought, the plans were made, and her daughter was heading out the door.

Ruth, the mother of seventeen-and nineteen-year-old daughters, found the "boy stuff" unsettling because it stirred unexpected feelings of sadness in her. She didn't have a first date until she was twenty-five. Her own girls had many friends, both boys and girls, and they did lots of group activities. Her daughters were having the fun she'd missed, and while she was happy for them, she felt sad for herself.

Anna and her thirteen-year-old daughter Julia had many conversations about sexual responsibility and waiting for the right time and place. Then, one day, Anna came home unexpectedly from work and found Julia in bed with the fifteen-year-old next-door neighbor. When confronted, Julia said she just wanted to know what all the fuss was about.

Watching our daughters become interested in boys, hang out with them, date them, fall in love, and break up with them can put us through considerable misery. My biggest fear was that Amanda would date a sleazebag. When she went to a girl-ask-boy dance with someone I could tell was not up to her level, I fussed and fretted all night. What if this turned into a real romance? What if she turned against me because she knew I didn't like him? What if they got married someday? That night of worry turned out to be nothing because she never mentioned him again. She probably decided he didn't have the qualities that mattered to her in a boyfriend.

According to Child Trends, Inc., younger teens in general are not sexually active. By age fifteen, only 18 percent of girls have had sex. By age seventeen, 52 percent of girls have had sex. Girls with highly educated parents are less likely to engage in sex early; only 10 percent of girls with college-educated parents have sex by age fifteen.

At fourteen Amanda and her boyfriend of five months broke up. I knew it was the first of many loves, but she was heartbroken and so was I. Since I was a single mom, I worried that maybe I hadn't provided an adequate role model for healthy relationships. It takes true grit to sort out all the issues so that you can see clearly and talk frankly with your daughter.

I'm frequently asked by mothers, "It is okay for girls to call boys?" This is one of those potential mother-daughter battle-grounds. Most mothers who ask this question grew up with the idea that if girl called boy, she was chasing him and that was a "no-no." Girls today live in a different culture. I think it is perfectly accept-able for girls to call boys. I like the fact that teenagers today hang out in groups more than my generation did. The more comfortable they are being around the opposite sex, the better decisions they will be making.

Like me, most mothers hope that their daughters will postpone becoming sexually active until they are mature enough to handle all the ramifications that come with sexual intimacy. Mothers want their daughters' first sexual experience to be in the context of a lov-ing, committed relationship.

In my opinion, teenage girls are not emotionally or intellectually prepared to cope with the feelings that sexual intimacy brings. They are too vulnerable to deal with the potential rejection and unhappiness, not to mention pregnancy or the possible health risks. Although girls today are inundated with messages about sexuality, they still lack information about their bodies and their own sexuality.

According to a study of 11,000 teens, reported by the Women's Sports Foundation, girls who play sports wait longer to become sexually active, are more likely to use contracep-tion, and are less than half as likely to get pregnant as are non-athletic girls.

✷ What's a Mother to Do?

Give Good Guidelines

As mothers, we must help our daughters make healthy sexual deci-sions. Before we talk with our daughters about sex, boys, and sleep-ing over, we owe it to both of us to know what our own attitudes are toward dating, boys, and sex. We seem to be flooded with sexually charged information, but at the same time we're highly squeamish approaching our daughters. For girls to make healthy choices, they need to know the following:

1. The facts about their bodies. Most mothers are not pre-pared to give all the information, so I suggest that you buy her a good book such as *It's a Girl Thing: How to Stay Healthy, Safe, and In Charge* by Marvis Jukes. Explain to her that since you don't have all the answers you thought this book would be helpful for you both. Tell her that you've read it and that you would like to know what she thinks about it. If this is an uncomfort-able subject for you, keep the conversation light and positive.

2. That they can say "No." Tell her she has the right to say "No" at any time. Just because she is kissing a guy doesn't mean she has to have sex. Just because she had sex once (or many times) doesn't mean she has to again. It's healthy for her to explore her developing sexual respon-siveness, but she can stop a sexual encounter whenever she wants. Tell her that it is okay to be up-front with boys about her feelings. Tell her to be open and honest with them.

3. That she can spend time with guys and develop male friendships. Girls need experiences with boys so that they can

> *Much experimenting with sex comes out of a hunger for touch, the need to be held and stroked. And much teen violence comes out of a desperate desire not to appear weak or needy, just as it does with adults.*
>
> *—Virginia Satir*

understand themselves. It is healthy for a girl to be able to date and have many different boys in her life because it teaches her how to relate to men and lets her learn what qualities are important in long-term, serious relationships without actually being in one.

Many mothers are uncomfortable with letting their daughters spend time alone with boys. They discourage their daughters from hanging out with a group of male friends, worrying that this might cause them to have early sexual encounters. However, making boys off-limits often has just the opposite effect. When girls are allowed to socialize with boys in safe settings, they are better able to understand their feelings toward the opposite sex and less likely to be sexually promiscuous. We all are more curious about the unknown than about the things we know and are comfortable with. The first of Amanda's girlfriends to have sex was the girl whose mother had made being with boys totally taboo. The mother's overprotectiveness totally backfired.

4. The criteria for good friends of both sexes. What are the qualities that make a good friendship?

5. That a healthy, loving relationship is based on friendship. Encourage her to know boys as friends. Allow her to get comfortable with boys so that she can talk, argue, play, and work side by side with them.

6. That it's important to make a well-informed decision about being sexually active. Tell her about the advantages of waiting to have sexual relations until she's in a committed, loving relationship.

7. That you'll keep *your* sexual behavior out of sight. Just as her emerging sexuality stirs anxiety in you, exposing her to your sexual behavior will stir overwhelming tension in her. I have counseled many single mothers who began dating when their daughters were teenagers.

Some let their boyfriends sleep over. This simply is not a good idea. Do not act out sexually in front of your teenager. Your daughter can accept displays of affection toward your husband but she can't stand it when it's toward a casual boyfriend.

Boys Are Friends Too

What is it that makes discovering boys so exciting and scary? It seems like once you reach adolescence, the wonderful world of boys begins to open up to you in new ways. When you were in elementary school, boys were considered anything but fun. Spitting on the playground at recess and chasing girls around with snakes that they had just caught, boys were really quite a nuisance. Girls usually wanted to have little to do with boys, and if your class was being too talkative, your teacher would make you sit in a boy-girl-boy-girl seating arrangement as punishment.

Seemingly overnight, all of this changes. Think of the first time when you realized that boys didn't have cooties and in fact were kind of cute. Remember how nervous you were the first time you talked on the phone with a boy you had a crush on? Once we reached junior high, my friends and I suddenly began to look at boys in a whole new way. We spent hours at night plotting out which boys we wanted to dance with at the next school dance, we would pass notes in class with lists of our current crushes (which usually never numbered fewer than three at a time), and we played games like M.A.S.H. and True Love. We spent countless hours gossiping about, staring at, or dreaming of boys.

This is not something unique to our generation. Our mothers got nervous before their first dates and spent hours sobbing when the boy they liked didn't like them back. The feelings remain the same, but many of the strategies regarding boys have changed.

Take dating, for example. I had always heard stories about dating, and I had this picture in my mind of what my first "real date" would be

In the "olden days" of the 1950s the average age for marriage was eighteen. What do you think the average age for marriage is now?

like. I imagined that I would get asked out by some good-looking, athletic guy whom I had a crush on. I would go to the mall and get a new outfit and spend hours getting ready. Then he would come to the door—with flowers, of course—meet my mother and we'd be off to dinner and a movie, just the two of us.

My imagined first date never happened. The only time I ever really had a "date" was when I went to organized school dances like homecoming and prom. I quickly learned I would not be doing a lot of dating during my teenage years, but instead would spend the weekends hanging out with friends—both guys and girls.

In our generation, the formal date has become almost obsolete. This may be why your mother has such a hard time understanding the way you choose to relate to boys. Whenever I think of my mother as a teenager, I think of the movie *Grease* or the television show *Happy Days*. I can just see my mom getting picked up by her current beau and scooting off to the drive-in movie or stopping at the soda shop for a milkshake.

Relationships between guys and girls today are generally much more laid-back than they were thirty years ago. Ask your mother if she ever had any really close guy friends, and I bet you'll find out that she didn't have guy friends in the same way you do. You mother probably didn't spend a whole lot of time hanging out with guys on a casual level,

The prom dates back to Yale in 1864, where it was called the Junior Promenade Concert.

and she may be more used to the idea that guys and girls spend time together because they are romantically interested in each other, not simply because they are friends.

I didn't have a high school sweetheart. Sure, I was together with different guys and had a few semi-long relationships, but I never got the "captain of the cheer squad dates football quarterback" high school experience that I had hoped for. Many times I felt like there was something wrong with me because I was always just the guy's friend. Looking back, I am glad I never dated one guy all through high school, and I realize that I learned a lot by getting the chance to know a lot of guys as friends. All girls go at their own pace, and having one serious boyfriend isn't always the right thing.

"My guy friends are so important to me," says sixteen-year-old Natasha. "Being able to just hang out with a bunch of guys is a lot of fun. It lets you get to know guys and learn to feel comfortable around them without the pressures of having to go out on a date."

Fifteen-year-old Becky adds, "Getting a group of guys and girls together to go to the movies is so much more fun than just going with one date. It's way more laid-back and you have a bunch of people to talk to instead of just one. It's also nice because if the boys are being dorks then you have your girlfriends there to save you."

According to Teenage Research Unlimited, boys and girls today become friends before pairing off. Formal dating is rarer than it was ten or twenty years ago, while group dating is more the norm.

According to Teenage Research Unlimited, teens are surprisingly traditional in their dating; they go to movies, restaurants, their boyfriend's or girlfriend's house, or a party. Although dating has evolved, teens still go to the same places as always on dates.

❀ *What's a Daughter to Do?*

Ease Your Mom's Worries

Many girls complain that their mothers get weird when it comes to their daughters' relationships with boys. Maybe your mother becomes over-protective and only allows you to spend a little time with guys, or maybe she is too pushy and is always encouraging you to get a boyfriend. Whatever it may be, mothers can put a real damper on your fun.

Your mother may have a hard time getting used to:

Coed slumber parties

Girls asking guys out on dates

Girls calling guys

The fact that your best guy friend is only a friend

If you want your mother to relax about the boy issue, you need to bring her up to date. Because the teen dating scene has changed so much since your mother was a part of it, she may be uneasy with how you relate to boys. Maybe she is worried that you don't know how to handle yourself with boys, or she thinks that you are getting too seri-ously involved and wants you to devote time to other things, or maybe she worries that you will get hurt, pregnant, or an STD. Maybe she didn't have the chance to date when she was a teen and doesn't want you to miss out too.

I never talked to my mom about boys. I hated it when she would ask me "Is he your boyfriend?" if I had been spending more time than usual with a certain guy. I never told my mom about my first kiss or filled her in on the details of a night I spent with a guy I really liked. I am amazed by girls who feel comfortable sharing every detail of their guy stories with their mothers, because although my mother and I are close, there are some things that I don't like to talk with her about.

There are somethings I learned to do to keep my mom happy when dealing with boys. Maybe they'll ease your mother's worries as well.

1. Always make time for introductions. I know introducing your mom to the guys in your life, whether they are just friends or potential boyfriends, is not always the easiest thing to do. I always hated it because I worried that my mother wouldn't like the boy and I was afraid that she would embarrass me. However, she insisted that before I went anywhere with a boy, he had to come inside and meet her first. I always had to spend few (sometimes embarrassing) minutes introducing her to guys and letting her make small talk with them. Although it was painful at times, I found that if I introduced guys to Mom, she felt better about allowing me to go out.

   Even though I tried to convince myself that my mother's opinion of the guys I hung out with didn't matter, if my mom wasn't particularly fond of a guy, I usually ended up realizing that I really didn't like him either. I learned that my mom is a good judge of character!

2. Find out about your mother. If your mother gets nervous about letting you go out with a boy, talk to her and figure out why she acts like that. Ask her if she was allowed to date as a teen and what her relationships were like with boys. This will give you a look inside her head, and may also remind her of how she felt as a teenager. Then ask her why she feels uncomfortable letting you go. Let her express her feelings without interrupting or arguing.

   My friend Amy's mom was always uneasy about letting her go out with guys, even when they were just friends. Finally she sat down with her mom and asked her why. Amy found out her mother had gotten herself into some uncomfortable situations with guys when she was a teenager and she was worried that Amy would do the same. By listening to her mom, Amy was able to not only understand her mother's unease, but learned a bit about the kinds of situations to avoid.

3. Reassure her. When your mother has finished telling you how she feels, explain your point of view. Let her know that having a coed slumber party at your friend's house after a dance is now normal. Reassure her that you'll all be sleeping in your own sleeping bags and that there isn't going to be any coupling off. It's important for you to calm your mother's unnecessary fears, but don't lie. Telling your mom that you are having an innocent, parentally supervised slumber party at your friend's house when you are actually renting a hotel room alone with your boyfriend is not calming your mother's fears. You want to show her you are trustworthy and responsible, not that you lie and sneak around behind her back. Try to come up with a compromise that's comfortable for both of you.

4. Respect her decision. Once you have both given your points of view, your mother still may not feel comfortable with the situation. If she doesn't allow you to go, respect her decision. Even if they seem ridiculous to you, your mother has valid reasons. One time I wanted to go camping with a group of guys and girls for the weekend. My mom said that she didn't feel comfortable letting me go. I didn't understand why and it bugged me that she wouldn't give me a reason, but I respected what she said and I didn't go camping. The camping trip turned out to be a disaster and I was thankful that I didn't go. Sometimes mothers do know what they are talking about!

5. Explain that guys are more than just boyfriends. Tell her that not every guy you hang out with is going to be a romantic interest. If your mother is too strict, letting her

know that hanging out with your guy friends is similar to hanging out with your girl friends may ease some of her worries about you becoming too involved too quickly. If your mother is pushy, telling her about the importance of guy friends will let her see that you don't always need a boyfriend to have fun with guys.

✳ Boy Tips for Moms

1. Boy-girl relationships in junior high should be viewed as friendships. Girls need good friends of both sexes.

2. Treat friendships with boys in a matter-of-fact way. Don't tease your daughter about guy friends. This makes her uncomfortable and promotes romance rather than friendship.

3. Encourage group dating and allow her to invite friends to your home.

4. Include her male friends on your family outings if she is comfortable with it.

✳ *Boy Tips for Girls*

1. Go at your own pace. If you aren't comfortable having a boyfriend, or if there is nobody you're interested in dating, that's okay.

2. Get to know guys and hang out with them as friends before you start dating.

3. Be open to all different types of guys. The "cool" guys aren't always the best ones to date or have as friends.

4. Don't lower your standards or morals just to have a boyfriend. Some time you will meet a guy who will like you for who you are instead of somebody whom you have lowered yourself for.

16

Getting High

Here are some questions about drugs and alcohol for both mothers and daughters to answer. There are no right or wrong answers; these questions are intended to stimulate your thinking and help you better understand your views on drinking and use drugs.

1. What do you do when you are at a party and all of your friends are drinking? Do you stay at the party and drink a little? Do you drink until you're drunk? Do you stay at the party but not drink? Do you leave?

2. When, if ever, you do drink, is your purpose to get drunk, buzzed, to relax, or to be social? Do you drink to loosen yourself up and feel more comfortable around people you don't know well?

3. What do you consider to be social drinking/drug use? How often do you participate in either of these?

4. Do you think of drugs and alcohol as a way to make you relax and forget about your worries?

5. How many times a week do you drink? Smoke? Use other types of drugs?

6. Have you ever used drugs or alcohol in front of your mother/daughter? Have you ever been under the influence of drugs or alcohol (having done them elsewhere) around your mother/daughter? Do you believe that it is ever okay for your mother/daughter to use drugs or alcohol?

7. What is your philosophy about a mother providing alcohol or drugs to her daughter? When, if ever, is it ever okay for a mother to allow her daughter to drink?

✳ One Party at a Time

We mothers can never know for sure if our daughters are drinking, taking drugs, or smoking. Teenage daughters don't announce to their mothers, "I drank a wine cooler" or "I smoked a joint." Experimentation with drugs, alcohol, and cigarettes is done with friends, in secret.

Amanda may drink at parties but she has never volunteered the information about when or how much. My gut feeling is that if she does, it's minimal. She can have a glass of wine or champagne at a family celebration, but she seldom wants to. My impression is that she doesn't really like the taste or the feeling that she gets. I would never allow underage teens to drink in my home. Amanda is adamantly against smoking and I don't think she's even tried that. She's made her own decisions about these things with only subtle guidance from me. Since there's never been a problem with substance abuse and I've never seen her high or drunk, I haven't had to harp, nag, or intervene. I simply ask her what she thinks about drinking, smoking, and drugs. I remember one conversation we had following her first high school house party.

Barely one month after school started Amanda, a sophomore, was invited to a party with her old friends from junior high, kids she'd just met, and kids she didn't know. As I dropped her off in front of the house, I could tell by looking at the kids arriving that the atmosphere of her first high school party would be much different than the ones she had attended in junior high. Other than the fact that a few kids were smoking openly, I couldn't put my finger on what exactly was different. I dropped her off and drove to the end of the street, where I watched the carloads of teenagers arriving. Hooting, hollering, waving their arms, laughing, and calling out to each other, many were older then I was used to seeing Amanda with. Up until that night, the parties she'd attended were with kids in the same grade. It looked to me like sophomores were mingling with seniors.

As I watched the kids jump out of the cars and bounce into the house, I could hear music blaring. I watched three guys get out of cars drinking beer. This was a new experience for me. My stomach did a flip-flop, and I drove home wondering if I done the right thing by allowing her to go. Should I have put my foot down and said, "No"?

This was the first of many hard calls. I knew from my experiences counseling that the kids who are the most rebellious and get into the most trouble with drugs and alcohol seemed to come from two opposing family structures where the level of parental involvement is inappropriate. The parent who doesn't know what's going on at all and doesn't care is at one extreme, and the overprotective parent who doesn't give the teenager any room to think is at the

QUESTION FOR MOM

Have you told your daughter what to do if she or her friends has been drinking and it isn't safe for her to drive? Can she call you no matter what?

other. I wanted to find a balance so that Amanda could exercise the good judgment she'd always shown, but in order to do that I had to keep the lines of communication open between us. I had to be aware, concerned, and appropriately involved.

Amanda got a ride home and when she came in to my bedroom to let me know that she was home, I said, "Hi honey, how was the party, did you have a good time?"

"Yup," she answered.

"Who brought you home?" I asked.

"Bryne," she replied. "You don't know her."

"I thought you were getting a ride with Justin."

"He was drunk, so I didn't want to ride with him," she said matter-of-factly as she went to get the phone.

"Wheeew," I thought to myself. "She's showing good judgment."

After that I made it my policy to handle "iffy" gatherings one party at a time. I warned her about drinking and driving and told her that I trusted her to use her very best judgment and never get into the car with some who'd been drinking. "Call me," I said. I told her stories about the crazy things folks do when they are high. That's about all I could do. As long as Amanda is making sound decisions and behaving herself, I'm satisfied.

> Researchers at the University of Minnesota report that when adolescents feel connected to their parents and their school, they are less likely to smoke cigarettes, abuse alcohol, or smoke marijuana.

✳ Double Messages

Laura and her fourteen-year-old daughter Simone were at odds over many issues when they came to me for counseling. Laura had

Did you know that the Marlboro Man died of lung cancer?

"busted" Simone for smoking on the street corner and was frantic. She didn't want Simone smoking and was trying everything she could from bribery and logic to threats and counseling to get her to stop. Simone said, "I'll stop if Mom will," and Laura replied, "I've been smoking too many years. I can't stop, but I want her to stop before she gets hooked like I am."

Our daughters get far too many double messages about smoking, drinking, and drug-taking. Recently, trendy fashion magazines have promoted the haggard, "drug" look on their models. For years the message has been "It's cool to smoke and drink," alongside the "Just Say No" campaign. An acquaintance of mine was concerned about her fifteen-year-old's heavy drinking and talked to me about it. "Do you think the fact that her father and I drink every night is influencing her?" she asked. I wanted to say "Duh," like the kids might, but I was more polite and said, "I think you're sending her a very confusing message." With double messages coming from her mother, your daughter is left on her own to sort out the whole range of drinking, drug, and smoking dilemmas.

Girls hate it when they see their mothers drunk or using drugs. I hadn't told Amanda that I smoked cigarettes in college because I gave it up years ago, but one night when my friend Linda was visiting, I smoked a cigarette with her to be "social." Amanda caught me and went ballistic. I had a lot of explaining to do and I did a lousy job of it. We mothers are often as confused as our daughters about the use of these substances. I learned from my own mistake that brushing off my smoking by saying, "Oh, honey, you know I don't smoke," did not constitute being accountable for my actions. Instead of trying to hide what I was doing, I should have acknowledged that on rare occasions I had smoked cigarettes. When I saw how upset Amanda was with me, however, I never smoked "socially" again.

Most girls prefer that their mothers don't smoke, drink, or use any drugs, but they can tolerate it as long as you don't get wasted. I tried to find a healthy balance with Amanda. She knew I drank in moderation and that I'd smoked in college and quit in my twenties. We didn't know then that smoking caused cancer, I explained. I'd told her that I smoked marijuana about four times in the '60s and since it only made me sleepy and hungry, I hadn't smoked it since, but she knew that I'd avoided all other drugs. I promote moderation rather than the rigid "Don't try anything" stand. In a way, this moderate and realistic approach dilutes the pleasure that comes with sneaking around.

Greta began experimenting with alcohol and cigarettes in junior high and by the time she was a senior in high school she was using cocaine. Her mother hadn't known anything about it until she was called to the emergency room where Greta was being treated for an accidental overdose. Both parents were stunned; they couldn't imagine their daughter doing such a thing. They told me that since their two older daughters "never got into any trouble" they'd expected the same from Greta. Greta told me, "My parents won't let me be my own person; they want me to be like my sisters and I'm not." Because Greta's parents could not tolerate any deviance from their picture of their daughters, they had blinded themselves to the reality of Greta's drug usage for years. By the time the three of them came to counseling, not only was their relationship very shaky, but Greta had developed a serious addiction to cocaine.

According to a study done by Washington State, one half of all the kids who drink get their alcohol from their parents.

❋ What's a Mother to Do?

Allow for the Possibility

While you can't be absolutely sure of what she's doing, you can be aware of what's happening in her social circle. By paying attention to the clues you're getting and asking your daughter what she thinks, you'll be aware of her decision-making process. That way you can handle your concerns before experimentation turns into a problem of habitual use or addiction.

A mother's job in this area is to find a balance between being completely naive and assuming the worst when it comes to her daughter's potential experimentation. There's also a balance between forbidding usage and promoting it.

Ellen told her fourteen-year-old daughter, "It's common that girls might drink at parties so I'd like to talk with you before you're presented with the drinking dilemma. I'm not suggesting that you will drink or get drunk, but if you ever do, call me and I will come to get you. I don't look forward to seeing you drunk and falling over, but I'd rather see you drunk than dead."

By allowing for the possibility that your daughter might drink, smoke, or try drugs, you address the issue without assuming that she will. Preventive mothering is teaching her how to handle those precarious situations *before* she's in the middle of them.

I talk with many teenage girls who tell me that they can't talk with their mothers about drinking or drugs because their mothers immediately "start the lecture" or say something like, "If everyone jumped off a bridge, would you?" Make sure your daughter has accurate information, which means you must first find out what she knows. The only way to do this is to listen without freaking out, butting in, lecturing, offering advice, or criticizing. Teenagers are curious about adult things. If you can stay open-minded and let her talk about concerns and ideas as they come up, not only will you find out what she is thinking, you can also throw in your two cents.

When thirteen-year-old Lily said, "I think smoking is cool," her mother responded, "You do?" which led to a friendly conversation debating the pros and the cons of smoking and drinking. This led to a conversation about decision making. Girls often make such dramatic statements, not because they believe the statement but because they want to engage in a congenial debate. It's a way of finding out all the facts while still having a say. By taking a stand against their mothers, they are asking to be "set straight" without a lecture. If you can talk about these highly charged matters in a warm manner, you can give help your daughter develop the willpower she'll need to stand up to peer pressure. If you can stay calm while she presents a viewpoint different from your own, you can drop a few suggestions without her becoming defensive.

Girls experiment to find out how alcohol, cigarettes, and marijuana taste and feel. Many stop at experimentation, deciding they don't like it and that they can have a good time without it. Many girls go on to light social drinking with friends at parties, but unfortunately others develop a substance dependency. Girls use substances to relieve anxiety, to fit in, and to feel better. You must be alert and aware of how your daughter is using substances; even if you can't stop your daughter from experimenting, you can assess how she is using substances. If she is using alcohol or drugs to cope with stress, low self-esteem, or uncomfortable feelings, you both may need assistance in treating the problem.

✲ Help Her Come Up with Excuses

It's very important to assist your daughter in developing some handy excuses to give her friends on why she isn't participating in the alcohol or drug scene. Telling her to "just say no" is too hard for many younger adolescent girls. Talk over what excuse she might give at a party where her friends are drinking but she doesn't want to. What excuse can she make without losing face in front of her friends so that she can call you to come get her?

✸ Don't Be in Denial

If your daughter comes home from a party high or drunk, pay attention. If your gut feeling is that your daughter is using drugs, drinking inappropriately, or smoking, don't ignore it. It won't go away by itself. If you don't know how to approach her, be sure to consult an expert. Each situation is different and you must decide what steps to take next. Educate yourself and keep the lines of communication open. Get professional consultation with a family counselor familiar with substance abuse. Don't kid yourself that you can hide your own misuse of alcohol or drugs; your daughter knows exactly what you are doing. If you have a problem, seek help now.

What about Mom's Drinking, Drugging, and Smoking?

My mother rarely drinks alcohol. She might have a glass of wine at dinner or a drink when we have dinner with her friends. When I was sixteen, I went to a party at a friend's house and saw her mother drinking. She was totally wasted. I couldn't believe it and it scared me a little bit. I couldn't even fathom what it was like for my friend to see her mother drunk at a party with all her friends. I had never seen my mom drunk and I hadn't realized that adults got drunk too.

My mother has done things I didn't like. When I was fifteen, I came home one afternoon and found my mom and her friend talking with an ash tray on the table in between them. Seeing my mom smoking a cigarette made me so angry. I had never seen her smoke before and I knew she wasn't planning on making a habit of it, but it hurt me just the same. I felt like my mother had betrayed me in some way. For an instant, I felt like the mother of a rebellious daughter, which was a role I didn't want to play.

Later that night, I bawled my mother out. I yelled, "I can't believe you! Smoking is so disgusting! Don't you know it is bad for you?" I wanted her to apologize for letting me down by making such a dumb decision and promise me that she wouldn't do it again. She just laughed it off and said, "Oh, Amanda. I never smoke. I was just doing to be social with my friend." Her response hurt me even more, and I stomped off saying, "That isn't an excuse!!"

✳ Peer Pressure

During alcohol education in sixth grade, we were taught a lot about peer pressure. We were given examples of types of peer pressure we might experience, and they showed us videos of teens pressuring their friends with clichéd lines like, "Everyone who is cool drinks," or "Just have one smoke. It's not that big of a deal." They would pack our brains full of comebacks like, "I don't think drinking is cool. If that's the way to be cool, then I would rather be uncool," or "Smoking is a big deal. It makes you smell bad, turns your teeth yellow, and worst of all, it can cause cancer." We would role play and practice using our strong rejections to learn how to avoid peer pressure.

Throughout junior high I took a strong stand against drinking. Thinking that only "bad" kids drank, smoked, or used drugs, I made pacts with my friends to never participate in these types of things. I never felt pressure because all of my friends were like me; none of them had ever done anything "bad," so I was rarely exposed to drugs and alcohol.

Since smoking stains your teeth and contributes to wrinkling, you'll be prettier if you don't puff. Once you've begun, it's hard to stop. According to the Center for Disease Control and Prevention, 72 percent of teens who smoke eventually try to quit. Most aren't successful.

Once I got to high school, this changed. I went to more parties where people were drinking and smoking, and people who were "good" participated in these things. Even my friends, with whom I'd solemnly sworn, were experimenting with drinking and smoking.

I quickly learned what real peer pressure is from these experiences. Peer pressure is often very indirect. It does not come from somebody backing you into a corner and trying to force you to drink. Watching everyone else at the party drinking and having a good time makes you feel pressured to join in. Being at a party where you don't know many people is awkward, but being one of the only sober people at such a party is much worse. Drinking together seems to create a bond between people, and when you aren't drinking, you feel you miss out on this "bond."

❈ What's a Daughter to Do?

Be Responsible and Be Safe

I did drink minimally in high school, but I have never smoked or used other drugs because I never wanted to. People experiment with alcohol for many different reasons, and I was mainly curious. I wondered what made it such a big deal and figured as long as I was responsible, it wouldn't be so bad to try it. I drank occasionally in high school, at parties, and hanging out with my friends; however, most of my good friends drank a lot more than I did. I spent many Saturday nights home alone because my friends were all going out to drink.

Looking back, I am very happy about the way I handled alcohol during my teenage years. After experimenting with alcohol my sophomore and junior years of high school, I had pretty much gotten the "party" thing out of my system and rarely drank during my senior year. I watch people who never drank in high school go crazy here at college because they didn't know how to handle alcohol and put themselves in dangerous situations.

I am not condoning underage drinking or saying you should use or abuse drugs and alcohol. I'm just saying that I know many teenagers are going to experiment. You have been slammed your whole life with adults telling you not to drink and are aware of all the consequences. If you decide to drink, be responsible, because drinking is a problem for more people than you may think and you could even hurt or kill yourself or somebody that you are close to.

Did you know that it takes thirty days for the 400 different chemicals in marijuana to leave the body? A joint a week means that you are always under the influence.

Here are some "rules" I used in high school to keep my attitude and ideas about alcohol positive.

1. **It's okay to say "No."** It is okay *never* to drink. People who have the courage to go against the norm and do what they know is best for themselves are very admirable. Just because you choose not to drink doesn't mean that you won't have a social life at all. It's okay to go to parties and not drink, and there are other people at your school who share your beliefs. Find them and make a point to do something non-alcohol-related when everyone else is going to get wasted. You are not alone in your stand against alcohol. Most people really respect those who are able to keep themselves under control and not let alcohol or partying consume their lives. Stay strong and remember it is always okay to not participate.

2. **Remember, puking sucks!** Why somebody would actually want to make themselves puke is beyond me. I hate throwing up and have never drunk so much that I made myself sick. Throwing up is sign that you've had way too much to

drink. I don't know enough about biology to know exactly what alcohol does to your body, but I know enough to know that if you are throwing up, something is wrong.

Know your body's limits and be good to yourself. Excessive drinking is terrible for you and can ruin your body; think about how bad you feel the morning after having too much to drink. I have seen many people go beyond the "buzzed" stage and have to be taken to the hospital, and I even know of somebody who died from alcohol poisoning. Alcohol can be very dangerous when not used in moderation, so know your limits, and don't get so drunk that you spend the night praying to the porcelain gods.

3. **Don't make a fool of yourself.** One of the first times I ever drank, I was at a party at my neighbor's house. I wasn't sure exactly how much I could handle and had a bit more than I should have, which made me more uninhibited than usual. I went around telling everyone that I was in love with a cute older guy named John and that I would do anything to be together with him. Everyone kept joking around and telling me, "Amanda, John's coming!" even though he was actually in California for the weekend. "He is?" I would ask, getting all excited and nervous waiting for him to walk in the door.

Of course, word of my behavior got back to John pretty quickly and I was humiliated, especially at school when he would pass me in the hall and give me a weird smile. I learned my lesson and never drank so much that I was out of control again, but it still took me three years to live down the "John" incident.

Mine was a pretty mild case of stupid things you can do if you drink too much. Not only may you end up puking, you may also get yourself into embarrassing or perhaps danger-ous situations. When you drink so much that you are com-pletely uninhibited, you lose all of your good judgment. You

might try to drive or get into a car with somebody who is
drunk, or you might get into a bad situation with a guy and
possibly get raped. Always be aware of your limits and keep
control of yourself. Getting drunk one night isn't worth making a fool of yourself or getting into a dangerous situation.

4. **Realize that your problems will still be there tomorrow.**
   I have always stuck to my rule of never drinking when I'm
   upset or depressed about something. I will not use alcohol
   as a way to fix my problems. Drinking can help you temporarily forget your problems, but when you sober up,
   your problems will still be there.

   Although using alcohol instead of dealing with issues may
   seem easier, it will just cause more problems in the long run.
   If you are upset about breaking up with a boyfriend, are
   having problems at home, or are just feeling depressed for
   no apparent reason, don't immediately run out and party.
   Find a more positive way to deal with your upset, like going
   out for ice cream with a friend, renting a movie, taking a
   bath, or going for a run. Repeatedly using alcohol to cope
   with problems can lead to alcoholism. If you find that you
   are constantly turning to alcohol to feel better, you may
   want to get help learning how to solve your problems.

5. **Know when you need to call for help.** If you find yourself
   in a situation where you have had too much to drink and
   there is nobody sober there to take you home, call somebody who can pick you up, or, if it's safe, stay the night
   where you are. Getting in trouble is worth the price of
   being alive, and your mother would rather see you drunk
   than dead. If you know that you can't call your mom, call a
   friend, a relative, or a neighbor, or, if you have money, call
   a cab. I've had friends call me late at night because they
   needed a ride home, and I was happy to go pick them up.
   The most important thing is to be safe and not do any-

thing that could put your life, or someone else's life, in danger.

❄ Reminders for Mom

1. Set a positive example and examine your own feelings about drug and alcohol usage. Be honest with both of you so that you don't send double messages.

2. Stay open-minded so that you can have open conversations. Allowing for the possibility that your daughter might drink, smoke, or take drugs lets you employ realistic preventative measures.

3. Most of the teenagers who drink a lot have parents who drink a lot. In general, parents who don't drink have kids who don't drink.

4. Don't let your house be a party house or supply kids with alcohol.

5. Know the signs of drug and alcohol use and pay attention when your daughter comes home from a party.

6. Discuss refusal techniques with her. Help her find a few excuses for not participating in the alcohol and drug scene.

7. If either of you has a drug or alcohol problem, seek professional help.

17

Privacy, Solitude, and Space

Leave Me Alone!

Sometimes I'm in no mood to talk to my mother. When I come home from school, work, or hanging out with my friends, all I can think about is going to my room, shutting the door, and listening to music—alone! Hoping my mom doesn't catch me before I make it downstairs, I'll sneak into the house and head straight for my room as quickly and quietly as I can. Nine times out ten, I fail.

"Amanda," she yells.

"What?" I yell back, hoping that the tone of my voice will tell her I'm in no mood for chit-chat.

"Come here and talk to me! I haven't seen you all day!"

I stomp into her room. "What do you want to talk about?" I ask. My arms are crossed, my shoulders tense, and my eyes are glaring, all to show her I'm not open to having a conversation at this moment. But she's already talking a mile a minute.

"How was your day?" she asks. "What did you do? Did you turn your French project in?"

"Fine. Not much. Yes." My short answers don't allow for any more conversation. "I'm going downstairs to my room," I say, and quickly leave the room.

As I enter my room, I shut the door behind me, plop down on my bed, and let out a sigh of relief. Finally I'm free to relax, be alone with my thoughts, and have quiet time to think about my day.

Soon, there's a knock on the door. "Honey," Mom says.

"What do you want?!" I reply, very annoyed by this interruption.

Opening the door, she asks, "Do you want to come to the grocery store with me? I'm going to get some food for dinner."

"No, Mom," I say, completely unable to hide my irritation. "Can't you just leave me alone for a little bit?"

"I haven't even seen you all day. I don't see how you can already be sick of me."

"I just want to be able to have some time without anybody bothering me. Is that so hard for you to understand?"

My mom looks a little hurt and says, "You always want to spend time alone in your room. I'll bet as soon as I leave, you'll be on the phone talking to your friends. You never want to spend time with your old mom anymore."

It is all I can do to keep myself from screaming at her, and I feel more stressed out and nervous than I did before I got home. She doesn't understand that I do want to spend time with her, I just want a few minutes to unwind before I do. Instead of telling her these things nicely, I scream, "Would you please get out of my room and leave me alone!"

Private Space

I t was hard for me to learn that once Amanda became a teenager, she needed her privacy. I think it's been challenging for me to leave her alone because I really like her company. Other times I've felt it was my motherly duty to know what's going on, and sometimes I was concerned that she was upset and might need my advice. I bugged her quite a bit until I learned that she really did benefit from her solitude.

Just as every women needs a space of her own, so does every girl. We all need places to get away, close the door, and have personal time. A place where, without interruption, we can daydream, write in a journal, paint our nails, or go inward and renew our souls. Teenage girls are so "other" driven, they need to balance all the stress of their lives with quiet time to reflect and center themselves.

Solitude is not a luxury. It is a right and a necessity.

—Anne Wilson Schaef

To everything there is a season, and a time to every purpose under heaven.

—Ecclesiastes

✴ What's a Mother to Do?

Take Time for Yourself

Set an example of what private time and space means. Try to take an hour of solitude, or even twenty minutes, each day for yourself. Take a bath, light candles, and soak. Go to bed early and read. Use the time you would have spent nagging her to really savor the joys of solitude. You'll be setting a good example.

✴ Help Her Create a Private Space

Once a girl hits thirteen, chances are she's spending more time alone in her room and less time with you. Help her create a space that reflects her personal style. Tell her that she needs a comfy corner where she can be away from family and friends. Although she may think you're a little weird, tell her that quiet time is for "discovering your soul." Even if she doesn't understand completely what you mean, you will be planting a seed. Girls have definite ideas on how they want to decorate their rooms. Usually it's a mélange of teddy bears, posters of "cool guys," pictures of friends, and, if they're lucky, a telephone. Let her decorations reflect her new stage of life.

Claudia gave thirteen-year-old Regan a bedroom-redecorating birthday present. She took her shopping at a linen outlet store to let Regan choose a comforter and matching sheets, then to a poster store for wall decor. "I let her choose whatever she wanted. I was surprised that she chose yellow and blue bed linen and flowery posters. I guess I was worried that she might choose something wild. When she finished decorating, her room was cozy and inviting."

Don't make her feel guilty about closing her door. Respect her privacy and knock before entering her room. After several scenes with Amanda, I gave her a velvet "Do Not Disturb" sign to hang from the doorknob of her bedroom door. Don't snoop in your daughter's drawers or clean out her closest. Let her space be truly private. Without interruptions she can unwind and quiet her mind, the beginning of meditation and prayer.

Girls will tell you more if you listen rather than ask.

Creativity needs silence to flourish. Talk to her about what solitude has done for you and that downtime is necessary. Her only obligation is to discover her inner world of imagination and daydreams. Soon she'll gain appreciation for solitude and be able to handle those times when her friends are busy and there's nothing to do. Remember, a girl who discovers her soul is on the path of happiness and is less likely to follow the crowd.

✸ Let Her Have Private Thoughts

One mother I know does not allow her teenage daughter to think for herself. She's constantly torturing her with impossible questions like, "Why do you think like that?" or scolds, "You shouldn't think that." She drives her fifteen-year-old crazy with this cross-examination.

Just as your daughter needs privacy, she also needs to have private thoughts and opinions. Whether she shares them with you or writes them in a diary, allow her the pleasure of thinking and expressing her own thoughts. Never violate her trust by reading her diary because that is where she sorts through mixed feelings or expresses her deepest doubts. Getting comfortable with the fact that you two have differences of opinions is a component of being "your own person" that you both must tackle. Don't go through your daughter's private things, don't read notes even if they're laying out, and don't open her mail. How would you feel if your daughter read your journal or opened your mail?

✳ Develop a Friendly, Unobtrusive Style

Even though I know that girls need privacy, I still want to know what's going on in Amanda's life. I want to know how her day was or to find out if Carrie, whom I've known since they were toddlers together, is going to the dance with Jason, whom I've known since they were in grade school.

Amanda can't understand why I want to know these things. Although she's never said so directly, I can tell by the look on her face that she's thinking, "Mom, get a life." Doesn't she understand that she is my life? She thinks most of her news is none of my business and even if it is, she doesn't want to pass it on to me daily. Trying to pry it out of her doesn't work because she clams up if I ask too many specific questions. But I have my ways and I've meticulously honed them since she hit junior high.

The first strategic maneuver is the greeting. Every morning, afternoon, and evening, I say in my most cheerful, friendly, non-intrusive voice, "Hi, honey, how's your day?" Regardless of her answer, I stay calm, centered, friendly, and effervescent. Even when she gives me that look and moans, *"Moooom!"* I remain unruffled. Instead of saying, "Don't talk to me in that tone," I breathe and count to ten. Before I'd developed this style, I tried to ply her with logic like, "I'm your mother, I need to stay informed," but it didn't fool her. "You're butting in," she'd reply, catching me every time.

When she does start talking, I'm nonchalant about it so she doesn't detect that I'm lapping up every word. I say, *"Mmmm,"* "Oh, that's nice," or ask casually, "What happened next?" Once she told me about a fifteen-year-old friend we've known since she was eight who thought she might be pregnant. Instead of freaking out, I asked my favorite leading question, "What do you think about that?" Her response, "It's not good to have sex so young. I told her she should talk to her mom," filled me with exhilaration because I'd gotten a glimpse into her problem-solving genius.

You probably also want to know what's going on around you—after all, staying in touch with your daughter's life is good parenting. There's a fine line between being in touch with what's going on and being snoopy or nosy. Here's a list of protocols I've used and passed on to the mothers I counsel:

1. Drop what you're doing, sit down, and give her your undivided attention when your daughter walks into the room.

2. Let her start the conversation. Avoid interrogation and cross-examination. If you ask too many questions, your daughter will avoid you.

3. Smile and look friendly. No one wants to talk to a person with a stern frown on their face.

4. If your daughter reveals startling information like the fact that her best friend has been smoking, don't use it against her by saying, "You can't spend the night at her house anymore." If she's sharing this with you, chances are slim that she's doing it herself.

5. Keep these conversations confidential. Don't repeat

what she has told you to other mothers. Show her that
you're trustworthy by keeping her secrets.

6. Provide a respectful forum. Listen carefully to find out
   what makes your daughter tick and to learn how her
   reasoning works.

7. Leave out the lecture. Conversations are not the time to
   deliver a discourse on the pitfalls of smoking. If you
   have a piece of advice or a warning you feel compelled
   to give, at least wait until she's through sharing. Better
   yet, wait a while then say, "You know, I was thinking
   about what you said about Sydney smoking and I wonder if you know that smoking causes permanent yellow-
   ing of teeth."

8. When she's finished talking, don't push her to continue
   or beg for more information. Let her be in charge of
   closing off the conversation.

9. If she's not in the mood for talking at all, smile and stay
   friendly just the same. Share a tidbit from your day.

✳ Remember the Natural Rhythm

A mother-daughter relationship has a natural rhythm, something
I've learned in over twenty years of counseling mothers and daughters. I want to share it with you so that you don't feel rejected when
it happens to you. Trying to alter this natural rhythm will only make
things worse. Here's how it works:

You come together—you go apart,

You come together—you go apart,

You come together—and so on.

It's like the ocean—the tide comes in and then it goes out.
Although every relationship has its own unique pattern, in general,

I received a birthday card from my daughter that said she loved me. When I opened it up, it continued: "But I never forgave you for cleaning my face with spit on your hanky."

—*Erma Bombeck*

the adolescent backs away momentarily, then reaches out. Your daughter wants to maintain a relationship with you and honoring her needs for privacy is one way to do this. Each of you will take time away, then come back together.

Once, when I was feeling particularly ignored by fifteen-year-old Amanda, I tried a little experiment. Instead of pushing her to spend time with me, I simply stopped seeking her out.

I refocused all my attention and energy onto myself. It wasn't out of meanness or desire to a get even, but more because I'd been neglecting myself. I smiled, answered her questions, and left her alone.

The first time I tried this, it took about three hours before she was sitting next to me trying to get our conversation going. At sixteen, she took two-and-a-half days before she had some time to sit down, but part of that was because of her busy school schedule and my work. I decided that if I insisted she be with me, she never had a chance to miss me, but when I allow her private time, soon she's wondering what I'm up to and seeks me out.

All living things have a rhythm. Your mother-daughter relationship is made up of two very alive women, so naturally your relationship has its own rhythm. Don't interrupt it. When a girl pulls away, it doesn't mean that she doesn't love her mother; she simply needs her privacy. Honoring the time apart will keep your bond alive.

No Privacy Anywhere

As a teenager, it probably seems like privacy is in scarce supply. At school, people's private lives are always being made public. Girls are the worst about this. Think about the number of times you and your girlfriends have sat around and discussed other people's lives. Conversations like, "I can't believe that Beth and Nick got together," or "Don't tell anyone, but I heard from Renae that Jill is going to break up with Craig!" are common among girls. Word travels fast and it's nearly impossible to escape gossip.

You may even find you don't have privacy away from school either. Mothers seem to believe that their daughter's business is their business as well. They can be nosy and ask too many questions, or snoop through your stuff and try to listen in on your conversations. Many times I've walked into the kitchen to get something to eat and heard my mom telling her best friend what I did with my friends last weekend. Sometimes she'll come into my room when I'm talking on the phone and want to know whom I'm talking to and what we're discussing.

It's good to let your mother know what is going on in your life, but sometimes all this nosiness can make you want to scream. You need some solitude and privacy.

Taking time to yourself is important because it allows you to unwind and collect your thoughts. After spending an entire day with people, you can get run down and stressed out. Everyone needs to have their private thoughts and space. When I feel the need to get away, I spend an afternoon at the art museum downtown by myself. There, I am free to be with my thoughts and do exactly what I want without pressure or disturbances. Private time is wonderful!

✷ *What's a Daughter to Do?*

Humor Your Mother and Teach Her Not to Snoop

"My mother will not give me any privacy," complains Marcy. "Whenever I'm on the phone in my room, she comes and opens the door so that she can hear what I'm saying. The other day I found her reading a note from my friend that I had left sitting out on my desk. It's driving me crazy." Your mother could have a reason for going through your stuff or listening to your phone conversations. Maybe she is worried that you are in trouble and wants to help but doesn't quite know how, or maybe she thinks you are keeping something terrible from her. It's also possible that your mother is just being nosy or that she doesn't trust you.

If you catch your mother going through your private things, you should sit down and have a serious talk with her about it. Although there is no excuse for snooping, try to understand your mother's point of view. Ask yourself, "Does my mother have a reason to be worried about me? Am I in trouble and hiding things from her?" Find out what she is looking for and why she is having a hard time trusting you. Tell her that it is important for you to be able to have your private thoughts and let her know how it makes you feel when she invades your privacy.

You may also want to reassure your mother that you will tell her if you're ever in big trouble or there's something she needs to know. Make sure she knows that wanting privacy doesn't mean you want to keep her in the dark, just that you need to have thoughts and experiences that stay personal.

Your mother may have gone through your stuff and gotten mad about something she found. Maybe she read your diary or the note from your friend talking about how the two of you snuck out to meet some older guys and has grounded you for it or become extra strict. Once your mother has snooped and found something that you wanted to keep private, there isn't much you can do. You both are feeling angry and betrayed and have probably lost respect and trust for one another.

The best way to deal with something like this is to put the fact that she invaded your privacy on the back burner for awhile. You have to deal with the issue your mother has found out about. Once you have worked through that, you can bring up the issue of privacy. You may want to wait a couple of weeks until your mother's anger has faded away and you've restored some of her trust in you. Then talk to her about how you felt when she went through your stuff and explain to her why it's important that she respect your private space.

You need to respect your mother's private time and space as well. She needs time alone to rejuvenate just as much as you do. If your mother doesn't take time for herself, you may want to encourage her to do so. Once she begins to understand the importance of being alone, she will respect your privacy more.

Learn to humor your mother a little bit too. Instead of fighting to keep her completely out of your life, tell her a little about what is going on in your friends' lives. It doesn't hurt to tell her that your best friend has a new boyfriend or that the boy who used to live next door got elected president of your school. Not only will you make your mother happy, she will feel more comfortable letting you go out with your friends if she feels like she knows something extra about their lives. You don't have to reveal any huge secrets, just give her a few tidbits of information so she'll feel like she's on the inside.

Being able to gossip a little with your mother is not only enjoyable for her, but it can be fun for you as well. The more I talked with my mother, the more I learned I could trust her. By testing her with small bits of information, I found she wouldn't divulge my secrets. I often found it refreshing to share things with my mother because she was able to give me a different perspective on things. Telling my mother about what was happening with my peers also gave her a better understanding of the pressures and issues I was dealing with every day.

You don't need to tell your mother everything. You don't need to tell her anything that makes you feel uncomfortable or that you know she won't understand. If your mother insists on interrogating you on things you really don't think she should know about, tell her politely that you don't feel like talking about that anymore or just say that you don't know.

If you do tell your mother something like your friends were drinking at the dance, and she gets angry, remind her that you are telling her these things as a friend. Let her know that if she's really interested in what's going on in your life, she is going to have to learn how to hear information without holding it against you. Communication will become much easier if you feel you are allowed to talk about what's going on in your life without restrictions.

PRIVACY QUIZ

Answer true or false.

For Mothers

1. I knock before entering my daughter's bedroom.
2. If my daughter leaves her diary on the counter, I will not read it.
3. I avoid eavesdropping on my daughter's telephone coversations.
4. I don't snoop in my daughter's drawers or closets.
5. I ask permission before I read her mail or yearbook inscriptions.

For Daughters.

1. I ask my mother's permission before I use her make-up or wear her clothes.
2. I knock before entering my mom's bedroom.
3. I avoid snooping in my mom's closets or drawers.
4. I ask permission before I take money from my mom's purse.
5. I leave my mom's mail and personal papers alone.

Reminders for Daughters

1. Take private time for yourself each day; it will keep you from getting stressed out.
2. If you don't feel like talking to your mother when you first get home, ask her if you can talk with her later.
3. Invite your mother to come into your room once in awhile and have a little friendly conversation. This will lessen her tendency to pry into your business.

Reminders for Moms

1. Pick the right time to talk to your daughter and don't play Twenty Questions. Let your daughter tell you about the school dance, her day at school, or the baseball game when she's ready. A story that comes from openness and willingness to share is a much better story. Respect the end of the story and don't ask for more details.
2. Not all business is a mother's business. You'll want to achieve a balance between respecting your daughter's privacy while still knowing what's going on.
3. If you should read a note, a diary, or a piece of mail and learn something disturbing, proceed with extreme caution.

18

Mom Embarrassment

How Could She Do That!

You're Embarrassing Me!

I ran downstairs to my room as soon as we got home from dinner. Reaching for the phone, I flopped down on my bed and pushed the first speed-dial button.

"Mothers can be so annoying!" I said as soon as my best friend, Sarah, answered the phone.

"You're telling me!" she answered. "What did yours do today?"

"We decided to go out to dinner tonight, and she insisted on wearing that big velvet hat."

"The bright purple one?" Sarah asked in shock.

"Yeah, the one with the big flower on front! I told her that it made her look ridiculous and she said, 'Amanda, I'm a free spirit and I don't mind if I look ridiculous.' So then we get to the restaurant and we get seated at a table across from these really hot guys. It was embarrassing enough that my mom was wearing that stupid hat, but when we sat down at our table she said, 'Those guys are *cuuuute!* Don't you think so, Amanda?' She said it so loud. They all looked over at us and I know that they heard her. I thought I was going to die!"

Sympathetic, Sarah said, "You're joking me. I can't believe she did that!"

"Yeah, well that's not all. My mom ordered linguine with clams as always, but when it came, it was different than she'd remembered. She was mad because the sauce was different or something. Anyway, she calls the waiter over to ask him why it was different but he didn't really know because he was new, so she insisted on talking to the manager! The manager comes out and explains to her that they changed the recipe a little. She gets all upset and says, 'That's what I really wanted to eat tonight.' So the manager and the waiter are apologizing like crazy, but there is really nothing that they can do because they don't have that meal anymore. I didn't understand why she couldn't just drop it and eat what they brought her."

"So what happened?"

"Well, she finally said that she would just eat it anyway, but she complained about it the rest of the night!" I said. "Then on the way home, she put on her favorite oldies tape and sang along the entire way home! I thought I was going to die! All I wanted to do was get home because I was so annoyed with her!"

"I don't understand moms," Sarah said. "They can be so weird sometimes!"

"How Could You?"

I don't remember the restaurant incident exactly the same way Amanda does. I do have a purple velvet hat with a pink flower but I didn't actually wear it during dinner. As soon as we got to the restaurant, I took it off because I know it embarrasses Amanda. The hat's really not as outrageous as it sounds. My girlfriends think it's attractive, but Amanda cringes whenever I put it on.

I did ask the waiter why they had taken my favorite linguini clam dish off the menu, but I never demanded to speak to the manager. I recall that the waiter was quite friendly and offered to ask the chef if he could make the dish

Age cannot wither her, nor custom sail her infinite variety.

—Shakespeare

for me. The chef said it would be no problem since fresh clams had just been delivered. The waiter and chef didn't mind, and it was all very pleasant, but fourteen-year-old Amanda was mortified. The most ordinary things tended to humiliate her. Once I ask the sales clerk if she could give me a reduced price since the dress I was purchasing was going to be marked down the next day anyway. Amanda shook her head in utter disbelief at my audacity. "How could you?" she scolded.

From age thirteen through sixteen-and-a-half, Amanda was humiliated by the tiniest thing I did. Once I accidentally spilled coffee on my blouse at a luncheon, and she could barely stand to be seen with me. Another time, I laughed at a joke and she gave me that wide-eyed stare that told me I was not behaving properly. I could never be sure what would set her off.

She had a strict dress code for me too. She always advised me, "Never wear sweatshirts," not that I'd ever worn sweatshirts, but she just wanted to make sure I didn't suddenly change my mind.

Most of the time I went along with her wishes. I knew these things were important to her and I could empathize with the trauma of associating with a mother who wasn't "with it." I'd felt the same shame when I was her age. Everything my mother did embarrassed me to death. I tried my best to do what Amanda expected, but no matter how hard I tried, I couldn't get it 100 percent right. Sometimes I'd give her a mini-speech on the advantages of maintaining my own style and personal freedom and say, "Honey, don't squelch me and I won't squelch you."

Eventually my idiosyncrasies didn't bother her as much. By seventeen, she had grasped that we were separate people and that if I made a fool of myself, it didn't reflect badly on her. By her senior year of high school, I'd learned the proper mother protocols so well

My love for her and my hate for her are so bafflingly intertwined that I can hardly see her. I never know who is who. She is me and I am she and we're all together.

—Erica Jong

that she actually invited me to chaperone the homecoming dance. I dressed up, put on my best public manners, and didn't talk to her unless she talked to me. I unobtrusively did my job guarding the back entrance and quietly took pictures as kids I'd known since grade school danced until midnight. At nineteen, she is very tolerant of my peculiarities. Now when I wear my black pants that she refers to as "high waters," she just shakes her head and smiles.

✳ What's a Mother to Do?

Meet Her Halfway

Your adolescent daughter is super self-conscious about both of you. She's realizing you aren't as perfect as she once thought you were, and she wants to protect you from embarrassment. When she corrects you she's often doing it out of concern for you. Thirteen-year-old Jesse said, "My mother is *soooo* embarrassing; she can't keep the names of my friends straight. She's called Melissa by a wrong name three times now. My friends are starting to wonder what's wrong with her. If she can't get her names right, I don't want her to come to school anymore." A younger girl would be delighted to have her mother come and would simply tell her mom the right name and move on, but an adolescent girl is concerned that her friends are noticing her mother as well. She wants her mother to blend in, in the same way she's trying so hard to do.

I'm sure you've noticed that your daughter doesn't want you to talk much around her friends. She can tolerate your presence if you're in the background, but if you're actively participating, then she's likely to feel humiliated by what you're wearing or what you're saying. When chauffeuring her and her friends, it's best to smile and listen rather than to get in the middle of their conversations. Console yourself knowing that you will learn much more by listening than you will by asking direct questions.

This ousting from center stage and into the wings can be difficult. Just a few years earlier, you felt confident as her mother, but now your identity is shaken. Your daughter not only sees your faults, she quickly points them out.

You'll get over the rough spots more easily if you cooperate in areas that really don't matter so much. For example, don't insist, as one mother I know did, on sitting in the front row for the play. When her daughter asked her to move to the back of the theater because she'd be nervous with her mother sitting close, her mother stubbornly refused.

The sacrifices I make. The other day, I was practicing the violin and my daughter came up to me and said, "Mom, can you pleeeeeze take that somewhere else?"

—Meryl Streep

Girls do not want their mothers looking too sexy, too sloppy, too hip, too out-of-style, or too conspicuous. They want you to look respectable and appropriate, conservative and "motherly" in a classy way. It takes several years of trial and error to get it just right, but respecting her wishes will make it easier to figure out. If your daughter wants you to wear your pantsuit instead of jeans, willingly do it for her. Your example shows her how cooperation makes life smoother. Most important, if you don't want her to stifle you, don't stifle her.

Moms Have Quirks

Inevitably, your mother will do things that will drive you crazy. My mother drives me crazy by wearing embarrassing clothes. She insists on asking, "Does my outfit look okay?" at least four times before we go anywhere. Even though I have already told her "Yes" at least twice, she keeps asking. The way she talks can bug me, too. She always asks, "Does Adrienne still go with Josh?" I correct her by saying, "Go where? The right way to say it is, 'Are Adrienne and Josh still together?'" Sometimes she talks too loud, she asks my friends weird questions, she smacks her gum, and she leaves the television on when she goes to bed. I know it's shallow to be so bothered by these things, but she can really

> *If it isn't one thing,*
> *it's your mother.*
>
> *—anonymous*

get on my nerves, and I sometimes wonder how I got stuck with the most embarrassing mother.

Maybe it was because I got older, but one day I finally realized that I had to accept my mother for who she is. She has thoughts, ideas, and feelings that are unique to her and she is her own person. You have to accept your mother too, and it will be a lot easier if you avoid the "grass is always greener" mentality. Your mother probably isn't any more embarrassing than other mothers. All of my friends have been annoyed with their mothers. Like every other mother, mine doesn't do things exactly the way want I her to. I wish she wouldn't wear her purple hat or that she would let me listen to music I like when we're in the car, but there are some things about her that I cannot change.

I realize now that there are many things about me that drive my mom crazy, like not filling up the ice cube trays after getting a few pieces of ice. I've figured out that if I want my mother to accept everything about me, then I need to accept her too.

✵ What's a Daughter to Do?

Focus on the Good Things

I know mothers can be very annoying at times. The clothes she wears, the way she talks, and the things she does can, at times, make it hard to keep from getting annoyed with your mother. But think of your mother as person for a moment; she has feelings as much as you do. Imagine how you would feel if somebody was always pointing out your flaws or sighed with exasperation every time you did something different from the way they do it.

Instead of focusing on your mother's negative traits, start noticing her good qualities and the things she does that you enjoy. You may be embarrassed by some of what your mother does and says, but most people probably don't even notice her behavior. Do you pay attention to other people's mothers and notice their embarrassing qualities? Many times, you exaggerate these things in your own mind.

I would get annoyed with my mother when she would talk endlessly with sales people at the mall or clerks at the grocery store. Usually I would hang my head in silence, praying that nobody would see me with this annoying woman. When my mother would say something I found extremely embarrassing, I would look at her wide-eyed with my mouth open in shock. "Mother!" I would scold her, and the stranger would look at us, a bit confused by my outburst. They would never notice the "embarrassing" thing my mother said, but they noticed my impatience and annoyance with her. In those situations, I ended up drawing the negative attention to myself, not my mother.

❋ Tell Her Nicely

If you feel completely humiliated by your mother, tell her tactfully. Yelling and rolling your eyes is not the best tactic to use to get your mother to change. If she does something you really don't like, explain to her what upsets you and give her an example of how she could change.

"My mother always comes to watch me cheer during our pep assemblies," says Laura. "For the first assembly, she sat in the student section. It was embarrassing for me because that's where all the kids sit and it was really out of place for my mother to be sitting there. I got really annoyed and told her not to sit there, but she thought I was just trying to be difficult and refused to move. The day before the second assembly, I explained to my mother why I didn't want her to sit in the student section and asked her if she would sit in the section that was designated for parents and other adults. After I explained to her how I felt, she was very understanding and cooperative."

❋ Reminders for Daughters

1. Finding out that your mother has faults is a sign you are growing up; accepting her quirks is a sign of your goodwill and maturity.

2. Relax. Most likely, nobody else even notices your mother's "embarrassing" behavior.

3. It's okay to ask your mother to change her behavior if you really believe that it's causing a problem.

✳ Reminders for Mothers

1. Your daughter can't stand anyone thinking and talking negatively about either of you. She doesn't want you to make a fool of yourself, so she tries to protect you with suggestions on how you should behave.

2. Be sensitive to the signals your daughter is sending you. You can talk, joke, and play around with her and her friends, as long as you don't go overboard.

19

Role Reversal

Who's The Mother?

"Where's your sister?" Kendra's mom stood in the doorway looking at her sixteen-year-old daughter sprawled out on the floor doing her homework.

Without looking up from her studying, Kendra said, "I drove her over to Emily's house to work on the science project that's due next week. Her parents are driving her home after they're done."

Carefully stepping over the piles of books that covered the floor, her mother walked to her bed, and, with a sigh, plopped face down into the pile of pillows.

Kendra glanced up from her reading. "Tough day?" she asked.

"Oh, it was just awful," her mother said. "Work can be such a pain. I really hate having to work. I think maybe I'll quit."

"I don't think that would be the best idea," Kendra replied.

"I know," her mother sighed "You're so lucky that you don't have all the responsibilities of taking care of a family. I wish I were your age again."

Kendra ignored her mother's last comment and said, "Erik's baseball coach called and said that his game is changed from Saturday to Monday night. You have to remember. I have play rehearsal."

"Just another thing to add to my list," her mother moaned. Then she added, "That reminds me of something I wanted to ask you. Erik wants me to let him spend the night at Ryan's house after their eighth grade dance. They're having a slumber party with girls too. Should I let him go? Ryan's parents are going to be there, but I'm not sure if it's such a good idea to let him go. What do you think?"

Kendra looked back down at her book, wishing her mother would understand she had a lot on her mind and wasn't in the mood to be her personal advisor. "It's up to you. That's not really a decision for me to make."

"Oh, I wish you would just help me a little. Can't you give me some input?"

Kendra sighed. "I don't think you should let him go. He's too young to be staying the night with girls there too."

"All right," her mother said. "But if he gets mad at me, I'm going to tell him it was your idea not to let him go."

"Fine," Kendra replied.

Kendra's mother sat up. "Gosh, you study a lot," she said, as she walked toward the door.

"I have to if I want to get into a good college."

"Well, when you're done," her mother asked, "will you come and help me make dinner?"

❋ Supermom

As children, most of us looked up to our mothers as incredibly wise women who were able to do everything. I know that when I was little I believed that all mothers knew special secrets about life and could solve any problem. Mothers seemed to know how to calm any worries and make you feel safe. In my mind, nobody could ever be as mature and responsible as my mother.

When I entered high school my glorified image of mothers came crashing down, and I began to see that they aren't always perfect. I remember my feelings of distress when my girlfriend's slumber party was crashed by her mother who had come home drunk and I watched my friend put her mother to bed. Slowly I came to the upsetting conclusion that many girls are more mature than their mothers. I learned that older doesn't necessarily mean wiser. "My mom is always telling me about her problems," says Carissa. "She always talks to me about how she is really stressed out or asks me for advice on what she should do about my little sister. Sometimes I feel like I'm more emotionally stable than she is. I try to help her as much as I can, but sometimes I don't want to worry about her problems and I want her to make decisions on her own without asking me."

Although it is important to help your mother out with things that need to be done, or allow her to openly express her feelings and even comfort her once in awhile, there is a difference between helping your mother and taking on her life. Many mothers don't face up to the responsibilities of motherhood. Liz complains that her mother is too caught up in her work and says, "My mom puts her job ahead of everything else. Sometimes I feel like she forgets she has kids who need to be taken care of."

"My mother acts like a teenager sometimes," says Marci. "She gets really caught up in her own social life and doesn't pay much attention to what is going on in the family. She hardly knows what's going on in mine or my brother's lives." Some of my friends' mothers aren't focused on being mothers. Their thoughts and emotions are tied up elsewhere and they don't seem to have the time and energy necessary for mothering.

❋ What's a Daughter to Do?

Acknowledge the Truth of the Situation

If you have a mother like this, you may find yourself feeling like you have to pick up where she slacks off. Maybe you worry that if you don't clean the house, it will never get done or you feel like you have to look out for your younger siblings and make sure that everything is okay in their lives. It's possible that you are more responsible and emotionally mature than your mother is and this has caused a reversal of your roles. Whether she is aware of it or not, your mother has put extra responsibility and pressure on you. Instead of asking you to help out around the house when she needs it, she has handed nearly all the work over to you; instead of expressing her concerns and upset feelings to you in a healthy manner, she looks to you to help solve her problems and get rid of her stresses.

If you have been taking on many of your mother's responsibilities, you are probably feeling very overwhelmed. Not only are you keeping track of your own life—your grades, your activities, your friends—but you're also trying to organize others' lives as well. Taking on your mother's problems and needs can be very exhausting. You may feel like part of your own life has been taken away because you are always looking out for somebody else.

❋ It's Okay to Act Like the Teenager You Are

If you often find yourself playing your mother's role, tell your mother how you feel. Maybe she isn't aware that she's putting so much extra pressure on you. Let her know you're willing to help out and are happy to comfort her when she is stressed out, but also tell her that you can't do everything. Explain to her that you have your own life with stresses and obligations and you feel overwhelmed by what she expects from you. Try to explain to your mother the difference between asking you to help out and dumping things off onto you. Telling your mother how you feel can be enough to make her aware of her own actions.

Talking to your mother may not work. It's possible that your mother is completely unable to understand what she is doing. She may be an alcoholic, a drug addict, or simply too self-involved. If you have a father you can talk to, see if he can help relieve some of your burden, or talk to a school counselor or another responsible, caring adult. They will help you understand. It is not your job to be your mother's caretaker.

✳ Don't Feel Guilty

Overly responsible daughters need to know that there is nothing you can do about your mother's actions. No matter how hard you try, you will never be able to fix your mother's problems, and it is not your responsibility to do so. It is not your fault if something in your mother's life is going wrong, and it isn't possible for you to take control of everything.

You are not a bad daughter if you don't feel like taking care of your mother, so don't feel guilty. As a teenager, you should be thinking about issues that are relevant to girls your age, not worrying about your mother's problems. It's natural to focus your energy on things like boys, sports, parties, and school, and you are not being selfish when you worry about your own problems instead of your mother's. You must find a healthy balance between helping your mother and taking care of your own needs.

You have proven you are a very hard-working and loving person. It takes a great deal of maturity, self-discipline, and caring to be able to take on your mother's problems. It is obvious that you care a lot about your mother and your family, because if you didn't, you wouldn't have taken on so much. You deserve to give yourself a break; remember that you are a teenager and it is okay to want to act like one.

Who's in Charge?

As a mother, it's normal to occasionally feel like you're the teenager and she's the grown-up, but it shouldn't be an everyday occurrence. I've counseled many women who were forced to take on motherly responsibilities as teenagers and have paid a high price. They were their mothers' caretakers, advisors, and confidantes. They stood in for her when she was hung over, out on dates, or simply too tired from working to run the household. Little by little, these girls lost their teen years and although they handled their responsibilities perfectly, they suffer from lingering anxiety. They feel anxious about leaving their mothers and since they felt emotionally responsible for their mothers' well-being, they remain emotionally crippled. They feel guilty for wanting their own lives.

Based on outward appearances, sixteen-year-old Kendra is a super-perfect teen. She's on the honor roll, sings in the choir, and serves on student council. She has lots of friends and is respected by both teachers and her peers. Her thirty-one-year old mother leans on her; they're more like sisters than mother and daughter. Kendra oversees her younger siblings' homework and mediates between her mother and father. Kendra manages it all but is under so much pressure that she's unable to let go and have fun. She suffers from migraines and worries about her mother.

Seventeen-year-old Matty gives the opposite impression. She skips school, gets poor grades, and talks back to teachers. She avoids going home as much as possible because she never knows if she'll find her mother drunk or unconscious from another overdose. Matty wants mothering and parental guidance, but since she's never had it, she withdraws instead of reaching out. She's full of rage and anger and doesn't trust adults. She's told me many times, "My mother doesn't care about me."

It takes huge amounts of energy to mother teenagers and it's especially hard if your own teen experience was cut short. Leanne said, "I had Syndey when I was fifteen years old and had to drop out of high school. When I was seventeen, her father left us and for two years I was so depressed I could barely get out of bed. All my friends were still in high school and I was tied down taking care of a baby. By age four, Syndey was cooking me breakfast. Without her, I don't know what I would have done. We grew up together; she's my best friend, but sometimes I wish I could trade places with her." If you had your daughter while you were still a teenager yourself, mothering your teenager will take extra effort. When you see her doing the things you missed, you might feel jealous or resent that she's having the fun you never had.

A mother who is bogged down with responsibilities of work and running the household might be tempted to rely heavily on her teenage daughter. "After their father died, there was no choice but for me to work," said Kathy, "which meant that Lea, who was thirteen at the time, had to do a bigger share of the housework and a lot of after-school baby-sitting for her nine- and seven-year-old brothers. She had to be a 'little mother.'"

A teenage girl in that position learns to take care of others before herself. She is in tune with her mother but not with herself. She can tell you what her mother and everyone else around needs to feel better, but she can't identify her own needs. She may be able to function this way for a long time, but eventually—perhaps when she's a mother with children of her own—she burns out and suffers from stress-related illnesses.

> *Through conducting hundreds of repair processes between parents and teenagers, I learned most parents have not completed their own adolescence. They really don't feel like the wise leaders they are supposed to be. Under these circumstances, it is hard for them to help their adolescents learn what they have not themselves yet learned.*
>
> —Virginia Satir

※ What's a Mother to Do?

Be in Tune with the Development Tasks

Just as you wouldn't want your little girl to miss the innocence of childhood, you don't want your teenager to miss the freedoms that come with her high school years. The carefree experience of having friends, slumber parties, and only taking care of yourself goes by very quickly. Before you know it, your youth has passed and your life is filled with adult obligations. Enjoying your adolescence has a significance later in life. A women who is loaded down with adult duties during her teen years often later has a midlife crisis or feels cheated out of her own life.

I'm not suggesting that you can't ask your teenager daughter to help out, but reversing roles is not the mature way to handle your problems. Even if your daughter is able to step easily into the mother role, if she does it all the time, you are shirking your responsibility. It's not healthy for a mother to go to her daughter with all her problems; placing that burden on her is too much. Your daughter has pressures too. A school day is not all play—it's full of stress and deadlines. She has to cope with teachers' personalities and demands, and making and keeping friends takes considerable time and effort.

Your daughter also has to cope with teenage developmental tasks. As a mother, it's essential that you be in tune with her present stage of life and that you're sensitive to both of your needs. It takes some women until their forties to come to terms with what they need to feel satisfied and content. When a mother understands the deeper issues of the teenage stage, she's able to allow her daughter the freedom to complete her developmental tasks. Just as a toddler learns to walk before she's ready to ride a bike, your teenager has certain skills to acquire before she can settle down to the responsibilities of adult life.

The developmental tasks of teenage girls are:

1. To be able to act independently from her mother while staying connected.

2. To remain curious and enthusiastic about life so that she continues growing, learning, and moving forward.

3. To play and taste excitement so that she can use her energy to achieve balance throughout her life.

4. To honor herself as a sexual and feminine young woman.

5. To learn to meet her needs in a healthy way.

AN IMMATURE MOM

- Is so wrapped up in her own life that she has no time or energy to be involved with her daughter.
- Immerses herself in the teen scene.
- Becomes so overwhelmed with responsibilities that she quits or relinquishes her role as mother.

A GROWNUP MOM

- Asks her daughter to help her out rather than dumping it all on her shoulders.
- Doesn't need to know all the details of her daughter's life, but is aware of her daughter's needs.
- Is actively dedicated to finding solutions to her own problems instead of looking to her daughter for help.

AN IMMATURE GIRL

- Is afraid to say "No." Tries to please others more than herself.
- Thinks she has to do everything on her own and gives up when she makes a mistake.
- Berates herself when she is slow to learn and gets discouraged easily.

A MATURE GIRL

- Makes choices based on what is best for herself. Can say "No" when appropriate.
- Gets assistance and asks for help when she needs it. Learns from her mistakes and goes on.
- Gives herself encouragement and says positive things to herself.
- Gives herself credit for trying and is proud of her smallest accomplishment.

When these tasks are thwarted, she will eventually feel that she missed out on an important aspect of her life and has to work much harder to compensate for that loss.

❋ Reminders for Moms

1. Remember the confusion you felt as a teenage girl and understand that this is what your daughter is going through.

2. Use your age, wisdom, and experience to help your daughter understand what she is unable to see. The feelings she is having are new to her but old to you. Make sure you understand yourself enough so that you can help her see clearly.

3. Confide your problems to an adult friend, not your daughter. Don't burden your daughter with a legacy of caretaking.

❋ Reminders for Daughters

1. Your mother's happiness is not your responsibility.

2. Your main job is to figure out who you are and what you need, not what your mother needs.

3. If you are concerned about your mother's well-being, talk to a counselor or trusted adult.

20

The Blues

Daughter's Down Days

I Don't Know What's Wrong

had slept through my alarm and didn't have time for a shower. Throwing on a pair of old jeans, I rushed quickly to school to make it just in time for first period. As I sat down at my desk, I knew that something was wrong. I felt a sadness inside of me that I couldn't explain; my heart was aching and my eyes were filling with tears. I had nothing in particular to be sad about, but for some reason something in my life didn't seem right. I had a lot of friends but I felt completely alone. I was getting good grades but I felt stupid. I was run down, stressed out, feeling unappreciated, sad, and completely vulnerable. All I wanted was for somebody to be kind and gentle to me, but nobody seemed to understand. They thought my quiet attitude was a sign of a bad mood and that I wanted to be left alone when the opposite was true. I wanted my friends to embrace me and tell me that everything was going to be okay and that they loved and appreciated me, but they didn't.

I had to leave the room. I was fighting my tears as hard as I could, but I knew that as soon as somebody talked to me, I would burst out crying.

Grabbing the bathroom pass, I quickly ran for the door. As I walked down the hall, the only thing I could think about was home. I wanted to bury my head in my pillow and weep until all of my hurt and sorrow went away. I wanted to be where I felt safe and was allowed to be sad and cry as much as I needed to. I had no strength to cover up my sadness.

I walked by the pay phone and had an immediate impulse to call my mother. I wasn't quite sure what I was going to say, but for some reason I longed for her. Picking up the phone, I dialed the number and crossed my fingers, hoping that she was home.

She answered after two rings. "Hello," she said.

"Mom, it's me." My voice was shaky, and immediately she knew something was wrong.

"What's the matter?" she asked, her voice full of concern.

I couldn't hold back my tears and burst out sobbing. "I don't know," I cried. "I can't stay at school, though. I'm so upset."

Hoping she could help me cure my problem, she asked, "What happened?"

"Nothing *happened*." I couldn't find the words to explain how I felt. "I'm just upset."

"What do you want me to do, honey?"

"Please come get me."

"Can you wait a half-hour?" she asked.

"Yes," I sniffled.

"Okay. I'll meet you in front of the school in a half-hour."

✳ What's Going On?

When I was younger and imagined my teenage years, I pictured going to the mall, dressing in cute clothes, and watching school football games. I saw myself going to school dances with hot guys and spending Friday nights with my girlfriends, laughing and always having a good time. I thought every day would be fun and that I would always feel carefree.

It's terribly amusing how many different climates of feeling one can go through in a day.

—Anne Morrow Lindbergh

I never anticipated the feelings of complete loneliness, uncertainty, and sadness that often come along with being a teenage girl. I didn't know there would be times when my best friend would talk bad about me behind my back or ditch me for the "cooler" kids. I never expected the first boy I ever loved to break up with me and go out with the one girl at school I disliked the most. I didn't know that I would hate the way I looked, or feel sad for no apparent reason, or struggle so hard when everyone else seemed to get what they wanted so easily. For every bit of excitement and joy I experienced from thirteen to nineteen, there was an equal amount of hurt and sorrow.

Adolescence is so much more complex than the stereotypical "glory days" picture we have in our minds. It is full of times of sadness and longing—longings that are hard to identify. Sometimes the cause to your sadness is obvious, like breaking up with a boyfriend or a death or divorce in your family. Other times, many little things, like a bad grade, a bad hair day, or friends acting weirdly, can mount up. Sometimes you feel depressed for no reason. You may feel an aching in your heart or a sadness in your soul and will have no idea what is causing these emotions inside of you.

The times you feel sad for no reason can be scariest. When you know what made you feel depressed, it's easier to ask for help because people can understand when there is a tangible cause to your sadness. However, when you are unsure why you feel the way you do or what would make you feel better, it is hard to ask for help.

"When I feel upset or sad for no reason, I don't really talk about it," says sixteen-year-old Hailey. "I become quiet and don't have a lot of energy. Usually my friends don't understand why I'm acting the way I am and instead of being nice to me, like I really want them to, they get mad because they think that I'm just in a bad mood or being a brat for no reason." Fourteen-year-old Krissy adds, "When I'm upset, I try to pretend like I'm happy. I don't want my friends to think that I'm weird or overreacting, and I know they don't want to be around me when I'm down in the dumps."

❋ *What's a Daughter to Do?*

Let Yourself Be Comforted

As a teen, it's natural to want to go to your friends for help with your problems. Usually they are the ones who understand you the best and can empathize with you the most. There are times when your friends won't be able to help you the way that your mom can, though. When you are feeling overwhelmed by sadness and aren't sure what to do to make them go away, your mother may be able to help you more than anyone else.

It can be scary to ask your mother for help or try to explain your feelings to her. Maybe you are afraid she won't understand. Maybe your mother isn't the soft, nurturing type. "My mom doesn't really like to talk about feelings, especially sad ones," says Mindy. "She keeps her emotions to herself, so I think that she probably wants me to keep mine to myself as well." Libby says, "My mom doesn't understand. She doesn't have any concept of what it's like to be a teenage girl today."

Your mother may not be the best listener and she may seem like she wouldn't understand, but you might be surprised by how she acts if you show her how you are feeling. Take a chance. Maybe she won't have great advice or completely relate to what you're going through, but she will be able to comfort you. There have been many times when I have been upset and felt better after crying to my mother. She didn't necessarily say or do anything, but she listened to me without interrupting or trying to change the subject. She was warm and gentle in a way that none of my friends ever were, and she allowed me to cry and get my feelings of sadness out in the open.

She became for me an island of light, fun wisdom, where I could run with my discoveries and torments and woes at any time of the day and find welcome.

—May Sarton

If you have tried going to your mother for comfort but she didn't help you in the way you would have liked, don't give up hope. It's possible that your mother doesn't know how to console you, but you can teach her how. Every mother has the ability to give her daughter amazing comfort and peace of mind, she may just need to learn how. Tell your mother what you need from her. Let her know that you need her to listen without giving advice or trying to fix your problem. Explain to her that when you are feeling unhappy the best way she can help is to be kind and gentle to you. Don't expect your mother to know when you are feeling upset—tell her when you need her to comfort you. If this is too difficult, simply ask her to read the mother section of this chapter. Hopefully she'll get the point.

Take a chance on your mother, give her the opportunity to help you, and accept the love and comfort that she gives you.

The Blues

The morning Amanda called in tears and asked me to come to get her, I knew she had the blues. The blues are those heavy feelings that come upon you when you least expect them. You've probably had them too. You wake up in the morning and don't feel like getting out of bed. You're not tired, but you want to pull the covers over your head. The blues can wash over you in the middle of the day and when someone asks what's wrong, you're not able to express it. Besides, even if you could put your finger on what's troubling you, it would take more energy than you have to clarify it. So you shrug your shoulders, sigh, and say, "Nothing." You feel discouraged and you're not sure why.

Teenage girls get the blues too, only the blues are more extreme because they're experiencing these complicated emotions for the very first time. Your daughter might not know the blues by name, but she still experiences them. Her heart is easily broken and she can feel shattered at the drop of a hat. Perhaps a friend at school ignored her or the boy she hoped would talk to her didn't. Maybe the effort she put in on the school project went unnoticed. Perhaps someone

According to Amy Wolfson, Ph.D., a sleep specialist at the College of Holy Cross, teens need from nine to nine-and-a-half hours sleep each night. Teens who said they weren't getting enough sleep also reported feeling of depressed, falling asleep at the wheel or in class, and, getting low grades.

spread an untrue rumor about her. Perhaps she heard a sad song on the radio or maybe she watched television and heard about another injustice. Maybe it's hormones or that time of the month. It could be spiritual stirrings.

You may think that because your daughter doesn't need you in the same way she once did, she doesn't need as much nurturing from you either. Let me reassure you that she still needs plenty. When I picked Amanda up from school that day, her eyes were sad and she looked small and fragile standing alone on the curb. I sensed that what she needed was the shelter of her mother. She jumped in the car and I asked, "You've got the blues?"

"I guess," she said, and immediately started sobbing.

"Want to talk about it?" I asked.

"I can't explain it," she said, "I'm just upset."

"You don't have the words right now," I said. "I understand, I've felt that same way myself."

It always troubles me to see Amanda discouraged and shaky. When she's hurt or upset, I'm immediately plunged into "mommy agony." Desperately wanting to relieve her load but knowing that I can't is torment. Pure instinct guided me that morning. I drove to a cozy bakery and we sipped freshly squeezed juice and ate a roll. We took a walk and, as we passed our favorite hair salon, I said, "Let's see if Rebecca can do your hair." Luckily she had a cancellation and was able to wash and dry Amanda's hair. By the time Rebecca was through, Amanda wanted to go back to school for the afternoon.

I wasn't always good at recognizing when Amanda was having the blues. Sometimes I mistook her crankiness for bad manners, but now I can see that there were times when a little more understanding from me would have been better. A friend of mine was really awful at comforting her daughter. She constantly made fun of her daughter's moods by saying, "Oh, she's just a moody girl." Her negative comments about her own daughter always made me and Amanda uncomfortable.

✳ What's a Mother to Do?

Show Her It's Okay to Feel Bad

Within each mother is a "little girl," tender, soft, and fragile, who gets the blues once in a while too. Even though we're able to run the office and cook gourmet meals, budget our finances and mow the lawn, or support our husbands and comfort our children, we still feel very small at times. Like everyone else, we're terrified of disapproval and rejection. We get sad and scared too. We're fearful that our daughters will abandon us and we'll end up lonely and alone. We also have disappointments.

Vulnerability is the ability and willingness to share your deepest feelings—your feelings of love and understanding—as well as your needs, fears, and doubts. Being able to talk freely about your vulnerabilities is the rarest of gifts. An authentic mother is willing to share the full spectrum of herself. "My daughter knows my shortcomings," admits Grace. "I have a myriad of misgivings about myself and I don't hide them from her."

By allowing your daughter to see your weaknesses and soft spots, you offer her the multidimensional you, faults and liabilities, thorns, warts, and all. Taking off the face you present to the world brings your daughter closer and gives

Our children, especially our daughters, watch us. They look to us to see what their own future may be like and what is possible. Even more important than what we tell our daughters is what we show them.

—Harriet Lerner, Ph.D.

her the larger view of both the "capable woman" and the "little girl" that you are. Doing this will help her realize that she does not have to be perfect and that it is okay to feel sad, alone, scared, or inadequate.

Tell your daughter directly how you're feeling and then give yourself what you need in order to feel better. Reveal your feelings but don't expect your daughter to make you feel better. Be sure to make time for what you need—whether it's quiet time to take a bath, an hour to read without interruption, an afternoon to yourself to play tennis, or a weekend away with your girlfriends. By taking care of your own needs, you're sending a healthy message to your daughter and showing her it's okay to have down days and that each of us is responsible for our own happiness.

✳ Offer Empathy

When you're plagued with the blues, isn't it comforting to be treated kindly? When you're sick with the flu, doesn't it lessen the ache to be handled gently? Your daughter needs solace just as much as you do. She still yearns for the comfort of her "mommy." When she suffers with soul malaise, she needs your kindness, special treatment, and a large dose of empathy.

"I can't imagine having my daughter turn to someone else to help her through her troubles. I didn't want her to have to keep her pain inside as I have always done. I wanted her to always know she could come to me," says Claudia. "So I had to get over my tendency to tell her to toughen up. I had to be soft even when it seemed like she didn't want it."

Kind words can be short and easy to speak, but their echoes are truly endless.

—Mother Teresa

Try to recognize the look on your daughter's face that says, "I'm having a really bad day." It's comforting to know your mother notices when you're down in the dumps. Comforting your daughter lets her know you care and gives her strength and the reassurance that no matter what happens, she'll be okay. Be warm toward her. The more you allow warmth to flow from you to your daughter, the richer your alliance will be. Reach out to her with warmth in your

A mother understands what a child does not say.

—Jewish proverb

words, "Sweetie, I'm sorry your having a tough day." Allow your heart, not just your mind, to respond. Serve her chicken soup, Popsicles, and sympathy, and you'll be giving her the reassurance that comes only with a mother's compassion. Reassure her that nothing is wrong with her or with what she's feeling. Tell her that upset feelings are normal: "It's natural to be disappointed that you didn't get asked to the dance."

Despair is intense in an adolescent girl. Although twenty years from now your daughter will have completely forgotten about her current boyfriend dilemma or the pimple on her face, at that very moment it is a huge problem to her. Whatever you do, don't belittle the intensity of her feelings. Virginia frequently says to her girls, "You don't even know what real problems are." While it may be true, this only adds to her daughters' sense that she is unable to care.

Your daughter's problems are very real to her. What upsets her is different from what upsets you. Girls hear their mothers talking about how taking care of a family, working, and paying bills is much harder than going to school, and they know that this is probably true. However, that fact doesn't lessen their current problems. The solution to her daughter's problem may seem simple to her mother, but it is not that way for the daughter.

No matter how insignificant you perceive her problem to be, your daughter needs a soft place to fall, a home where she can be completely herself and where it's safe to let out all her tears and sorrow. Healing comes with crying. If your daughter can't turn to you, she'll keep it knotted up inside or, in desperation, turn to someone or something else to release her pain.

When she's in the throes of negativity, it's important to remember that an adolescent girl who is allowed to freely express the full range of her emotions eventually learns to sort them out and manage them appropriately.

✳ Show Her Warmth

When you daughter was young, she probably allowed you to hold her hand and give her a hug. Now that she's an adolescent, you may have to experiment to find creative ways to comfort her. She isn't holding onto her teddy bear or a tattered security blanket anymore, but the signs that she needs tender loving care are still there.

When Amanda turned thirteen, it seemed like she didn't want me to hug or cuddle her like she had when she was younger. For several years, whenever I'd attempt to comfort her by giving her a hug, she'd stiffen. I'd try to hug her and even when she let me, she wouldn't allow me to come too close or hug for very long. She needed her distance from me, yet I knew she still needed my comfort, so I gave her invisible hugs instead. I'd put a flower by her bedside with a note that said, "Here's an invisible hug." When I could see that she was upset, I might say, "Honey, is there anything I can do? Come sit beside me," or I'd remind her, "It's okay to cry." Even though she wouldn't snuggle up, I was letting her know that it was safe to cry and be "little" in my presence.

Part of comfort is surprises. If you've ever walked on the seashore when the tide is out, you know the wonderful surprises waiting for you. Your daughter loves to be remembered by you in small ways.

COMPILE A COMFORT LIST

Write down seven things that make you feel comforted, have one for every day of the week. What little thing can you add to your environment, such as a candle or a flower bud in a vase on your desk, to help you feel better? What sounds, smells, and sights do you like? What can your mother/daughter do when you need to be comforted? What do you do to comfort yourself?

It's the little things you do that let her know you care. You can't solve her problems for her, but you can let her know you're supporting her.

Let the delight of having a such wonderful daughter shine through what you say and what you do. Allow the thrill of loving her to show on your face. Pamper her by doing one of her chores: "You're having a hard week; I'll do the dishes for you." Fuss over her. Ask her if she could use a little downtime or give her a bottle of bubble bath and a candle and tell her to treat herself to an hour in the tub.

Your love and comfort through the turbulence is the safety net that allows your daughter to emerge strong and whole; she stays connected to her soul through your reassurance.

> *Keep me from the wisdom that does not weep, and the philosophy that does not laugh, and the pride that does not bow its head before a child.*
>
> *—Kahlil Gibran*

✳ Signs That Your Daughter Needs Time to Recoup and Refresh Herself

1. Mood swings and tantrums.

2. Lots of tears for no apparent reason.

3. More arguments than usual.

4. Depression and edgy nerves.

5. Sleeping too much or not enough.

6. Change in eating habits.

7. Exhaustion or physical illness.

PART 3

Flying into the Future

21

Finding Your Passion

"What Does It Mean to You to Be Happy?"

"Today we will be talking about happiness." My favorite class of the day was Leadership because we talked about issues that were relevant to our everyday lives. Each day after class ended, I realized that I had learned something new about myself.

As my classmates began to talk about what in their lives made them most happy, I sat trying to think of something to say. "What does it mean to you to be happy?" asked the teacher. "What makes you the most happy in life? What is the importance of happiness?" The more my teacher and classmates talked, the more I realized that I had very little to say on the subject. I agreed with what everyone said—that it was important to be happy and everybody had different things that made them happy. And I knew that I was a happy person. But I couldn't define what it was that made me the most contented. Feeling uncomfortable and a bit out of place in this conversation, I imagined everyone thinking to themselves, "Why doesn't

Amanda have anything to say? Doesn't anything make her happy?"

Then my teacher handed us a blank sheet of paper and told us to write down what made us the happiest in our lives and then illustrate it. Eagerly starting the assignment, everyone in the class began to write what things they valued and what brought them the most joy in life. I watched as people drew smiling stick figures holding hands and wrote, "Being with my friends," or "Spending time at the beach," with a drawing of the sun and beach balls. Watching my peers do this boggled my mind as I sat back and wondered, "How can they all do this so quickly while I am stuck?" Sure, the things that my classmates were writing were important to me too. Of course I loved spending time with my friends and lying on the beach, but for me there was much more to life than that. These things didn't bring me true happiness.

I sat for the entire period trying to put something on my paper. I couldn't bring myself to write down anything less than what I really valued as most important in my life. I felt that there was something wrong with me because I didn't find complete happiness in the same things that my peers did. I racked my brain for an entire hour, and the only realization that I came to was that I didn't have a clue what I really wanted for my life and I didn't know myself as well as my peers seemed to know themselves. So when class was over, all I handed in was a blank sheet of paper.

❋ The Best Time of Your Life

Whenever adults would tell me to enjoy my youth while it lasts and that high school would be the best time of my life, I would be a little bit scared. I thought to myself, "If this is the best time of my life, I'm in serious trouble!" There were many times when I felt lost and unsure of myself. I was much better at finding talents and strengths in my friends than I was at seeing them in myself. Everyone around me had qualities that made them stand out in some way. They all seemed to know exactly what they were good at, what they wanted for their lives, and what was important to them. Everyone, that is, but me. I often found myself feeling lost and desperately searching for that one thing that made me special. All I wanted was to find one thing that filled my heart with joy; something that I could immerse myself in and feel satisfied and completely happy.

You know why adults are always asking kids what they want to be when they grow up? 'Cause they're looking for ideas.

—Paula Poundstone

I had all of the things that you are told will make you happy. I was a cheerleader I was involved in honor society, and I was an editor on the school newspaper. I got good grades and was loved by all my teachers. I had a lot of friends and I always had something social to do if I wanted. But there was still something missing. I wanted to find my passion—the one thing that I could merge my whole self into and come out feeling a renewed excitement for life.

Finding your passion means finding the thing that you can put your whole heart and soul into. More than liking to shop or hanging out with your friends, your passion is something that fills your life with joy, meaning, and excitement.

It took me a while, but I came to see that for me it's painting, reading, and writing. Whenever I am upset about something going on in my life or feel like I need some time to myself, I dive into one of these three things. Many nights, after an especially rough day at school, I sit in the art room and paint until 6 P.M. After an hour of melting into the canvas, I feel renewed. I am able to think more clearly and have a better outlook on myself and my life. It is a profound secret that devoting time to doing what you love can really uplift your view of life. Your passion is something that allows you to "escape" from difficult circumstances in a positive, healthy way.

Remember always that you have not only the right to be an individual, you have an obligation to be one.

—Eleanor Roosevelt

What's a Daughter to Do?

Say "Yes, yes, yes!" to Your Passion

Don't feel like you have to love the same things that your friends do; everyone's passions are different. Some girls feel passionate about sports and athletics; others love the arts such as music, photography, and theater. Everyone has a special talent that makes them especially happy; if you haven't found it yet, don't worry. Try many different things because you might be surprised at what you find interesting. Think back to when you were younger and what you really enjoyed; this may remind you of an interest that you forgot you had.

> Kristi Yamaguchi was born with a club foot but overcame it. She started skating at age six. She won the World Junior Pairs title in Figure Skating in 1985 at the age of fourteen and the World Junior Singles title at age seventeen.

The wonderful thing about being a teenager is that we have the time and freedom to devote to finding our passion. It is okay for us to experiment and find what really fills our hearts. However, some girls are not allowed to experiment as freely as others because their mothers hold them back. Maybe their mothers haven't discovered their own passions or they don't know how to encourage their daughters to find what they love in life. Often our mothers push us towards their own interests.

"My mother made me take dance lessons from the time I could walk," says fourteen-year-old Michelle. "I enjoyed it as a child, but as I got older, I realized that dance wasn't something I wanted to devote all my time to. I wanted to spend my time doing something that made me happy, but when I told my mom about my decision to quit dance, she got really upset. I didn't understand why she wanted me to continue doing something that didn't make me happy."

Sometimes mothers push daughters to do things because they didn't get to do what they dreamed of when they were younger. Maybe she always wanted to learn to ride a horse but nobody let her, or she wanted to be an excellent trumpet player but she didn't have anyone to encourage her to practice and keep going with it.

Often girls resent this pushing, as Lee notes: "Whenever I want to quit piano lessons, my mom says to me, 'When you're older, you'll be happy that I made you learn to play the piano.' I don't understand why something that I hate to do right now will bring me joy as an adult."

If your mother is pressuring you to do something that you don't really enjoy, or has become overly involved in your passion—always volunteering to make costumes for the play you're in or insisting on being the assistant coach of your softball team—you might suggest that she find her own passion. Your mother has spent the last thirteen or more years raising you. She has devoted so much of her life to looking after your needs and making sure that you are happy that maybe she has forgotten how to make herself happy.

"From the time I was young, my mom wanted me to learn how to ski," seventeen-year-old Kara says. "I was never interested in skiing and I never understood why she wanted me to do it so badly until one day when she said, 'I always wanted to ski when I was a teenager, but I never got the chance to take lessons.' I realized then that she was trying to live a dream through me. I suggested that she sign up for skiing lessons. I even found a morning class listed in the newspaper. She was a little reluctant because of her age; maybe she was afraid that she wouldn't be able to learn. I kept encouraging her and when she signed up for lessons not only was she happy that she had finally gotten to do something that she had always wanted to, but I was relieved because she stopped trying to get me to do it."

Once in a while I still remind my mom, "It's okay for you to do something for yourself."

According to the State of Our Nation's Youth Survey, three times as many teenage girls as boys say their top career choice is medicine. Girls work harder at their studies—averaging nearly ten more hours of homework per week—and receive better grades than boys the same age.

Light My Fire

Lasting self-esteem comes from believing in yourself, achievement, and passion. Passion is the boundless enthusiasm that we are all born with; it keeps us active participants in life. We lose touch with it when it isn't nurtured. Just think about the good-natured hopefulness of a ten-month-old baby—that's the curiosity, cheerfulness, and optimism that you want to sanction, guide, and direct in your daughter. Passion is the burning desire that propels each of us forward. It gives our lives meaning and purpose. It keeps us reaching for our dreams even when we're afraid, keeps us on course when others say it's not possible. Passion makes the mundane meaningful and keeps our outlook fresh.

Teenage girls are full of passion. If you've ever stood in the stadium at a rock concert, you know what I mean. Advertisers target the teenage girl market; if they can spark girls' interest, the product will be a monetary success.

Because teenage girls want to fit in, they often lose track of their own talents. While quick to recognize the talent and capabilities of others, they doubt their own. Comparing themselves to their schoolmates, they inflict torture upon their fragile egos. "All my friends are prettier, smarter, and skinner than I am," said Shaye. "I can't do anything right." They aren't yet able to distinguish their own unique genius. Their lack of self-confidence haunts them. They wonder if they have anything to offer; they worry about the future. It takes very little to ignite their insecurities. They don't have a clue as to how to direct all their energies. Unless someone—a mother, father, or a mentor—lovingly guides her, a girl's passion for life can be misdirected, or worse it can, burn out.

Every child is an artist. The problem is how to remain an artist once he grows up.

—Pablo Picasso

That's where you come in. The teen years are your peak opportunity to help your daughter find out what she's good at and what makes her heart sing. For this is the prime time for her to discover, understand, and use her fire.

❄ What's a Mother to Do?

Encourage Her Zest for Living

Treat your daughter as the most brilliant person you know. Boast about her. Acknowledge her dreams, however small they might seem, and tell her, "Go for it!" If she wants to be on crew, tell her you think it's a wonderful plan. Whatever you do, don't tread on her inspirations by saying, "That's impossible." If she says she wants to be an astronaut, a doctor, an actress, a fireman, or a mommy, tell her, "You can." She may change directions many times before she's clear, but that's okay. You need to highlight the joy that comes with searching for and following her natural inclinations. Give her a glimpse of all that's possible for her. Show her the delight of living a passionate life.

Mary Shelley wrote *Frankenstein* at age nineteen.

Encourage her to tackle new things. Don't push what makes you happy onto her. Don't live out your unfulfilled passions through her. I made this mistake myself: When Amanda was in the seventh grade, I persuaded her to go out for track. "She's a natural," the coach told me and soon she was not only running hurdles, she was placing in the top three. I envisioned college scholarships, but Amanda protested after winning her fourth meet. Finally she told me that she was going to quit, saying, "Mom, if you like track so much, why don't you do it?'" I had to admit it was my favorite sport, but since I hurt my hip running and couldn't continue, I was living out my dream through her.

Develop your own passions, and teach her by example the "hows" of fulfilling hers. Encourage your daughter to explore what she loves, whether as a career goal or just a hobby. What's important

We cannot give the butterfly of happiness to another: each must catch it alone.

—Sister Wendy Beckett

is that she is exposed to lots of options. Allow her to try a variety of things—complicated mathematical equations, ballet, ceramics, Web page design. Don't force her; instead simply allow her to explore the possibilities. Give her your quiet support. You can be enthusiastic without taking over. Go to her events and watch, but don't give orders from the sidelines. Standing back gives her the room to figure out if this is what she really wants.

Encourage her to stick with the things that she likes. Tell her that perseverance is what's needed to make any dream come true. Ease her fears about trying new things. Tell her "You learn quickly" and "Everyone starts at the bottom."

Notice how your daughter spends her free time. Is a special interest blooming? Notice her schoolwork. What is her natural bent? What subjects does she do well in? Emphasize the merits of her intellect; encourage her artistic and creative abilities.

When Amanda was in the second grade, she brought home her English papers. I was amazed to discover how well she could punctuate sentences. I knew then that she could be a writer if she wanted to be, and told her, "You can write a book someday if you want to, or you could be an editor of a newspaper, or you could be a copy editor." It wasn't a long conversation, but something stuck, because she wrote her first book, *Landera, The Green Giraffe,* that very same year. Throughout her teen years, I'd remind her of her talents and point out her options. "If you want to," I'd say, "someday you could work on newspaper or write copy for brochures, or be a freelance writer for a magazine." You recognized the brilliance in your daughter when she was in grade school. Let her know you still see her talent; cheer her on and she'll have one less hurdle to get over.

The best way to teach your daughter to follow her passion is by following yours. Have you been so focused on your career and family that you've lost touch with your own passion? Perhaps you've been so busy paying the bills and keeping the house running that you've neglected yourself, or you don't know anymore what excites you. Is there is something you want to do in life? There is no reason at all why you can't begin now. Your daughter is watching you. If you have zest for living, so will she.

DISCOVERING YOUR PASSION QUIZ

Take this quiz and compare your answers. Talking about your answers may help both of you discover something about yourselves that you may not have known.

1. What is your mother's/daughter's favorite song? Food? Movie?

2. How does your mother/daughter spend her free time?

3. What would your mother/daughter consider to be a good time?

4. Who is a person that your mother/daughter admires? Why do you think she admires that person?

5. What has your mother/daughter done in her life that she is proud of?

6. Does your mother/daughter have a hobby? What is it? How much time does she devote to this hobby?

7. When your mother was a teenager, what did she see herself doing as an adult? What does your daughter want to do when she is an adult?

8. If your mother/daughter could travel to any place in the world, where would she go?

9. How often does your mother/daughter do something spontaneous and unplanned?

❋ Create a Daydreaming Circle

I once led a group for high school girls and their mothers called the Daydreaming Circle. Daydreaming isn't just for kids; we all have secret dreams of how we'd like our life to be when we grow up. Some of our dreams are so hidden that we can't remember them; others are dormant because of our obligations; and others are right under the surface waiting to be launched.

The Daydreaming Circle originally came together as a therapy group because of broken relationships between these seven girls and their mothers. But the group didn't stay focused on repairing relationships for long. As a getting acquainted exercise, I gave each mother and daughter two sheets of paper. On the first sheet, I ask each mother and daughter to write a secret wish or goal that they had. On the second sheet, I asked each of them to write about how they'd like their lives to be ten years from now. At the end of two weeks, I collected the writing assignments and typed them onto separate pieces of paper without names. I brought the sheets to the group and read each dream, goal, or wish out loud. As we went along, the group gave each dream a title—"The Silver Kitty," "The Movie Star," "The I Don't Know," "The Graduate," "The Hair Salon"—until we had fourteen dreams and fourteen ten-year goals. Then we began the detective work of figuring out which dream went with which person.

It was an amazing process. Girls learned that their mothers were "people, too" and mothers saw their daughters in a whole new light.

After the owners of the dreams were identified, we began a seven-month process of brainstorming strategies to launch each person's dream. Each group member made a poster with her dreams pasted in the middle. Around the edges they pasted pictures that they'd cut from magazines to help them see the dream more clearly. Mothers and daughters supported each other in designing action plans that consisted of small steps each needed to take to make their dreams come true. The "The Hair Salon" dreamer researched the requirements for cosmetology school. "The Movie Star" dreamer joined the drama club. As the girls and the mothers participated in the Daydreaming Circle, the troubles between them lessened. When you're launching your dream, you're a happier person. And when you have a purpose that's close to your heart, you don't waste time or energy focusing on what's wrong. As each mother and daughter launched their dreams, they felt better about themselves as well as less critical of each other.

It is not because things are difficult that we do not dare, it is because we do not dare that things are difficult.

—Seneca

We began our meetings with a positive reading or quote. Each member reported about her success or setbacks for the week, and we gave each other pats of the back for both. We initiated a complaint corner so that each member could voice her negativity, discouragement, and frustrations. We asked for input and advice. We made adjustments to action plans and ended each meeting with jokes.

It's been over fifteen years since that first Daydreaming Circle and I no longer have contact with all the dreamers. But I do know about a few: "The Silver Kitty" went to veterinary assistant school, "The Mommy" adopted a child, and "The Writer"—that's me—has written seven books and many articles.

A Daydreaming Circle is an incredible process. Because not only are dreams launched, mother-daughter relationships grow stronger. When you're supporting each other's dreams and encouraging each other with jokes and praise, the strain and distance between begins to melt away.

Why not launch your dreams together?

❋ Five Ways Mothers and Daughters Can Develop Their Passions

1. Experiment with many different activities and hobbies.
2. Don't spend time doing something that you don't enjoy just because you feel obligated to.

3. Listen to your heart. If something is right for you, your heart will tell you.

4. Try to remember some of the things that you enjoyed doing as a child, and start doing them again.

5. Find somebody who shares your passion to support you.

✳ Five Ways to Help Your Daughter Develop Her Passion

1. Encourage her to spend time doing something that she loves to do, even if it takes time away from things she feels obligated to do.

2. Support her when she shares her dreams with you.

3. Don't pressure her to continue something if she doesn't enjoy it.

4. Give her encouragement by reminding her of her strengths and complimenting her on the things that she does well.

5. Tell her it makes you happy to see her happy.

22

Legacy of Love

The Intangibles

As I was writing this book, I shared several passages that Amanda had written about me with colleagues and friends. "Ouch!" one person said. Another asked, "Doesn't it hurt to read what she's writing about you?" "Not at all," I answered. It makes me laugh to read her descriptions of me. It tickles me to see that she can describe my quirks. By seeing my flaws she'll learn to face her own. Writing so openly about what we've been through has expanded the borders of our connection. Finding out that we don't remember the same event in exactly the same way, rehashing the touchy moments, laughing about the glitches, have given us a fresh perspective—we've become more familiar with each other. Our mother-daughter bond is not ending, it's stretching.

As mothers we don't know for sure what we've imparted to our daughters. We're competing with many intangibles: her personality and temperament, peer groups, and many other circumstances

When you're a caregiver, you feel like you're putting your hands on something every day and that you're making it better. Even if you're not, you think you are. So you live in a very fulfilled space.

—Meryl Streep

beyond our control. We use all our skills to get our points across. We harp, nag, lecture, plead, and cajole. We show her how to bake a cake, load the dishwasher, paint a picture, think for herself, follow through, and budget her allowance. We advise her to use common sense, study, and be honest. We build her up, support her, set her straight, and keep our fingers crossed. We tell her that with hard work and determination she can do anything that she sets her mind to. We know that there are more ups and downs ahead for her, and we pray that we've instilled the strength to face whatever challenges life presents. Whatever she wishes for, we wish for her. We don't want her to just get by, we want her to soar. We want her to be at ease with herself; we hope she finds contentment.

Thinking of nineteen-year-old Amanda I picture the little girl in the photo album *and* the beautiful young women she's become. She believes in herself; she has character, soul, and spunk. I know that she will make contributions to the world and have fun. She's able to bounce back from her disappointments and appreciate her blessings. When I doubt myself, I see the goodness in her and know that it's a reflection of the goodness in me. I'm proud of her and I think to myself, "Job well done."

Amanda is at the beginning of her adult life and I am at the other end of mine. As I reflect on where we've been and where we're going, I realize I need to tell her one more thing. "Honey," I say, "I want you to listen carefully to what I'm telling you. I'm not plan-

Without mentioning what your mother/daughter does, how would you describe her? The look on her face, her philosophy, her special attributes.

ning to die right away, but I will someday and when I do, I know that you will be sad and miss me, but there's no need for you to suffer. I will never be far away. Death is an illusion, you know. When I die, I'll be close by, surrounding you in love and light, cheering you on. Even though I'll be out of sight, be still, and you will find me in your heart and in your memories. Plant sunflowers and pansies in my honor. Plant them in unexpected places, by the side of the road, on hilltops, and in pots at your doorstep. My love surrounds you always. You and I are one." She listened and gave me the greatest gift by saying, "I know, Mom."

Life with those we love is very short. Recognizing that you and your daughter will someday part puts the struggles in perspective, washes away the hurts, and clarifies misunderstandings. Treat your daughter kindly, laugh with her, love her well, and let nothing come between you. Point out the things in life that truly matter—the birds, the blue sky, the fluffy clouds, the smell of rain. If you can do that, you'll be a source of lasting joy that she can call upon and be comforted by.

✳ What's a Mother to Do?

Show Your Soul

As mothers we frequently get so focused on imparting practical information that we forget to hand down the spiritual tools our daughters need for a joy-filled life. Here are six simple ways to show your daughter how to connect with Spirit.

1. Point out the miracles, the lucky breaks, the magic, the funny coincidences in your everyday life so that she can recognize the miracles operating in her own life. Point out the full moon, the angel-shaped clouds, the magnificent sunset so that she can see the beauty in nature.

2. Girls respond to music, and I when I play beautiful music to wake Amanda our days start out peacefully. A simple piece of heartwarming music can change our

mood in just seconds. By listening to fifteen minutes of soul-moving music each morning and evening, we melt into serenity and find peace amid the hustle and bustle of our busy schedules. Introduce your daughter to heart-moving music that speaks to you. Ask her to play one of her favorites for you.

Amanda's high school teacher, Ms. Matheson, showed the class overheads of paintings and drawings while playing Pachelbel's *Canon*. Amanda was so moved by that music that she shared it with me, and *Surfin' Pachelbel* by Liv & Let Liv became a standard in our household.

3. You can show your daughter how to bring harmony into her everyday life using candles, fragrances, and incense. Ask your daughter to light the candles for dinner and point out the soothing effect of candlelight. When you eat more slowly by candlelight, you're giving her permission to indulge in the pleasures of slowing down. Ask her to choose a fragrant incense stick to burn outside the window or on the front porch. The smell helps her to focus on the pleasures of all her senses. A potpourri pot simmering on your stove and a gentle comment on how the fragrance softens the energy in your home helps her become aware of her own energy. Give her bath oils so that she can bathe in waters steeped in aromatic essences and learn how to treat her body kindly.

4. Teach your daughter about perseverance and patience. Your "to-do" list is likely longer than the hours in your day and so is hers. When she's frustrated because she has two tests, a paper due, a band concert, doesn't understand her chemistry assignment, and her best friend isn't speaking to her; when you're frustrated because you have a boss who wants you to work overtime, a garage that needs cleaning, out-of-town guests

arriving, and you're coming down with the flu, remind yourself and her that problems aren't solved all at once, but one by one. Take a deep breath, choose one problem to solve, solve it, and go on to the next. Tell her: One step at a time, one breath at a time, perseverance, and patience. That's the way we reach our goals.

5. Watch your attitude. If the day is gloomy and so are you, you send a gloomy message to your daughter. But when the day is gloomy and you say out loud, "This is great day to be alive," you put a healthy spin on life. Say it even if you don't feel it; soon you'll both believe it.

6. If you want your daughter to appreciate her advantages and blessings, don't preach or lecture to her that she has it better than you did at her age. Instead thank God openly for all the blessings you have now. "I'm grateful for clean sheets and fresh towels," Marianne told her thirteen-year-old daughter, Emily. "What are you grateful for?" she asked. "Lime Kool-Aid and felt-tip pens," Emily answered. While driving in the car, let your daughter hear you giving thanks. Tell her often that you are grateful to have her as your daughter. If your attitude is one of gratitude soon she'll be focusing on what she has, not what she lacks.

Hard to Put into Words

Learning doesn't always come from being taught; we learn some things without even realizing it. My mother teaches me best when I'm watching her and seeing her view of the world and the way she lives her life, not by reminding me to get my homework done on time, nagging me to do the dishes, or yelling at me to drive slowly.

She has taught me that my life is a gift and that I should enjoy it, both the good and the bad times. My mother lives in the moment and

I still call her every day. Whether she wants to pick up the phone and call me back isn't my concern. No matter what, she has only one daughter. And regardless of how close I get to other people, she's my only mom. I'm not going to let go of that.

—Brooke Shields

notices beauty all around her. "We may not be rich with money, but we are rich with love," she says when I complain about not getting new jeans. She writes me little notes that say, "There is beauty in the simple mundane of everyday life," when I've complained about being bored. Her attitude has taught me that my life is a treasure, and this has helped me to appreciate the wonderful things I have, even when it seems like I have nothing to be thankful for.

I see how my mother has persevered through tough times, and I learn never to give up, even if I don't succeed or things don't go the way I wanted. Her life hasn't turned out the way that she planned, but when she says, "Life has brought me greater things than I ever could have imagined," I know that even when she felt like giving up, she kept going. When I look at my mother, I see that I can do amazing things. My mother has shown me that life is full of possibility, and that I must be aware of and open to my potential.

My mother taught me that it's okay to be myself and that I shouldn't follow the crowd. She openly accepts differences in people. "He's a 'character,'" she says about somebody that I might call weird. And when I complain that she's acting like a goof, or dressing funny, or doing something out of the ordinary, she responds, "I'm a free spirit, Amanda!" Her spirit shines through everything she does, teaching me that it's better to follow my heart and be myself even if that means going against the norm. My mom follows her instincts, and in doing so, she encourages me to listen to my own.

I don't know if my mom even knows that she has taught me these lessons. I rarely tell her that I admire how hard she has worked, or how much I appreciate all that she has given me, or how I love the spirit that shines through her personality. I watch my mom and see her beautiful view of the world and think, "If I have a daughter someday, I want to raise her exactly how she raised me." Now, instead of pointing out how different we are, I like to notice our similarities. I see some of my mother's spirit in myself, and that makes me happy.

❋ What's a Daughter to Do

Give a Handmade Gift

On your mother's birthday, Mother's Day, Christmas, or any day at all, give your mother a handmade gift. I've done this several times and my mother always cries. "This is the best gift you could give me," she says. A handmade gift from you means much more to her than something you bought, because she knows that you are thinking of her the entire time you are making it. A handmade gift takes effort, and that means a lot to our mothers, especially since they often are convinced that we aren't thinking about them at all.

Here are some gift ideas that don't cost much, but your mother will probably remember the rest of her life.

1. Buy a small double frame and put pictures of you and her at the same age in it. Perhaps it might be baby pictures of the both of you or a picture of you both as teens. If you can't find matching pictures, call your grandmother for help. There's something sentimental for your mother about seeing pictures of the two of you side by side.

More than forty-six countries celebrate Mother's Day. In the United States, Mother's Day is always the second Sunday of May. When Anna Jarvis' mother died in 1904, Ms. Jarvis sought a special memorial Mother's Day service at a small chapel in West Virginia. It took three years, but eventually she got her wish. The first Mother's Day was held May 10, 1907.

2. Write your mother a poem or make her a card. I know I gave my mom lots of handmade cards when I was in grade school because she still displays them. I don't do it as much now, but when I do she keeps them in a drawer in her bedroom. When I went away to college, I put a handmade card on her dresser; it's been there now for over a year. The card can be funny, deep, or thankful, but if you made it, she'll love it.

3. Give her a certificate proclaiming her "Mother of the Year" or "The Funny Mother of the Year." Make her a coupon book with coupons like "I'll do the dishes once without you asking," or "I'll answer one question about my friends," or, "Good for three hours of not talking back."

As silly as all this might sound, making the effort to please your mother can improve relations between you. When my mother is in a bad mood, a little effort on my part can change things so that she doesn't take all her frustrations out on me. I gain respect for myself when I make the effort to be kind to her.

23

A New Spin on an Old Struggle

Mothers Can Be So Irrational

"Mothers can be such a pain," I said as my friend Sarah got into my car. I knew she would be able to understand my mother frustrations, and empathize with my side of the story.

Giving me a sympathetic look to let me know that she understood my upset she asked, "What happened?"

With a sigh, I began to tell her the story of the fight my mother and I had just had.

"Mothers can be so irrational," Sarah said.

"I know it. If she would have asked calmly, 'Amanda, could you be home by six so that we can have dinner together?' things would have been so much simpler, but she has to make everything crazy by freaking out for no reason. I really don't understand her."

"I completely understand," Sarah said. "It's like we're the adults in the family. Mothers get so worked up about the littlest things and they fly off the handle without even talking calmly first. When we're moms, we'll definitely be much more rational than our mothers."

"Yeah, definitely," I said. "But with our luck, we'll probably get daughters who are as irrational as our mothers."

✻ We Get Along

By the time I reached my senior year of high school, my mother and I had mastered the art of getting along. After five intense years of working it out, we finally understood each other. I know not to leave unwashed dishes lying in the sink, always to call if I'm going to be home late, and that saying, "You're right and I'm sorry" (even if I believe that I've done nothing wrong), is the best thing to do when my mom is angry at me. My mother accepts that I want her to knock when I in my room with the door closed, that some nights I want to stay out extra late with my friends, and that I will never tell her about some things, no matter how much she asks. She no longer embarrasses me, and we rarely get into the screaming matches or the earth-shaking battles that we once did.

Although everything was working out wonderfully between us, I was ready to be away from her. I wanted to be independent and it was time for my life to take on a fresh beginning. Feeling ready to conquer whatever challenges the world would throw me, I couldn't wait to take complete control of my life. I was ready to break free, and even though it seemed as if my mother and I had just begun to really understand each other and had learned how to live happily and peacefully together, it was time for me to leave. I packed all of my clothes, photos, books, CDs, and everything else that I couldn't live without and with the car stuffed full to the ceiling, my mother drove me to another state and dropped me off at college.

Mamas only do things cause they love you so much. They can't help it. It's flesh to flesh, blood to blood. No matter how old you get, how grown and on your own, your mama always love you like a newborn.

—Ntozake Shange

During my first year at college, I realized what my mother meant to me. After I left home, I quickly saw what a wonderful relationship my mother and I had created—and how so many other girls were disconnected from their mothers. Some dreaded having their mothers come for parents' weekend, while I couldn't wait to have her there. Living in the dorm allowed me to appreciate her in a whole new light.

The daughter never gives up on the mother just as the mother never gives up on the daughter. There is a tie here so strong that neither can break it. I call it the "unbreakable bond."

—*Rachel Billington*

Now, in my sophomore year, I still get homesick and I long for my mother—especially on Sunday afternoons, the time we spent running errands, going out to lunch, or just hanging out together. I enjoy keeping my mother updated about my life and I call her three times a week to let her know what's going on. My mother and I can communicate about all kinds of stuff—from feelings to great literature, from boyfriends to finances. She respects my opinions and I ask for hers. We laugh, make plans to hang out together, and I hoping she'll come visit while I'm studying abroad in France.

I feel a little heartsick when I realize that my relationship with my mother will never be quite the same as it once was. Never again will she be the first person I talk to when I wake up every morning nor will she be the last person I say goodnight to before I go to sleep. She won't be there every day to ask me how my day was when I walk in the door from school. She won't always be there to make me my favorite dinners or take me to the mall for a spur-of-the-moment shopping spree.

My life is different now, and we can never go back to the way things once were. But one thing I can say for certain is that no matter how far apart we live, or how much we disagree, no matter what changes our relationship undergoes, my mother and I will always be connected by a strong and powerful invisible bond. I'm glad we have worked together to create a good relationship and I can honestly say, "I like you, Mom."

✳ What's a Daughter to Do?

Know That Hard Work Pays Off

During the times when you are struggling to get along with your mother, you may wonder why you put so much effort into having a good relationship with her. Why do you continually sacrifice things that you want in order to compromise with your mother, even though it seems like you're the one who gives the most? Why do you try desperately to express your feelings and point of view to your mother when it seems as if she will never understand you?

Don't let feelings of desperation get you down. You may not see the results of your efforts immediately, but your hard work will pay off. When you are in the midst of living the struggles, it is difficult to see the good in your relationship. The benefits of hard work may be clouded by arguments, hurt feelings, and misunderstandings.

Working to have a good relationship with your mother is worth it, I promise. I know, because it worked for me. If you keep working at it, by the age of nineteen or twenty, you and your mother will truly enjoy one another and will be able to laugh and have a good time. You will feel happy and safe knowing that she's your mother.

The Emptying Nest

While Amanda was looking forward to packing up her belongings and going off to college, I was not exactly dreading it, but I was definitely circumspect as I reviewed our last five years. While I was excited for her, I was uneasy about what changes this would bring for me. I cherish having her around. She's added sparkle to my routine. While she's at college, I can't be there in person to partake in the delights. I won't meet her friends or hear about her studies as often. I won't know her professors or be assured that she's eating well. What if she gets sick, who will bring her orange juice and chicken soup? She won't be flopping on my bed for midnight chats and we won't have our Sunday routine any longer. As we shopped for a trunk, sheets, towels, an iron, and a small refrigerator, I wondered how I would fit into her life in the future. In twenty short days, my only child, my little love object, would be leaving my nest, venturing into an exciting, new world. With all the new friends she'd be making, would she still have time for me? Starting college was another rite of passage, the springboard to adulthood and total independence. What seemed like a glorious beginning for her, left me feeling more alone than I'd been in eighteen years. She'd been my whole focus. Every decision I made was made with her in mind. How could I protect her when she was in another state? What would our relationship be now?

A daughter in her mid-twenties once hesitantly confessed that whole days go by without her thinking of me. She was startled when I burst out laughing: "Whole days go by without my thinking of you." She and I did a little dance of liberation.

—June Bingham

We both cried as I drove away from campus, and although I didn't cry during the five-hour drive home, I was in a daze. I was stunned; I couldn't think or feel. I was in shock for a week. What would I do if I wasn't a mother? I'd been looking forward to the time when I no longer had to cook dinner every night, I'd dreamed of stocking the refrigerator with sparkling water and take-home containers from my favorite restaurants, but I hadn't comprehended the emptiness I'd feel as I stared at the bare refrigerator. As I wrote Amanda's name and phone number in my address book, I couldn't be brave any longer. "My little girl has her own page in my address book!" I sobbed to my friend, Gethen.

I think Amanda and I are just about over the adolescent phase of our relationship because she's giving up on her tendency to point out that she's nothing like me, and I'm getting over my tendency to give her advice on every aspect of her life. But we're not over it completely, and I don't mind. While writing this book, I told her that the hard chair she was using at the computer wasn't good for her back. She gave me that look and said, *"Mooom!"* but a day later she had propped herself with pillows. I didn't say a word. It was satisfying

Mothers are spiritual teachers. We teach love to our children by showing them respect and patience and tenderness. They will learn to give love in the ways they receive it from us and see us give it to others. It is not enough for us to know that we love our children. We must ask ourselves very seriously what this means.

—Marianne Williamson

enough that she still lets me mother her once in a while.

Recognize the Treasure You've Been Given

It's not easy to describe the relationship between a mother and a daughter because it's more than you imagine it to be. It's intense. It's an eternal spiritual involvement between two distinct feminine spirits. It's a reverence for the separateness of the two of you and the divine connection that is always present.

Love between a mother and a daughter is beautiful as long as it does not bind or hinder the growth of the other. For many years, mother love is so active that almost seems unnatural for you not to take the lead. That's the work in it. Learning when to direct her and when to step back, when to give her advice and when to be quiet. Mother-daughter love is a spiritual undertaking filled with pain and glory.

When you view your daughter from this vantage point you see that she's not only your daughter, she's a child of God and so are you. When your daughter came into your life, your heart was opened; you aren't the same person that you once were. Your spiritual obligation is to remain open to her—no matter what. She was given to you, not to mold to please you, but to hold her in the light so as her life unfolds she can be all that she's meant to be. She will take the best of you, improve on it, and become better. Her bright spirit reflects the essence of you.

Mother-daughter love goes beyond our understanding; it transforms our heart and our life. Mother–daughter love stands firm, yet for your relationship to hold up through the adulthood challenges that are ahead, love must branch into the sweetness that comes when you're enjoying each another. Liking one another is basis for a lasting connection. In bowing to the mystery of your child, who is now a teenager and will soon be a young woman, you allow all that she is to shine. When she can be who she is in your presence and when you can be who you are with her, you are at ease with one another. When you can talk openly together without either one of you being offended, you've unlocked the richness and joy in your alliance, and you've found the holy treasure.

We are together, my child and I, mother and child, yes, but sisters really, against whatever denies us all that we are.

—*Alice Walker*

Afterword by
Mavis Gruver
founding editor of
New Moon Magazine

I'm eighteen, still live at home, and my mother and I don't always get along. We get on each other's nerves a lot, and the two of us argue more than any other two people in our family. It used to be much worse. We would be talking about something, and I would get frustrated and say something hurtful. Then my mom would get mad at me, and I would feel like I couldn't do anything right. Things between us would be strained for (what felt to me like) a long time afterward. We've worked on our relationship, and it's really helped. I'm trying not to take everything she says personally and to bite my tongue instead of saying something rude. I don't know what my mom's been doing differently, but she doesn't grate on my nerves the way she used to. Maybe I've grown up. Maybe my mom and I have realized that while we have a strong, close relationship, we can't always get along, and that when we're mad at each other it's better to express our feelings and move on. We listen more and try to understand each other's side of the story.

Because I think listening to other perspectives is so important, I really like the two distinct voices and points of view in *Between Mother and Daughter*. It's great to have a book about mothers and daughters actually written by a mother–daughter team. So many books about mothering only have one perspective: the mother's. That makes it hard for the reader to remember that there are two people and two perspectives in mother–daughter relationships. Judy and Amanda Ford's reflections and confessions will give mothers a better understanding of their daughters, and daughters a better appreciation of their mothers' point of view.

Working together with my mom has helped us stay close. We started *New Moon: The Magazine for Girls and Their Dreams* together, and even when we can't agree about anything else, we agree about what's best for the magazine. I think it's because we both really care about it, and we can listen to each other's ideas and criticism without feeling personally hurt. Respecting and truly listening to each other at *New Moon* has helped us do that in the rest of our lives. We're always trying to listen more, trust more, and understand each other better.

Reading *Between Mother and Daughter* gave me new insights into my relationship with my mother. It put our relationship into perspective for me and showed me that our big problems weren't so big after all. What's improving between us now will continue to get better and better as we go along, as long as we remember to respect and make an effort to understand each other. And aren't respect and understanding what relationships are all about?

Resource Guide

Books

Nathalie Bartle with Susan Lieberman, *Venus in Blue Jeans: Why Mothers and Daughters Need to Talk about Sex*

Evelyn Bassoff, *Cherishing Our Daughters: How Parents Can Raise Girls to Become Confident Women*

Ann F. Caron, *Don't Stop Loving Me: A Reassuring Guide for Mothers of Adolescent Daughters*

Sean Covey, *The 7 Habits of Highly Effective Teens: The Ultimate Teenage Success Guide*

Shireen Dodson, *The Mother-Daughter Book Club: How Ten Busy Mothers and Daughters Came Together to Talk, Laugh, and Learn Through Their Love of Reading*

Gladys Folkers and Jeanne Engelmann, *Taking Charge of My Mind and Body: A Girl's Guide to Outsmarting Alcohol, Drugs, Smoking, and Eating Problems*

Will Glennon, *200 Hundred Ways to Raise A Girl's Self-Esteem: An Indispensable Guide for Parents, Teachers, and Other Concerned Caregivers*

Mavis Jukes, *It's a Girl Thing: How to Stay Healthy, Safe, and in Charge*

Mary Motley Kalergis, *Seen and Heard: Teenagers Talk about Their Lives*

Vimala McClure, *The Tao of Motherhood* and *The Path of Parenting*

Cristina Page, editor, *A Smart Girl's Guide to College: A Serious Book Written by Women in College to Help You Make the Perfect College Choice*

Bonnie M. Parsley, *The Choice Is Yours: A Teenager's Guide to Self-Discovery, Relationship, Values, and Spiritual Growth*

Hugh and Gayle Prather, *Spiritual Parenting: A Guide to Understanding and Nurturing the Heart of Your Child*

Virginia Beane Rutter, *Celebrating Girls: Nurturing and Empowering Our Daughters*

Varla Ventura, *Sheroes: Bold, Brash, and Absolutely Unabashed Superwomen from Susan B. Anthony to Xena*

Carol Weston, *Girltalk: All the Stuff Your Sister Never Told You* and *For Girls Only: Wise Words and Good Advice*

Web sites

www.americangirl.com

www.bluejeanmag.com

www.girlzone.com

www.go-girl.com

www.gURLwURLd.org

www.hues.net

www.intelligent-living.com

www.newmoon.org

www.teenvoices.com

www.themint.org

American Girl
8400 Fairway Place
Middleton, WI 53562

Family Life
P. O. Box 52220
Boulder, CO 80322
(800) 879-3661

Girls' Life
4517 Harford Road
Baltimore, MD 21214
(888) 999-3222

Journal of Family Life
22 Elm Street
Albany, NY 12202
(518) 471-9532

Mothering Magazine
P.O. Box 1690
Santa Fe, NM 87504
(800) 984-8116

New Moon Magazine
P. O. Box 3587
Duluth, MN 55803-3587
(800) 381-4743

Teen Voices
515 Washington Street, 4th Floor
Boston, MA 02111
(617) 426-5505

Tools
529 South 7th Street,
Suite 570
Minneapolis, MN 55415
(800) 328-0417

Acknowledgments

To my high school teachers, Ms. Heather Matheson and Mrs. Lois Judd, for inspiring me, guiding me, and believing in me. I'm grateful for your lasting influence and the knowledge that you've shared with me. The world needs more teachers like you!

To my three beautiful friends, Sarah, Adrienne, and Jocelyn: I feel so blessed to have been able to share my life with you amazing girls. You all have taught me more lessons about friendship, love, life, and happiness than you probably realize.

Thank you,
Amanda

To my dear friend Gethen Bassett, who has walked with me through the most difficult moments and who is always available as needed for commiserating and movies. I cherish you.

To Barbara Deede, a beacon of perseverance, good humor, and spunk, for backing us all the way.

Thank you,
Judy

About the Authors

Judy Ford, M.S.W., is a family counselor in Kirkland, Washington. Amanda Ford is a college student at Willamette University in Oregon.

We would like to know about your mother-and-daughter struggles and the solutions you're finding. Write us with your trials, tirades, and triumphs at the address below:

Judy Ford and Amanda Ford
P.O. Box 834
Kirkland, WA 98083
e-mail: JFordBooks@aol.com

Books by Judy Ford

Wonderful Ways to Love a Child

Wonderful Ways to Love a Teen...Even When It Seems Impossible

*Blessed Expectations: Nine Months of Wonder,
Reflection & Sweet Anticipation*

Wonderful Ways to Love a Grandchild

Wonderful Ways to Be a Family

Wonderful Ways to Be a Stepparent

For workshops and speaking information, write:
Judy Ford
P.O. Box 834
Kirkland, WA 98083
e-mail: JFordBooks@aol.com

About New Moon Publishing

"New Moon Publishing has an agenda for girls and young women that's refreshingly different from mainstream corporate media. New Moon is building a community of girls and young women intent on saving their true selves. New Moon's magazines are a godsend for girls and young women and the adults who care about them."

—Mary Pipher, Ph.D., author of Reviving Ophelia:
Saving the Selves of Adolescent Girls

New Moon: The Magazine for Girls and Their Dreams Edited by girls ages 8-14, *New Moon* is the ad-free, international, bi-monthly magazine that is an inspiration at any age.

New Moon Network: For Adults Who Care About Girls Share the successes and wisdom of a worldwide network of parents, teachers, and other professionals committed to raising healthy, self-confident girls. Between the Moon and You A catalog of valuable resources and special gifts that educate and celebrate girls and women. Online at www.newmooncatalog.com.

New Moon Education Division A variety of participatory workshops and compelling speakers for conferences, conventions and meetings.

For information on any of these resources, contact:

New Moon Publishing
P.O. Box 3620
Duluth, MN 55803-3620
Phone: 800-381-4743   Fax: 218-728-0314
Email: newmoon@newmoon.org   Web: www.newmoon.org

Conari Press, established in 1987, publishes books on
topics ranging from psychology, spirituality, and women's history
to sexuality, parenting, and personal growth. Our main goal is to
publish quality books that will make a difference in people's
lives—both how we feel about ourselves and
how we relate to one another.

Our readers are our most important resource,
and we value your input, suggestions, and ideas.
We'd love to hear from you—after all,
we are publishing books for you!

To request our latest book catalog,
or to be added to our mailing list, please contact:

CONARI PRESS
2550 Ninth Street, Suite 101
Berkeley, California 94710-2551
800-685-9595
510-649-7175
fax: 510-649-7190
e-mail: Conari@conari.com
http://www.Conari.com